SVG Colors, Patterns & Gradients

Painting Vector Graphics

*Amelia Bellamy-Royds
& Kurt Cagle*

Beijing · Boston · Farnham · Sebastopol · Tokyo

SVG Colors, Patterns & Gradients

by Amelia Bellamy-Royds and Kurt Cagle

Printed in the United States of America.

Published by O'Reilly Media, Inc., 1005 Gravenstein Highway North, Sebastopol, CA 95472.

O'Reilly books may be purchased for educational, business, or sales promotional use. Online editions are also available for most titles (*http://safaribooksonline.com*). For more information, contact our corporate/institutional sales department: 800-998-9938 or *corporate@oreilly.com*.

Editor: Meg Foley	**Indexer:** Amelia Bellamy-Royds
Production Editor: Colleen Lobner	**Interior Designer:** David Futato
Copyeditor: Jasmine Kwityn	**Cover Designer:** Ellie Volckhausen
Proofreader: James Fraleigh	**Illustrator:** Rebecca Demarest

October 2015:   First Edition

Revision History for the First Edition
2015-10-02:   First Release

See *http://oreilly.com/catalog/errata.csp?isbn=9781491933749* for release details.

978-1-491-93374-9

[LSI]

Table of Contents

Preface. vii

1. Things You Should Already Know. 1
   SVG Is Drawing with Code   1
   SVG Is Always Open Source   2
   SVG Is XML (and Sometimes HTML)   2
   SVG Is Squishable   2
   Pictures Are a Collection of Shapes   3
   Images Can Have Images Inside Them   3
   Text Is Art   3
   Art Is Math   4
   An SVG Is a Limited View of an Infinite Canvas   4
   SVG Has Structure   4
   SVG Has Style   4
   Behind All Good Markup Is a Great DOM   5
   SVG Can Move   5
   SVG Can Change   6

2. The Painter's Model. 7
   Fill 'Er Up with the fill Property   8
   Stroke It with the stroke Property   12
   Stroking the Fill and Filling the Stroke   17
   Take a Hint with Rendering Properties   26

3. Creating Colors. 31
   Misty Rose by Any Other Name   31
   A Rainbow in Three Colors   36

Custom Colors   40
Mixing and Matching   48

4. Becoming Transparent. 53
   See-Through Styles   53
   The Net Effect   58

5. Serving Paint. 63
   Paint and Wallpaper   64
   Identifying Your Assets   65
   The Solid Gradient   68

6. Simple Gradients. 75
   Gradiated Gradients   75
   Transparency Gradients   78
   Controlling the Color Transition   79

7. Gradients in All Shapes and Sizes. 85
   The Gradient Vector   85
   The Object Bounding Box   90
   Drawing Outside the Box   94
   Gradients, Transformed   100

8. And Repeat. 111
   How to Spread Your Gradient   111
   Reflections on Infinite Gradients   113
   Repeating Without Reflecting   114
   Using (and Reusing) Gradients in HTML   118

9. Radial Gradients. 133
   Radial Gradient Basics   134
   Filling the Box   135
   Scaling the Circle   140
   Adjusting the Focus   144
   Transforming Radial Gradients   147
   Grand Gradients   149

10. Tiles and Textures. 163
   Building a Building Block   164
   Stretching to Fit   171
   Laying Tiles   175

Transformed Tiles   181

11. **Picture-Perfect Patterns**. **189**
    The Layered Look   189
    Preserved Patterns   193
    Background Images, SVG-Style   197

12. **Textured Text**. **207**
    Bounding Text   208
    Switching Styles Midstream   214

13. **Painting Lines**. **221**
    Beyond the Edges   221
    The Empty Box   224
    Using the Coordinate Space   231
    Patterned Lines   235

14. **Motion Pictures**. **239**
    Animation Options   240
    Coordinated Animation   247
    Animated Interactions   251

A. **Color Keywords and Syntax**. **269**

B. **Elements, Attributes, and Style Properties**. **277**

Index. **285**

Preface

This book takes a deep dive into a specific aspect of SVG: painting. Painting not with oils or watercolors, but with graphical instructions that a computer can transform into colored pixels. The book explores the creative possibilities, and also the potential pitfalls. It describes the basics, but also suggests how you can mix and match the tools at your disposal to generate complex effects.

This book was born from another project, an introduction to using SVG on the Web. In order to keep that book a manageable length—and keep it suitable for introductory audiences—many details and complexities had to be skimmed over. But those details and complexities add up to the full, wonderful potential of SVG as a graphics format. Once you understand the basics of SVG, you can start thinking about creating more intricate drawings and more nuanced effects.

What We'll Cover

If you're reading this, hopefully you're already familiar with the basics of SVG—how to define a graphic as a set of shapes, and how to use that graphic either as a standalone image file or as markup in an HTML page. If you're not sure if you're ready, Chapter 1 reviews the basic concepts we'll expect you to know.

The rest of the book focuses on the *Colors, Patterns & Gradients* described in the title:

- Chapter 2 discusses the rendering model used to convert SVG code into visual graphics, and introduces the basic properties you can set on your shapes and text to control how they are painted to the screen.

- Chapter 3 focuses on color: how it works in nature, how it works on the computer, and how it can be specified within your SVG code.

- Chapter 4 discusses transparency, or more specifically, opacity; it introduces the many ways you can control the opacity of your graphics, and how these affect the end result.

- Chapter 5 introduces the concept of a paint server: complex graphics content that defines how other SVG shapes and text should be painted to the screen. It also introduces the solid color paint server, which is actually more useful than it may seem at first.

- Chapter 6 looks at gradients, with a particular focus on the different color transition effects you can achieve by adjusting color stop positions and properties.

- Chapter 7 explores the ways in which you can manipulate a linear gradient to move it within the shape being painted.

- Chapter 8 covers repeating linear gradients and some of the effects you can create with them. It also includes some practical examples and tips on using gradients (and other paint servers) for inline SVG icons in an HTML page.

- Chapter 9 looks at radial gradients, including repeated radial gradients, and concludes with some examples of creating complex effects with multiple gradients.

- Chapter 10 introduces the <pattern> element, which creates repeating tiles and textures.

- Chapter 11 shows how a pattern can be used to define a single image or graphic that can be used to fill shapes or text.

- Chapter 12 examines in more detail how paint servers are applied to text.

- Chapter 13 looks at some of the issues that come into play when using paint servers to paint strokes instead of fill regions.

- Chapter 14 gives some examples of animated paint servers and discusses the benefits and limitations of the different animation methods available in SVG.

At the end of the book, two appendixes provide a quick reference for the basic syntax you'll need in order to put this all to use:

- Appendix A recaps the many ways you can define colors, including all the predefined color keywords.
- Appendix B summarizes all the paint server elements, their attributes, and the related style properties.

About This Book

Whether you're casually flipping through the book, or reading it meticulously from cover to cover, you can get more from it by understanding the following little extras used to provide additional information.

About the Examples

SVG images are displayed and manipulated with many different types of software, and each program interprets the SVG code slightly differently. This is particularly an issue when graphics files are distributed on the Web; you hope that the person on the other end sees something fairly close to what you thought you created!

The examples in this book have therefore been tested on the latest stable, desktop versions (as of July 2015) of Chrome, Firefox, Internet Explorer, and Safari browsers. Quirks, bugs, and lack of support are noted in the text; in addition, expected changes in support for the Microsoft Edge browser are mentioned.

Nearly every other browser uses a variation of one of the main open source rendering libraries: Gecko (Firefox), WebKit (Safari and iOS devices), or Chromium/Blink (a fork of WebKit, primarily developed for Chrome). You can therefore use the major browsers' support levels as a guideline, but be aware that not all software updates at the same time. For mobile browsers, there are also often practical performance limitations even if features are technically supported. Certain mobile browsers (e.g., Opera Mini) intentionally limit which web features they support in order to improve performance.

SVG is also used in graphics programs such as Adobe Illustrator and Inkscape. There are a number of tools, such as Apache Batik or libRSVG, that convert SVG code into other vector graphics formats, such as for PDF documents. These all introduce whole new areas of compatibility issues, which have not been detailed in this book. Test carefully in any tool you need to use!

Using Code Examples

Supplemental material (code examples and figures) is available online at the following URLs.

Download from:

https://github.com/oreillymedia/SVG_Colors_Patterns_Gradients

View live at:

http://oreillymedia.github.io/SVG_Colors_Patterns_Gradients/

This book is here to help you get your job done. In general, if example code is offered with this book, you may use it in your programs and documentation. You do not need to contact us for permission unless you're reproducing a significant portion of the code. For example, writing a program that uses several chunks of code from this book does not require permission. Selling or distributing a CD-ROM of examples from O'Reilly books does require permission. Answering a question by citing this book and quoting example code does not require permission. Incorporating a significant amount of example code from this book into your product's documentation does require permission.

We appreciate, but do not require, attribution. An attribution usually includes the title, author, publisher, and ISBN. For example: "*SVG Colors, Patterns & Gradients* by Amelia Bellamy-Royds and Kurt Cagle (O'Reilly). Copyright 2016 Amelia Bellamy-Royds and Kurt Cagle, 978-1-4919-3374-9."

If you feel your use of code examples falls outside fair use or the permission given above, feel free to contact us at *permissions@oreilly.com*.

Conventions Used in This Book

The following typographical conventions are used in this book:

Italic
  Indicates new terms, URLs, email addresses, filenames, and file extensions.

`Constant width`

> Used for program listings, as well as within paragraphs to refer to program elements such as variable or function names, databases, data types, environment variables, statements, and keywords.

`Constant width bold`

> Shows commands or other text that should be typed literally by the user.

`Constant width italic`

> Shows text that should be replaced with user-supplied values or by values determined by context.

> Tips like this will be used to highlight particularly tricky aspects of SVG, or simple shortcuts that might not be obvious at first glance.

> Notes like this will be used for more general asides and interesting background information.

> Warnings like this will highlight combatibility problems between different web browsers (or other software), or between SVG as an XML file versus SVG in HTML pages.

In addition, sidebars like the following will introduce supplemental information:

A Brief Aside

There are two types of sidebars used in this book. "Future Focus" asides will look at proposed features that aren't yet standardized, or new standards that aren't widely implemented. "CSS Versus SVG" asides compare an SVG graphical effect with the CSS styles (if any) that could create a similar appearance.

Although the sidebars are not absolutely essential for understanding SVG colors, patterns, and gradients, they will hopefully add important context when planning a complete web project.

Safari® Books Online

 *Safari Books Online* is an on-demand digital library that delivers expert content in both book and video form from the world's leading authors in technology and business.

Technology professionals, software developers, web designers, and business and creative professionals use Safari Books Online as their primary resource for research, problem solving, learning, and certification training.

Safari Books Online offers a range of plans and pricing for enterprise, government, education, and individuals.

Members have access to thousands of books, training videos, and prepublication manuscripts in one fully searchable database from publishers like O'Reilly Media, Prentice Hall Professional, Addison-Wesley Professional, Microsoft Press, Sams, Que, Peachpit Press, Focal Press, Cisco Press, John Wiley & Sons, Syngress, Morgan Kaufmann, IBM Redbooks, Packt, Adobe Press, FT Press, Apress, Manning, New Riders, McGraw-Hill, Jones & Bartlett, Course Technology, and hundreds more. For more information about Safari Books Online, please visit us online.

How to Contact Us

Please address comments and questions concerning this book to the publisher:

O'Reilly Media, Inc.
1005 Gravenstein Highway North
Sebastopol, CA 95472
800-998-9938 (in the United States or Canada)
707-829-0515 (international or local)
707-829-0104 (fax)

We have a web page for this book, where we list errata, examples, and any additional information. You can access this page at *http:// bit.ly/svg-colors-patterns-and-gradients*.

To comment or ask technical questions about this book, send email to *bookquestions@oreilly.com*.

For more information about our books, courses, conferences, and news, see our website at *http://www.oreilly.com*.

Find us on Facebook: *http://facebook.com/oreilly*

Follow us on Twitter: *http://twitter.com/oreillymedia*

Watch us on YouTube: *http://www.youtube.com/oreillymedia*

Acknowledgments

This book would never have come into being without the patience and persistence of a series of editors at O'Reilly: Simon St. Laurent, Meghan Blanchette, and (last but not least!) Meg Foley. Much appreciation goes to the technical reviewers, who did their best to minimize the number of errors and incomprehensible statements that made it through to the final copy: David Eisenberg, Dudley Storey, Robert Longson, and Sarah Drasner.

Appreciation is also due to the O'Reilly team who do their best to make the final book elegant and professional. In particular, thanks to Sanders Kleinfeld for adapting the Pygmentize syntax highlighters to play nicely with SVG code, and to production editor Colleen Lobner for managing many custom requests.

Thanks also to the wider community of SVG developers, both those of you creating with SVG and those of you building the underlying software. Many of the tips, tricks, and warnings highlighted in this book were collected from discoveries made by others and shared through blog posts, live demos, Q&A forums, and mailing lists.

CHAPTER 1

Things You Should Already Know

This book is written with the assumption that you already know something about SVG, web design in general, and maybe even a little JavaScript programming.

However, there are always little quirks of a language that some people think are straightforward while other, equally talented, developers have never heard of. So this chapter gives a quick review of topics that you might want to brush up on—if you don't already know them.

SVG Is Drawing with Code

An SVG is an image file. It is perfectly possible to only use it as an image file, the same way you would use other image formats, such as PNG or JPEG. You can create and edit an SVG in a visual editor. You can embed it in web pages as an image.

But SVG is more than an image. It is a structured document containing markup elements, text, and style instructions. While other image formats tell the computer which color to draw at which point on the screen, SVG tells the computer how to rebuild the graphic from its component parts. That has two main consequences:

- The final appearance of an SVG depends on how well the software displaying it follows the SVG instructions. Cross-browser compatibility is often a concern.

- It is easy to edit parts of an SVG—to add, remove, or modify particular pieces—without changing the rest. You can do this in your editor, but you can also do it dynamically in your web browser to create animated or interactive graphics.

SVG Is Always Open Source

Not only is an SVG a set of coded instructions for a computer, it is also a human-readable text file. You can edit your SVG in a text editor. Even better, you can edit SVG in a code editor with syntax highlighting and autocomplete!

The examples in this book all focus on the basic SVG code. You can, of course, use a visual editor to draw shapes, select colors, and otherwise fuss with the appearance of your graphic. But for full control, you will need to take a look at the actual code that the editor creates.

SVG Is XML (and Sometimes HTML)

The SVG code you view in your text editor looks an awful lot like HTML code—full of angle brackets and attributes—but a standalone SVG file is parsed as an XML document. This means that your SVG can be parsed and manipulated by tools meant for XML in general. It also means that your web browser won't display anything if you forget to include the XML namespaces or mix up an important detail of XML syntax.

Nonetheless, when you insert SVG code directly in HTML 5 markup, it is processed by the HTML parser. The HTML parser forgives errors (like missing closing tags or unquoted attributes) that would halt the XML parser (or most SVG-only graphics editors). But it also ignores any custom namespaces, downcases any unrecognized attribute or tag names, and otherwise changes things up in ways you might not expect.

SVG Is Squishable

The syntax for SVG was—for the most part—designed to make it easy to read and understand, not to make it compact. This can make certain SVG files seem rather verbose and redundant. However, it also makes SVG very suitable for gzip compression, which should always be used when serving SVG on the Web. It will usually reduce file sizes by more than half, sometimes much more. If storing a gzipped SVG on a regular file server, it is typical to use the *.svgz* extension.

SVG is also bloatable, which makes it squishable in another way. Most SVG editors add their own elements and attributes to an SVG file by giving them unique XML namespaces. A class of optimization tools has developed that will strip out code that does not affect the final result. Just be careful about the settings you use—optimizers can remove attributes you might want later if you're manipulating the code yourself!

Pictures Are a Collection of Shapes

So what does all that code represent? Shapes, of course! (And text and embedded images, but we'll get to those in a moment...) SVG has only a few different shape elements: `<rect>`, `<circle>`, `<ellipse>`, `<line>`, `<polyline>`, `<polygon>`, and `<path>`. Nonetheless, those last three can be extensively customized to represent any shape you can imagine, to a certain degree of precision. The `<path>`, in particular, contains its own coded language for describing the curves and lines that create that shape.

Images Can Have Images Inside Them

Each SVG is an image, but it is also a document, and that document can contain other images, using the `<image>` element. The embedded images could be other SVG files, or they could be raster images such as PNG or JPEG. However, for security and performance reasons, some uses of SVG prevent those external images (and other external resources such as stylesheets or fonts) from being downloaded. In particular, external files will not be used when an SVG is displayed as an embedded image (`<img>` element) or background image in an HTML page.

Text Is Art

The final building block used in SVG is text. But text isn't an alternative to graphics—the letters that make up that text are treated like another type of vector shape. Importantly for this book, text can be painted using the exact same style properties as vector shapes.

Art Is Math

The core of all vector graphics (shapes or text) is that the end result can be defined using mathematical parameters (the XML attributes) to the browser's SVG rendering functions for each element. The most pervasive mathematical concept in SVG is the coordinate system, used to define the position of every point in the graphic. You can control the initial coordinate system by setting a `viewBox` attribute, and you can use coordinate system transformations to shift, stretch, rotate, and skew the grid for certain elements.

An SVG Is a Limited View of an Infinite Canvas

There are no limits on the coordinates you can give for your vector shapes, except for the practical limits of computer number precision. The only shapes displayed, however, are those that fit within the particular range of coordinates established by the `viewBox` attribute. This range of coordinates is scaled to fit the available area (the "viewport"), with accommodations for mismatched aspect ratios controlled by the `preserveAspectRatio` value.

You can create nested viewports with nested `<svg>` elements or reused `<symbol>` elements; in addition to providing regions of aspect ratio control, these redefine how percentage lengths are interpreted for child content. Other elements use `viewBox` to create a scale-to-fit effect (as we'll see when we get to the `<pattern>` element in Chapter 11), although without re-defining percentages.

SVG Has Structure

The structure of an SVG includes the basic shapes, text, and images that are drawn to the screen, and the attributes that define their geometry. But SVG can have more structure than that, with elements grouped into logical clusters. Those groups can be styled and their coordinate systems transformed. But they can also be given accessible names and descriptions to help explain exactly what the graphics represent.

SVG Has Style

SVG graphics can consist solely of XML, with all style information indicated by presentation attributes. However, these presentation styles can also be specified with CSS rules, allowing styles to be assigned by class or element type. Using CSS also allows conditional styles to depend on media features or transient states such as :hover or :focus.

The strict separation between geometric structure (XML attributes) and presentation style (presentation attributes or CSS style rules) has always been a little arbitrary. As SVG moves forward, expect the divide to collapse even more. The SVG 2 draft specifications upgrade many layout attributes to become presentation attributes. This opens these properties to all the syntactic flexibility CSS offers: classes of similar elements can be given matching sizes with a single style rule, and those sizes or layout can be modified with CSS pseudoclasses or media queries.

Behind All Good Markup Is a Great DOM

The SVG markup and styles are translated into a document object model (DOM) within a web browser. This DOM can then be manipulated using JavaScript. All the core DOM methods defined for all XML content apply, so you can create and re-order elements, get and set attributes, and query the computed style values.

The SVG specifications define many unique properties and methods for SVG DOM elements. These make it easier to manipulate the geometry of a graphic mathematically. Support for SVG DOM in web browsers is not as good as one might hope, but certain methods —such as determining the length of a curved path—are indispensable for SVG designs.

SVG Can Move

In a dynamic SVG viewer (e.g., a web browser) with scripting support, you can use those scripts to create animated and interactive graphics. However, SVG also supports declarative means of interaction, whereby you define the scope of an entire interaction and the browser applies it with its own optimizations. There are two means of doing this:

- Using animation elements in the markup, with a syntax borrowed from the Synchronized Multimedia Integration Language (SMIL)

- Using CSS animations and transitions of presentation styles

At the time of writing, scripted animation is supported in all web browsers, but may be blocked for certain uses of SVG. Declarative animation (SMIL and CSS) is supported in most browsers, but not all (Internet Explorer being the most notable exception). In addition, browsers are starting to implement the new Web Animations API, which allows a script to define and trigger an animation that will then be run independently, similar to a declarative animation.

SVG Can Change

Not only can individual SVG graphics change as you interact with them, but the definition of SVG can change too. The established standard (at the time this book was written) is SVG 1.1, but work is ongoing to develop a level 2 SVG specification with new features and clearer definitions of some existing features. Furthermore, because SVG uses CSS and JavaScript, and because it is heavily integrated in HTML, it inherits changes to those languages as well.

CHAPTER 2

The Painter's Model

If I asked you to draw a yellow circle with a blue outline, would it look the same as if I asked you to draw a blue circle and fill it in with yellow?

If I asked you to draw a red pentagon and a green square centered on the same spot on a page, would most of the image be red or green?

There are no hard-and-fast rules when you're drawing things by hand. If someone gives you ambiguous instructions, you can always ask for clarification. But when you're giving instructions to a computer, it only has one way to follow them. So you need to make sure you're saying exactly what you mean.

Even if you use SVG a lot (and we're going to assume you use it at least a little), you probably haven't given much thought to how the computer converts your SVG code into colored patterns on the screen. If you're going to really make the most of those colored patterns, however, you need to know how your instructions will be interpreted.

This chapter discusses the basics of the SVG *rendering model*, the process by which the computer generates a drawing from SVG markup and styles. It reviews the basic `fill` and `stroke` properties that define how you want shapes or text to be painted. The entire rest of the book can really be summed up as different ways you can specify fill or stroke values.

The SVG rendering model is known as a *painter's model*. Like layers of paint on a wall, content on top obscures content below. The SVG specifications define which content gets put on top of which other content. This chapter also discusses z-index and paint-order, two properties that allow you to change up the rendering rules. These properties are newly introduced in SVG 2, and are only just starting to be supported in web browsers. We therefore also show how you can achieve the same effect with SVG 1.1 code.

Fill 'Er Up with the fill Property

The basic elements and attributes in your SVG code define precise geometric shapes. For example, a one-inch square, positioned with its upper-left corner at the coordinate system origin, looks like this:

```
<rect width="1in" height="1in" />
```

A circle 10 centimeters in diameter, centered on the middle of the coordinate system, is created with the following code:

```
<circle cx="50%" cy="50%" r="5cm" />
```

 This book isn't going to spend much time on the geometry of the shapes you are painting. But as a reminder, Scalable Vector Graphics are often, well, *scaled*. Inches and centimeters will not necessarily match the distances on your real-world ruler. They can be affected by the resolution of your monitor, zoom level of your browser, and of course any viewBox or transform attributes on your SVG elements.

The scale affects all units equally, however; there will always be the same number of centimeters per inch (2.54) as on your ruler. In all except the oldest web browsers, 1in will also always be equal to 96px (CSS pixel units). It will also be equal to 96 of SVG's unitless user coordinate values, which are always interchangeable with px. Other SVG software is also switching over to this standard, established by the CSS Values and Units Module Level 3.

If you include either the circle or the rectangle markup (or any other shape or text) in an SVG without any style information, it will be displayed as a solid black region exactly matching the dimensions you specify. This is the default fill value: solid black.

The fill property tells the SVG-rendering software what to do with that geometric shape. For every pixel on the screen—or ink spot on the paper—the software determines if that point is inside or outside of the shape. If it is inside, the software turns to the fill value to find out what to do next.

In the simple case (like the default black), the fill value is a color and all the points inside the shape get replaced by that color. In other cases, the fill value is an instruction to look up more complicated painting code. Where to look it up is indicated by a URL referencing the id of an SVG element representing the instructions (a *paint server*, which we'll talk more about starting in Chapter 5).

 If you *don't* want the software to fill in the shape, the fill property also takes a value of none.

A final option for fill (and also stroke) is to use the keyword currentColor. This keyword always evaluates to the current value of the CSS color property on any given element. The color property itself has no direct effect in SVG, but in combination with currentColor, it has two main uses:

- To coordinate inline SVG icons with surrounding HTML text. The color property's primary use is for setting the color of CSS-styled text. An inline SVG graphic that uses currentColor will therefore inherit the text color from the surrounding HTML markup.

- To provide an indirect inherited style value for reused content. SVG graphics duplicated with a <use> element inherit styles, including fill and stroke, from the context in which they are used. By setting accent details on the reused graphics to use currentColor, this can be manipulated separately from the main fill and stroke when the graphic is reused by changing the color value on the <use> element.

By default, the fill is painted solid and opaque (unless there are different instructions in the paint server). The fill-opacity property can adjust this. It takes a decimal number as a value: values between 0 and 1 cause the shape's paint to be blended with the colors of the background. A value of 1 (the default) is opaque, while a value of 0 has much the same effect as fill: none. We'll discuss opacity in detail in Chapter 4.

When it is not clear which sections of the shape are inside versus outside, the fill-rule property gives the computer exact instruction. It affects <path> elements with donut holes inside them, as well as paths, polygons, and polylines with crisscrossing edges.

The fill-rule property has two options:

- evenodd switches between inside and outside every time you cross an edge.
- nonzero (the default) gets "more inside" when you cross an edge that is drawn in the same direction as the last one, and only gets back to outside again when you have canceled them all out by crossing edges in the opposite direction.

Example 2-1 draws a crisscrossed <polygon>, first with the default nonzero fill rule and then with an evenodd fill rule; Figure 2-1 shows the result. The shapes have a thin stroke around the edges so you can see them even when the shape is filled on both sides of the edge.

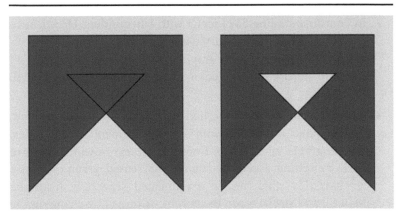

Figure 2-1. A polygon with nonzero fill rule (left) and with evenodd fill rule (right)

Example 2-1. Modifying the fill region with the fill-rule property

```
<svg xmlns="http://www.w3.org/2000/svg"
     xmlns:xlink="http://www.w3.org/1999/xlink"
     viewBox="0 0 400 200" width="4in" height="2in">
    <title xml:lang="en">Fill-rule comparison</title>
    <rect fill="lightSkyBlue" height="100%" width="100%" />        ❶

    <polygon id="p"
             fill="blueViolet" stroke="navy"
             points="20,180 20,20 180,20 180,180 60,60 140,60" />  ❷
    <use xlink:href="#p" x="50%" fill-rule="evenodd" />            ❸
</svg>
```

❶ The opening <svg> element establishes the coordinate system
   and sets the default size of the printed figure. A <rect> element
   adds a solid-color backdrop. For this simple SVG code, styles
   are set with presentation attributes.

❷ The basic polygon has fill and stroke styles, but the fill-
   rule property will inherit the default nonzero value.

❸ A duplicated copy of the same polygon is offset horizontally by
   half the width of the SVG. The copied polygon will inherit the
   fill-rule="evenodd" value set on the <use> element.

No matter how many times the edges or subpaths cross over each
other, each point is either inside or outside the shape. Areas are not
painted twice just because they are inside two different subpaths.
That may not seem like a relevant distinction when the fill is a solid
color, but it becomes important when the fill is partially transparent.

Future Focus
Filling in the Future

The discussion of the fill property in this section has focused on the way it is
currently defined in the stable SVG 1.1 specifications. The in-progress SVG 2
specifications will offer more flexibility to the way shapes are filled, most nota-
bly by allowing a single shape to have multiple fill layers. These proposed features will be discussed in more detail elsewhere in the book, in "Future Focus"
sidebars such as this.

Every shape in SVG, as well as text, can be filled—and will be filled by default. This includes open-ended `<path>` elements and `<polyline>` elements, which define a shape where the end of the line does not connect with the beginning. The fill region of these shapes is created by connecting the final point back to the beginning in a straight line. If it ends up crossing other edges as it does so, the `fill-rule` calculations apply.

> Open segments within a `<path>` are closed by connecting them back to the initial point on that subpath: the last point created by a move-to command.

Even a straight `<line>` element is technically filled in by default: however, because the return line that connects the end point to the beginning exactly overlaps the original line, the resulting shape does not enclose any area. No points are inside the shape, and so no points are affected by the fill value. You need to *stroke* the line if you want to see it.

Stroke It with the stroke Property

In computer graphics, stroking a shape means drawing a line along its edge. Different programs have different interpretations of what that can mean.

In SVG (currently, anyway), stroking is implemented by generating a secondary shape extending outward and inward from the edges of the main shape. That stroke region is then painted using the same approach as for filling the main shape: the software scans across, and determines whether a point is inside or outside the stroke. If the point is inside, the software uses the painting instructions from the `stroke` property to assign a color.

> Each section of the stroke shape is only painted once, regardless of whether the strokes from different edges of the shape overlap or cross each other.

The default for stroke is none, meaning don't paint a stroke region at all. Just like for fill, the other options are a color value or a reference to a paint server element.

Just as fill-opacity can modify fill, there is a stroke-opacity property to modify the stroke paint. Both fill-opacity and stroke-opacity will be discussed in more detail in Chapter 4.

There are many other stroke-related properties. We're not going to talk about them much in this book, but they control the geometry of the stroke region. As a quick reference, they are as follows:

stroke-width

The thickness of the stroke, as a length, number of user units, or percentage of the weighted width and height of the coordinate system. In SVG 1.1, the stroke region is always centered on the edge of the shape, so half the stroke width extends outside it.

stroke-linecap

The approach to use for stroking around open ends of a path or line; the default butt trims the stroke tight and perpendicular to the endpoint. The other options, round and square, extend the stroke by half the stroke width, in the specified shape.

stroke-linejoin

The approach to use for stroking around corners in the shape; the default miter extends the strokes in straight lines until they meet in a point. The other options are round (use a circular arc to connect the two strokes) and bevel (connect the two strokes with an additional straight line).

stroke-miterlimit

The maximum distance to extend a mitered line join beyond the official edge of the shape, as a multiple of the stroke width (default 4 times the width). If the stroke edges don't meet in a point within that distance, a beveled line join is used instead.

stroke-dasharray

A pattern of distances (dashes and gaps) for stroking and not stroking the shape. The default, none, creates a continuous stroke over the entire shape. The ends of each dash are affected by the stroke-linecap setting.

Figure 2-2. A polyline with various stroke shapes—left to right: round, beveled, and mitered line joins; top to bottom: round, butt, and square line caps; bottom row: square line caps and a thicker stroke-width

stroke-dashoffset
> The distance into the dasharray pattern at which to position the beginning of the path. Default is 0.

Example 2-2 mixes and matches various stroke line join and line cap options on copies of the same polyline, to generate the effects shown in Figure 2-2.

Example 2-2. Controlling the geometry of the stroke region

```
<svg xmlns="http://www.w3.org/2000/svg"
    xmlns:xlink="http://www.w3.org/1999/xlink"
    viewBox="0 0 400 400" width="4in" height="4in"
    xml:lang="en">
```

```
<title>Stroke join and cap styles compared</title>
<style type="text/css">
    .backdrop {                                         ❶
        fill: peachPuff;
    }
    .shapes {
        fill: none;
        stroke: indigo;
        stroke-width: 8px;
    }
    .join-round {
        stroke-linejoin: round;
    }
    .join-bevel {
        stroke-linejoin: bevel;
    }
    .join-miter {
        stroke-linejoin: miter;
        stroke-miterlimit: 10;
    }
    .cap-round {
        stroke-linecap: round;
    }
    .cap-butt {
        stroke-linecap: butt;
    }
    .cap-square {
        stroke-linecap: square;
    }
    .wider {
        stroke-width: 14px;
    }
</style>
<defs>
    <polyline id="p2"
        points="20,20 20,80 100,80 40,20 100,20" />    ❷
</defs>
<rect class="backdrop" height="100%" width="100%" />

<g class="shapes">
    <g class="cap-round">
        <title>Round line caps</title>
        <g id="row">                                    ❸
            <use xlink:href="#p2" x="0"   class="join-round">
                <title>Round line joins</title>
            </use>
            <use xlink:href="#p2" x="35%" class="join-bevel">
                <title>Beveled line joins</title>
            </use>
            <use xlink:href="#p2" x="70%" class="join-miter">
                <title>Mitered line joins</title>
```

```
            </use>
        </g>
    </g>
    <g class="cap-butt">                                         ❹
        <title>Butt (cropped) line caps</title>
        <use xlink:href="#row" y="25%" />
    </g>
    <g class="cap-square">
        <title>Square line caps</title>
        <use xlink:href="#row" y="50%" />
    </g>
    <g class="cap-square wider">                                 ❺
        <title>Square line caps with a wider stroke</title>
        <use xlink:href="#row" y="75%" />
    </g>
    </g>
</svg>
```

❶ For this more complex example, a `<style>` block of CSS rules is used to set fill and stroke properties on the elements according to their classes.

❷ The basic shape, a `<polyline>`, is predefined in a `<defs>` section.

❸ Three copies of the polyline are arranged to form each row in the comparison grid. Each one will have a different `stroke-linejoin` style.

❹ The row as a whole is then duplicated and shifted vertically, assigning a new `stroke-linecap` style each time.

❺ The final row also inherits a different value of `stroke-width`.

Unlike `fill`, the stroke region *is* affected by open-ended paths. Stroked `<polyline>` elements look different from a `<polygon>` with the same points. A `<path>` element (or subpath thereof) that is closed with a `Z` command has a line join at the final point, while open subpaths start and end with line caps.

Stroking the Fill and Filling the Stroke

When a shape has both `fill` and `stroke` paint, some pixels are included in both the fill area and the stroke region, and therefore have two different colors specified. As with all of SVG, the painter's model applies: if both colors are opaque, the color of the layer on top replaces the color of the layer below.

But which layer is "on top"?

By default, the stroke is painted on top of the fill. This means that you can always see the full stroke width. It also means that if the stroke is partially transparent, it will appear two-toned. The fill paint color will be visible under the inner half of the stroke region but not under the outer half.

Stroke markers—symbols that display on the corners of custom shapes—are painted after the fill and stroke, in order from start to end of the path.

In SVG 1.1, the only way to draw a stroke underneath the fill is to separate it into two shapes: one with stroke only, and then the same shape duplicated in the same position (with a `<use>` element), filled but not stroked:

```
<g stroke="blue" fill="red">
    <g fill="none">
        <path id="shape" d="..." />
    </g>
    <use xlink:href="#shape" stroke="none" />
</g>
```

The preceding snippet makes extensive use of inherited styles. The `<path>` itself does not have any fill or stroke values directly set; it inherits from its surrounding. The overall stroke and fill values are set on the containing `<g>`; one or the other is then canceled out on the nested group and the `<use>` element.

SVG 2 introduces the `paint-order` property to make this effect much easier to achieve. Its value is a list of whitespace-separated keywords (`fill`, `stroke`, and `markers`) that indicate the order in which the various parts of the shape should be painted. So the same effect could be created with a single element:

```
<path id="shape" d="..." stroke="blue" fill="red"
      paint-order="stroke fill" />
```

Any paint layers you don't specify in the `paint-order` property will be painted later (`markers`, in this case), in the same order they normally would be. This means that to swap fill and stroke, you only need to specify the stroke:

```
<path id="shape" d="..." stroke="blue" fill="red"
      paint-order="stroke" />
```

The stroke will be painted first, then fill, and finally any markers. The entire fill region will always be visible, even where it overlaps the stroke.

The default value of `paint-order` (equivalent to `fill stroke markers`) can be explicitly set with the `normal` keyword.

 At the time of writing, `paint-order` is supported in the latest Firefox (since version 31), Blink (since Chromium version 35), and WebKit (since March 2014) browsers. Internet Explorer/ Edge and older versions of the other browsers use the default paint order.

The ability to control painting order is especially important with text. Text in SVG can be stroked just like shapes can, to create an outlined effect. However, all but the thinnest strokes tend to obscure the details of the letters.

By painting the fill region overtop of the stroke—in a contrasting color—you can reinforce the shape of the letters and restore legibility. Example 2-3 uses `paint-order` and a thick stroke to create a crisp outline around heading text. Figure 2-3 shows the result in a supporting browser.

Figure 2-3. Outlined text with strokes painted behind the fill

Example 2-3. Stroking without obscuring the finer details of text

```
<svg xmlns="http://www.w3.org/2000/svg"
    viewBox="0 0 400 80" width="4in" height="0.8in"
    xml:lang="en">
  <title>Outlined text, using paint-order</title>
  <rect fill="navy" height="100%" width="100%" />
  <text x="50%" y="70"
        text-anchor="middle"
        font-size="80"
        font-family="sans-serif"
        fill="mediumBlue"
        stroke="gold"
        stroke-width="7"
        paint-order="stroke"
        >Outlined</text>
</svg>
```

If you relied solely on `paint-order` to achieve this effect, your text would be a blocky mess on unsupporting browsers, as shown in Figure 2-4. Some fallback strategies are in order.

Figure 2-4. Outlined text with strokes painted using the default order

One solution is to use the CSS `@supports` conditional rule to only apply the outline effect if `paint-order` is supported. In other cases, use different styling that provides legible text, if not the desired effect.

Example 2-4 provides a modified version of the code from Example 2-3; the styles have been moved from presentation attributes to a <style> block so that conditional CSS can be applied. The basic styles include a much narrower stroke when painting order cannot be controlled; the @supports block replaces this with the thick stroke and paint-order option.

Example 2-4. Testing support before using paint-order

```
<svg xmlns="http://www.w3.org/2000/svg"
    viewBox="0 0 400 80" width="4in" height="0.8in"
    xml:lang="en">
    <title>Using @supports to adjust paint-order effects</title>
    <style type="text/css">
        .outlined {
          text-anchor: middle;
          font-size: 80px;
          font-family: sans-serif;
          fill: mediumBlue;
          stroke: gold;

          /* fallback */
          stroke-width: 3;
        }

        @supports (paint-order: stroke) {
            .outlined {
              stroke-width: 7;
              paint-order: stroke;
            }
        }
    </style>
    <rect fill="navy" height="100%" width="100%" />
    <text x="50%" y="70" class="outlined"
          >Outlined</text>
</svg>
```

The result looks like Figure 2-3 in browsers that support paint-order (all of which currently also support the @supports rule). Figure 2-5 shows how the revised code looks in other browsers.

Outlined

Figure 2-5. Text with a narrower outline when paint-order is not supported

The `stroke-width` has been cut by more than half between Figures 2-3 and 2-5. However, the stroke only appears slightly narrower, because the inside half of the stroke is now visible on top of the fill.

If changing the appearance with `@supports` is not acceptable to you, the only alternative is to duplicate the elements to create one for stroke and one for fill. Depending on the way you are using your SVG, and how much control you have over its styling, you may be able to use a script to perform the conversion for you when necessary. Because `paint-order` is a new style property in CSS, browsers that do not support it will not include it within the `style` DOM property of each element. You can therefore detect these browsers and generate the extra `<use>` elements as required.

Example 2-5 provides a sample script that identifies elements by class name and performs the manipulations if required.

Example 2-5. Simulating paint-order with multiple elements

```
<svg xmlns="http://www.w3.org/2000/svg"
    xmlns:xlink="http://www.w3.org/1999/xlink"
    viewBox="0 0 400 80" width="4in" height="0.8in"
    xml:lang="en">
  <title>Faking paint-order with JavaScript</title>
  <style type="text/css">
    .outlined {
      text-anchor: middle;
      font-size: 80px;
      font-family: sans-serif;
      fill: mediumBlue;
      stroke: gold;
      stroke-width: 7;
      paint-order: stroke;
```

```
        }
    </style>
    <rect fill="navy" height="100%" width="100%" />
    <text x="50%" y="70" class="outlined"
            >Outlined</text>
    <script><![CDATA[
(function(){
    var NS = {svg: "http://www.w3.org/2000/svg",
                xlink: "http://www.w3.org/1999/xlink"
            };
    var index = 10000;

    var t = document.getElementsByClassName("outlined");      ❶
    if ( t &&
        (t[0].style["paint-order"] === undefined )){          ❷
        Array.prototype.forEach.call(t, fakeOutline);         ❸
    }

    function fakeOutline(el){
        el.id = el.id || "el-" + index++;                     ❹

        var g1 = document.createElementNS(NS.svg, "g");       ❺
        g1.setAttribute("class", el.getAttribute("class") );
        el.removeAttribute("class");
        el.parentNode.insertBefore(g1, el);

        var g2 = document.createElementNS(NS.svg, "g");       ❻
        g2.style["fill"] = "none";
        g2.insertBefore(el, null);
        g1.insertBefore(g2, null);

        var u = document.createElementNS(NS.svg, "use");      ❼
        u.setAttributeNS(NS.xlink, "href", "#" + el.id);
        u.style["stroke"] = "none";
        g1.insertBefore(u, null);
    }
})();
]]> </script>
</svg>
```

❶ The elements to modify are identified by a specific class name, "outlined", for easy access in the script.

❷ The style property of *any* element (here, the first element selected) can be examined to determine if it supports the paint-order property. A strict equality test (===) is used to distinguish an empty value (no inline style was set on the element) from an undefined value (the property name is not recognized).

❸ If the fallback is required, the fakeOutline() method is called for each element that had the class name. The forEach() array method is used to call the function as many times as needed. However, the list returned by getElementsByClassName() is not a true JavaScript Array object, so t.forEach(fakeOutline) cannot be used. Instead, the forEach() function is extracted from the Array prototype and is invoked using its own call() method.

❹ The fakeOutline() function will duplicate the outlined element with a <use> element, so it will need a valid id value; if it doesn't already have one, an arbitrary value is added with a unique index.

❺ The element is replaced by a group that is transferred all of its classes. This of course requires that all fill and stroke styles are assigned via class, and not by tag name or via presentation attributes. The insertBefore() method is used to ensure that the new group will have the same position in the DOM tree as the element it is replacing.

❻ A nested group will hold the original element, but will prevent it from inheriting the fill style.

❼ Finally, a <use> element duplicates the element, but cancels out the stroke style so that it only inherits fill styles. It is inserted into the main group as the last child ("before" nothing), so that it will be drawn on top of the version with no fill.

The result of running the script (in a browser that does not support paint-order) is shown in Figure 2-6. Although it appears identical to Figure 2-3, the underlying DOM structure is much more complex.

Figure 2-6. Text duplicated to mimic a stroke-first paint order

As you can tell, the script is rather convoluted for such a simple effect. Creating a more generic fallback script—a complete polyfill for the property—is even more difficult, as you need to account for all the different ways in which a style property can be applied to an element. Effectively, you need to re-create the work of the CSS parser, indentifying all the style rules it discarded as invalid.

In most cases, if the final appearance is essential in all browsers, it is easier to create the layered stroke and fill copies of the object within your markup, directly creating the structure that would be generated by the script:

```
<g class="outlined">
    <g style="fill: none;">
        <text id="el-10000" x="50%" y="70">Outlined</text>
    </g>
    <use style="stroke: none;" xlink:href="#el-10000" />
</g>
```

Regardless of whether you are hard-coding the markup or dynamically generating it with a script, the more complex DOM structure must be considered in any other scripts active in the document.

Future Focus
Additional Ordering Control with z-index

When different shapes (or other content) overlap, the painter's model again comes into effect: the graphic is painted element by element, and the last element shows up on top.

The order of the layers in an SVG document is therefore defined by the order of the elements in the code: shapes, text, and images are layered together in the exact order they are specified in the markup. In SVG 1.1, the only way to change the order in which elements are painted is to change the order of the elements in the DOM.

There are two main problems with this:

- It forces you to break up logical groupings of your content. For example, instead of using a <g> element to group a text label with the graphic it describes, you often need to move all your text labels to the end of the file so they aren't obscured by other shapes.

- You cannot change the visual layering of elements using SMIL or CSS animations; you must use JavaScript to manipulate the DOM—which can have a negative impact on performance and interrupts user-input focus.

In contrast, CSS layout (since version 2) uses the `z-index` property. Elements within the same CSS layout stacking context that overlap (due to fixed or relative positioning or negative margins) are ordered from bottom to top according to the value of the `z-index` property. The exact values aren't important, only the order.

SVG 2 adopts `z-index` for rearranging SVG layers. The default value is 0, and individual elements can be given positive integer values to pull them in front of the rest of the graphic or negative integer values to drop them behind.

At the time of writing, none of the major browsers have implemented `z-index` stacking for SVG elements.

The ability of `z-index` to reorder elements is constrained when certain style properties are used on a parent element. Filters, masks, and **opacity** values less than 1 all cause child content to be flattened into a single stack that is then layered as a whole.

Unlike in CSS layout, a two-dimensional coordinate system transformation would *not* create a new stacking context for SVG. This reflects the fact that transformations are a normal part of SVG layout.

Again, replacing the functionality of `z-index` with JavaScript would require a complex polyfill that scanned all stylesheets and calculated the final cascaded value for each element. It only gets more complicated from there: because most browsers *do* support the `z-index` property on elements controlled by CSS layout, you cannot use the **@supports** rule or simple JavaScript checks to determine whether it is supported for SVG.

Even with a working script, you would not be able to replace the most important benefit of `z-index`: the ability to separate the logical organization of your DOM from the painting order. Your markup might be written in a logical order, but if you are using scripts to reorder it, the shuffled version will be used by accessibility tools such as screen readers, or when copying and pasting text.

Unfortunately, therefore, current best practice is to organize the code so that elements are in the order you want them to be painted. For screen readers, you can indicate the logical grouping and order of elements with ARIA attributes: `aria-owns` to create a virtual parent-child relationship, and `aria-flowto` to define the reading order. Dynamic changes to the painting order of interactive elements are nonetheless likely to cause problems with user-input focus.

Take a Hint with Rendering Properties

One final class of style properties helps control *how* the browser applies paint data to graphics. After that, the rest of the book will focus on *what* you are painting in those shapes.

These final properties are considered to be "hints" from you—the author of the SVG—to the browser or other software converting your code into colored pixels. They offer suggestions as to which features you consider most important, if the browser has to compromise performance or appearance in some way. From most to least likely to have a consistent impact, they are:

`shape-rendering`
How the browser should adjust the edges of the shape to accommodate limitations in the screen resolution. There are four options:

- `auto`, the default, which instructs the browser to select the best optimization.

- `optimizeSpeed`, which indicates that fast rendering is the most important feature (probably because the graphic is being animated); the edges of the shape may not be drawn precisely. However, the exact changes may vary by browser and in many cases will be the same as `auto`.

- `crispEdges`, which indicates that the browser should maximize contrast around the edges of the fill and stroke regions. This usually means the edges will be *aliased* to the nearest pixel boundary, instead of having edge-pixels partially colored (*anti-aliased*). For vertical and horizontal lines, this can create a sharper image, but results for curves and diagonal lines are usually less satisfactory.

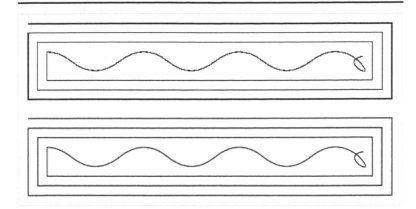

Figure 2-7. Effect of the shape-rendering property on a thin-stroked path: crispEdges (top) and geometricPrecision (bottom)

- geometricPrecision, which indicates that the browser should represent the exact shape as precisely as possible, and may use anti-aliasing to do so if required.

Figure 2-7 compares the crispEdges and geometricPrecision values for both straight and curved sections. Each shape consists of a single path with a 1px-wide stroke. The crisp-y straight edges are sharp and clean, but uneven: the stroke rounds up or down to either one or two full screen pixels depending on the exact position of the line (narrower strokes may round down to nothing). The curves are aliased into sharp steps. In contrast, with geometrically precise rendering, the same amount of color is allocated to each point in the path, but that color may be blurred across multiple device pixels if required.

text-rendering
How the browser should adjust the shape and position of letters within text. The four options are:

- auto (the default)
- optimizeSpeed, which is the same as auto in most browsers; for large text, this might turn off text layout adjustments (Firefox by default uses legibility adjustments for text larger than 20px).

- `optimizeLegibility`, which indicates that the browser should use all information at its disposal to adjust the rendering of individual letters and the layout of strings of text to make it easier to read. In practice, some browsers adopted this as a suggestion to turn on letter kerning and non-essential ligatures specified in the font file.

- `geometricPrecision`, which indicates that the browser should treat the letters as if they were geometric shapes, and draw them exactly without adjustments from resolution-based font hinting.

In SVG 1.1, the exact impacts of `text-rendering` were not well defined. It was not consistently implemented for SVG text; however, the property was adopted by some browsers to apply to non-SVG content for kerning and ligature control.

The exact impact of the different options will likely be clarified in future specifications (SVG 2 or a CSS module). The introduction of the `font-variant-ligatures` and `font-kerning` properties should help separate those features from rendering quality (although speed-optimized rendering may still cause those settings to be ignored). Figure 2-8 shows the effect of the settings on common system fonts in Firefox 39 on a Windows computer; optimized speed and optimized legibility look the same, but at small font sizes can be quite different from geometrically precise rendering.

`color-rendering`
How precise the browser should be about calculating colors, particularly when blending elements or generating gradients. The options use the standard hint keywords:

- `auto`
- `optimizeSpeed`
- `optimizeQuality`

Browsers do not currently change any behavior in response to this setting.

`image-rendering`
How the browser should calculate the appearance of raster images when the displayed size of that image does not exactly

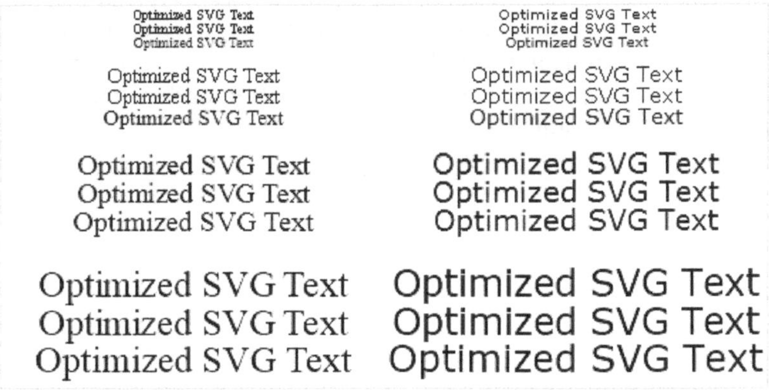

Figure 2-8. Effect of the text-rendering property on text of different sizes in Times New Roman (left) and Verdana-system fonts (right)— top to bottom in each set: optimizeSpeed, optimizeLegibility, geometricPrecision

match the number of pixels defined in the image file. In SVG 1.1, the options were the standard `auto`, `optimizeSpeed`, and `optimizeQuality`. However, in practice it became clear that there was not always agreement on how to create a "quality" scaled-up image. The algorithms that create the best results for photographs can create a blurred effect when the image contains sharp edges.

The CSS Image Values and Replaced Content Module Level 3 has adopted the `image-rendering` property and deprecated the `optimizeSpeed` and `optimizeQuality` values. The `optimizeSpeed` option is replaced by a `pixelated` value (scale up each pixel as a square). An additional option, `crisp-edges`, would apply some smoothing but maintain high-contrast edges.

At the time of writing this book, the `optimizeQuality` option, which had recommended smooth interpolation for photos, is covered under the default `auto` setting, reflecting the practice in existing browsers. There is some discussion of having a separate `smooth` property, to allow alternative `auto` options.

A distinct but related set of properties are the color-interpolation instructions, which we'll discuss in more depth in Chapter 3. The color-interpolation setting is not (supposed to be) a hint, but rather a requirement. However, a value of `optimizeSpeed` for `color-rendering` gives the browser permission to ignore the color-interpolation mode if it would slow down the rendering. In practice, however, low support for the color interpolation options makes this distinction irrelevant.

Creating Colors

In this chapter, we more thoroughly examine the options for filling your graphics with solid blocks of color. It starts by outlining how color works on the Web, and describes the different ways in which you can specify colors on the Web: from the very readable (but not very rational) color keywords, to RGB and HSL color functions.

The color basics will be complemented by a discussion of partially transparent colors in Chapter 4. Color concepts are also an essential prerequisite for the colored gradients that will be introduced starting in Chapter 6.

Misty Rose by Any Other Name

When writing code for other people to read (for example, the examples in this book!), it is nice to be able to use human-readable color names like red or gold or aquamarine.

It is even nicer if a computer can read the same values. And with SVG, they can. Web browsers and SVG editors should all understand red, gold, and aquamarine. They will also recognize more fanciful names like mistyRose, peachPuff, and mediumSeaGreen.

Where do these names come from? There are two sources: a very simple set of color keywords that was introduced in early versions of HTML and CSS, and a much more extensive set of keywords that were adopted by SVG (and later CSS) from the X11 windowing system for Unix computers.[1] Both sets of keywords are supported in all major SVG viewers. In addition, all but the oldest browsers in use also support them for other CSS properties.

As user-friendly as they are, the keyword system has a number of limitations.

For starters, the 147 keywords only describe a small fraction of the millions of possible color variations that a modern computer monitor can display.

The keyword choices are also rather inconsistent and arbitrary. The original web colors and the X11 colors sometimes conflict. The colors cyan (from X11) and aqua (from CSS 1) are identical—but different from aquamarine. The color darkGray (from X11) is actually *lighter* than the color gray (from CSS 1).

All the gray keywords are also duplicated using the spelling grey. But that's a feature, not a bug!

Nonetheless, some older browsers only accepted the American gray spelling, so use it for optimal support.

The X11 color names themselves are not particularly systematic, either: some have dark, medium, and light variants, while others have pale variants. And the variations aren't always logical: darkSeaGreen is not really *darker* than seaGreen, lightSeaGreen, and mediumSeaGreen; it's just *duller*.

Nonetheless, if you enjoy the ease of using readable color names, all the recognized keywords are listed in Appendix A along with their numeric equivalents. Figure 3-1 shows the resulting colors as an alphabetical patchwork from AliceBlue to yellowGreen.

The keyword names, like most CSS keywords, are case insensitive. You could write them in all caps if you feel very strongly about your colors. Most official references use all lowercase, but this book uses

---

1 If you're interested in how these keywords ended up as the standard for X11 in the first place, Alex Sexton has dredged up the history from old Unix forums. His presentation "Peachpuffs and Lemon Chiffons" from CSSConf 2014 can be watched online (*https://www.youtube.com/watch?v=HmStJQzclHc*).

camelCase (capitalizing the start of subsequent words) to make them easier to read.

The code used to create Figure 3-1 is provided in Example 3-1. It uses XMLHttpRequest to load a separate file with the list of color keywords in alphabetical order, and then creates rectangles filled with each color. Each rectangle has a child <title> element containing the color name; if you run the code in a browser, these will be available as tooltips when you hover over each color swatch.

Example 3-1. Creating a color keyword patchwork

SVG MARKUP:

```
<svg xmlns="http://www.w3.org/2000/svg"
     xmlns:xlink="http://www.w3.org/1999/xlink"
     width="400px" height="650px"
     xml:lang="en"
     viewBox="0 0 7 21" preserveAspectRatio="none" >   ❶
  <title>SVG Color Keywords</title>

  <script><![CDATA[
      /* script goes here */                            ❷
]]> </script>
</svg>
```

❶ There are 147 keywords in the SVG specification (including the variant spellings for gray), which is conveniently 7×21. The viewBox creates a grid of 7 columns and 21 rows, and uses preserveAspectRatio="none" to make that grid stretch to fill the entire <svg>.

❷ The graphic is drawn entirely by the script. Because this is an SVG file, an XML <!CDATA[…]]> block is required to contain any special characters in the code.

JAVASCRIPT:

```
(function(){
    var svgNS = "http://www.w3.org/2000/svg";
    var xlinkNS = "http://www.w3.org/1999/xlink";
    var svg = document.documentElement;

    var dataFileURL = "color-names.csv"              ❶
    var request = new XMLHttpRequest();
    request.addEventListener("load", draw);
    request.overrideMimeType("text/csv");
```

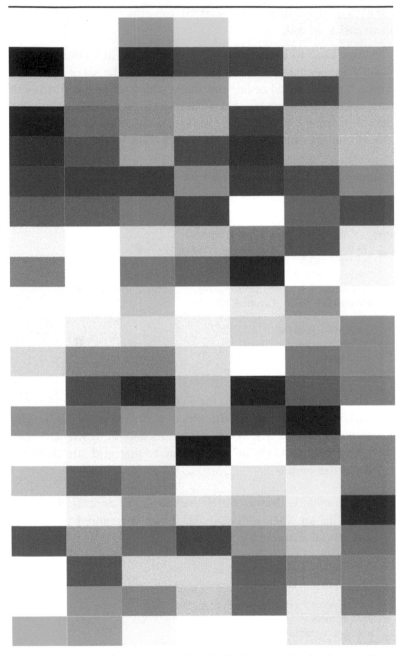

Figure 3-1. The colors associated with all the named color keywords

```
request.open("GET", dataFileURL);
request.send();

function draw() {                                          ❷
    var w = 7; //swatches per row

    var colors = request.responseText.split("\n");         ❸

    for (var i=0, n=colors.length; i<n; i++){
        var c = colors[i].trim();                          ❹

        var swatch = document.createElementNS(svgNS, "rect");
        swatch.setAttribute("width", 1);
        swatch.setAttribute("height", 1);
        swatch.setAttribute("x", i % w );
        swatch.setAttribute("y", Math.floor(i / w) );      ❺

        swatch.style.setProperty("fill", c);               ❻

        var tip = document.createElementNS(svgNS, "title");
        tip.textContent = c;
        swatch.insertBefore(tip, null);                    ❼

        svg.insertBefore(swatch, null);                    ❽
    }
}
})();
```

❶ The XMLHttpRequest object is used to load a separate datafile
with a list of color names. An event listener is used to call our
drawing function when the file has been loaded. The MIME
type, "text/csv", indicates that we're expecting a delimited text
file; that way, the browser won't try to parse it as XML.

❷ The draw() function is called when the requested file has been
downloaded. The datafile has each keyword on a separate line; it
was created by making a spreadsheet with a single column, and
then saving that as a comma-separated values (CSV) file.

❸ The request's responseText property is used to get the entire
file as a single JavaScript string. The split(*token*) method creates an array from a string, broken around that token—in this
case, the newline character, escaped in Javascript as \n.

❹ A for loop cycles through each string in the array (i.e., each line from the datafile). The trim() method gets rid of any errant whitespace.

❺ Each rectangle is set to a width and height of 1 in the stretched SVG coordinate system; the horizontal and vertical positions are calculated from the index and the number of swatches per row.

❻ The fill style property is set using the keyword name.

❼ The keyword is also used as the text content of a <title> element, which is then added as a child of each <rect> to create the tooltips.

❽ Finally, the styled <rect> (with its tooltip) is added to the SVG.

Looking at Figure 3-1, it becomes clear that the color keywords are not a representative sample of all possible colors. In addition to the duplicated grays, there are quite a number of off-white colors, and relatively few dark tones.

Sensibly, there are many more options for defining colors than the 147 keywords. To fully understand how custom colors work, however, we're going to first diverge into a little bit of physics and a little bit of biology.

A Rainbow in Three Colors

In physics, color is a property of the wave frequency or energy level of light. Visible light itself consists of a specific range of frequencies within the much wider spectrum of electromagnetic radiation. At lower energies, electromagnetic radiation creates radio waves; at much higher energies, it becomes X-rays.

The spectrum of light is continuous. There are no clear distinctions between colors, just a smooth rainbow from red through orange, yellow, green, blue, and violet—and beyond, to the ultraviolet lights that our eyes cannot see. Each color is associated with a specific frequency and energy level.

Just as you can tune your radio to be sensitive to one radio frequency and not others, so colored pigments are sensitive to specific frequencies of light. They absorb energy from light of the correct

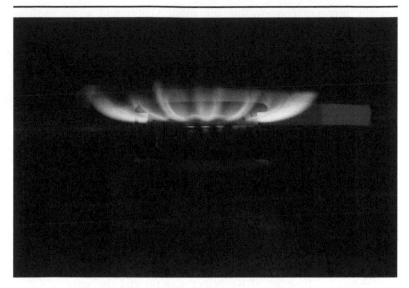

Figure 3-2. The blue flame of a gas burner (public domain photograph by Wikimedia Commons user Sapp)

frequencies—colors—and reflect other light. Similarly, chemical reactions that *emit* light do so at specific frequencies—colors—based on the energy released by the reaction. Heat-based light sources can nonetheless be "tuned" to adjust the color. As the efficiency of a flame's combustion reaction increases with different fuel or oxygen levels, the energy per photon (unit of light) increases and the color changes from a dull red, like glowing coals, to yellow, to a bright blue, like the gas flame shown in Figure 3-2.

The frequencies in light don't mix any more than different radio stations do. Each photon preserves its own energy level and color. You can separate the many colors of sunlight into a rainbow, by shining the light through a prism or a fine mist.

So why, then, does sunlight normally look white, and not technicolor? That's where the biology comes in.

Your eye is sensitive to a certain range of the electromagnetic spectrum—the part we call visible light—because of pigment molecules that absorb the energy from that light and convert it to chemical signals in your brain. Most human beings have four types of light-sensitive pigments in their eyes: a very sensitive but not color-specific pigment (responsible for night vision and some motion detection), and three color pigments. Each color pigment is sensitive to different but overlapping regions of the spectrum.

Our eyes, therefore, *don't* see color as a continuous spectrum of every possible frequency of light. They only see how much light is absorbed by each of the three colored pigments. Your brain compiles this information into the full range of colors that you see.

The pigments in our eyes are usually associated with the colors blue, green, and red, but that's an oversimplification: the green and red pigments are sensitive to blue light as well, and all three are sensitive to medium-green light. Another naming system describes them as S (for short wavelength), M (medium), and L (long wavelength), as the frequencies of light are usually defined by the light wavelength.

 Because light has a fixed speed, the frequency (number of waves per second) and the wavelength (distance between subsequent waves) are directly interchangeable. Higher energy light has a higher frequency and a shorter wavelength.

Because the eyes see color as a mixture of three different values, we can "mix" colors in art if not in physics. Figure 3-3 outlines how it works. When your eye is exposed to pure yellow light, *both* the M and L pigments are triggered in equal measure, but the S pigment is not. Your brain constructs the sensation of the color yellow from this information.

If your eye is exposed to an equal mixture of bright green and bright red light from the same location, the same pattern of pigment activation is created, and your brain still thinks it is looking at yellow.

Nearly every form of color communication in use, both print and screen, takes advantage of color mixing. The colors involved differ between print and screen, however.

Printed pigments, like the pigments in our eyes, absorb specific frequencies of light. When a pigmented ink or paint absorbs part of the light shining on it, it removes that frequency from the colors that reflect back to your eyes. Mix in another pigment, and another color is removed. This is called *subtractive* color mixing, and is the color mixing you learned in kindergarten. Yellow paint absorbs most blue-violet light, reflecting greens, yellows, and reds; blue paint

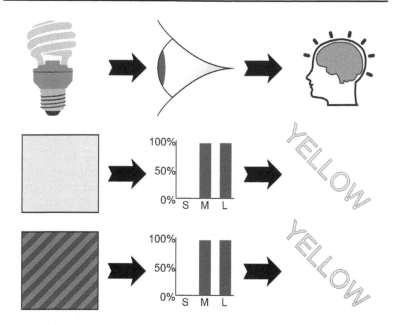

Figure 3-3. How the three-color system fools our mind (clip art icons from openclipart.org by users jhnri4, pnx, and benoitpetit)

absorbs the reds. Mix yellow and blue together, and the result absorbs both red and blue, reflecting back the green that you see.

As you might remember from kindergarten, mixing deep-colored paints often creates a muddy mess. Modern printers therefore use bright pigments that reflect more light than they absorb: cyan (blue-green), magenta (with both blue and red reflected) and yellow (red through green reflected). Blend all three together and all colors of light will be absorbed, creating a black ink; however, printers usually include an intense black ink separately. Graphics intended for high-quality printing use a CMYK (*C*yan, *M*agenta, *Y*ellow, and blac*K*) color model that defines each color as the combination of the four inks.

A computer screen, in contrast, shines light directly to your eyes. Multiple colors combine to increase the total amount of light that reaches your eyes. This is, therefore, an *additive* color model. Color computer monitors—like color TVs before them—use red, green, and blue light of frequencies that capitalize on the differences between the pigments in your eyes. The finely spaced red, green, and blue lights that make up each pixel are modulated to re-create nearly every pattern of activation in your eye that natural light could simulate.

 Because of the unevenly overlapping patterns of color sensitivity between the different pigments in your eye, there are some colors—certain saturated greens, intense blues, and deep reds—that can never be accurately represented by RGB light. Similarly, colored printing methods have certain natural colors that they can never completely re-create. The spectrum of possible colors that can be represented by a color system is known as the *gamut* of that color system.

Digital graphics systems have a fixed number of brightness levels for each color in a pixel. Early color computers had 4 levels for each color—including off—resulting in 64 (=4×4×4) colors overall. The original list of "web safe" color keywords used in HTML can all be mapped to a 64-color monitor. However, most modern computer displays support 256 levels (0–255) for each color, more than 16 million combinations. This is the basis of the color encoding used on the Web.

Custom Colors

There are two ways, in CSS or SVG, to define a custom color as a set of RGB values:

- Function notation, like rgb(*red,green,blue*)
- Hexadecimal notation, like #*RRGGBB* or #*RGB*

The values used in the function notation may be either integers between 0 and 255 or percentages. You can't mix integers and percentages—all values must be the same type.

The values in a six-digit hexadecimal format also represent the numbers from 0 to 255, but do so using hexadecimal numbers. In hexadecimal, each digit can be a value between 0 and 15, instead of only 0 to 9 (*hexa* is 6, *deci* is 10, so *hexadecimal* is a base-16 number system). The extra digits are indicated by the letters A (10) to F (15).

The three-digit hexadecimal format is a shorthand for colors where both hexadecimal digits in each color are the same.

Hexadecimal digits are case-insensitive in CSS and SVG; #ACE and #ace are equivalent (and represent a light blue color that can also be written #AACCEE).

The following color definitions all specify the same RGB values:

- rgb(102, 51, 153)
- rgb(40%, 20%, 60%)
- #663399
- #639

In some of the latest web browsers, you can also represent the color #639 with the keyword RebeccaPurple. The name was added to the CSS Color Module Level 4 in tribute to Rebecca Meyer, who loved the color purple and who died on her sixth birthday; her father, Eric Meyer, is a former member of the W3C CSS working group and the author of many books on CSS. It is the only color keyword that has been added since the SVG 1 specifications.

The CSS Color Module Level 3 introduced an alternative way of describing colors, based on a more universal color theory instead of the RGB computer monitor. The hue-saturation-lightness (HSL) color model describes colors as a mixture of a "pure" color and black, white, or gray. Specifically, the three values are as follows:

Hue
  The pure color, defined as an angle on a color wheel where pure red is 0°, pure yellow is 60°, intense green is 120°, and so on: 300° is magenta and 360° is red again.

Saturation

The intensity of the pure color (adjusted for lightness) in the mixture, where 0% saturation is a shade of gray and 100% saturation is a vibrant color.

Lightness

The level of white or black in the mixture, where 0% lightness is pure black, 100% lightness is pure white, and 50% lightness is the most intense color.

Unlike RGB values, HSL values are not always unique; different HSL combinations can create the same color. For example, any value with 0% saturation will be a gray, regardless of the hue, and any value with 100% lightness will be white, regardless of the hue *or* saturation.

 Two other color models are confusingly similar to HSL: the hue-saturation-value (HSV) model and the hue-saturation-luminance (unfortunately, also abbreviated HSL) model. The definitions for hue and saturation are the same, but the values for the third measure are not interchangeable. If you're trying to match colors defined in other graphics software, be sure you're using the same color model.

Figure 3-4 uses circular color wheels to demonstrate the relationship between hue angle and color, with different lightness values shown at different radii and different saturation values shown in separate wheels.

The brightest, most intense colors are created when saturation is 100% and lightness is 50%. In the RGB model, these colors have at least one color channel at 100% and one channel at 0%. In general, when converting from RGB to HSL:

- The saturation value is calculated as 100% minus the percentage of the *maximum* channel made up by the *minimum* RGB channel:

    ```
    S = (1 - min/max) × 100%
    ```

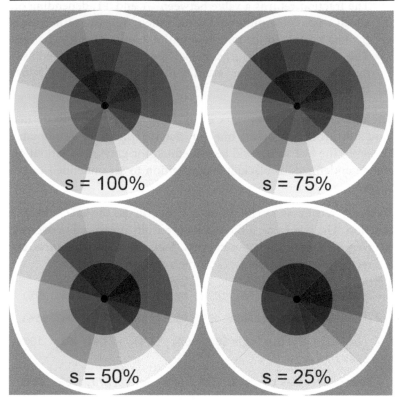

Figure 3-4. The hue-saturation-lightness (HSL) color model; hues increase clockwise from 0° on the right; lightness levels are 25%, 50%, and 75%, from the center; saturation values are as indicated

- The lightness value is the *average* between the minimum and maximum color channels (as a percentage):

  ```
  L = (min% + max%)/2
  ```

- The hue is determined from the ratio of the medium to the maximum color channels, *after* subtracting the value from the minimum channel from each:

  ```
  H =   0 + 60 × ([G-B]/[R-min]), if max is R
  H = 120 + 60 × ([B-R]/[G-min]), if max is G
  H = 240 + 60 × ([R-G]/[B-min]), if max is B
  ```

The fraction returns a value between –1 and +1, depending on which color is the minimum, which then increases or decreases the hue relative to the pure hue of the dominant color channel. The first formula returns negative hue angles for reddish-purples; these can be converted to the equivalent positive values by adding 360.

The conversion formulas work even if two color channels are tied (you can arbitrarily select one for the maximum or minimum). However, the hue values will be undefined for grays, and saturation will be undefined for black; it is convention to set undefined values to zero.

To specify a color as an HSL value in CSS, you use the hsl(h, s%, l%) function. The hue value, although theoretically measured in degrees, is given as a number without units. Saturation and lightness are always expressed as percentages. Some examples:

- The color lime, rgb(0%, 100%, 0%), is hsl(120, 100%, 50%)

- The color green, rgb(0%, 50%, 0%), is hsl(120, 100%, 25%)

- The color purple, rgb(50%, 0%, 50%), is hsl(300, 100%, 25%)

- RebeccaPurple, rgb(40%, 20%, 60%), is hsl(270, 50%, 40%)

 Although hsl() color functions are supported in all modern browsers (Internet Explorer 8 being the only browser in common use without support), they may not be supported in other tools for editing, displaying, or converting SVG. The same is true for the CSS 3 partially-transparent color functions, which will be discussed in Chapter 4.

Example 3-2 presents the SVG and JavaScript code used to create Figure 3-4. It creates <use> elements for each colored pie segment, and uses the style object to set the fill to an hsl() color value. Each piece is also rotated into place using the hue value as the parameter to a rotate() transformation function.

Example 3-2. Building an HSL color wheel using scripted SVG

SVG MARKUP:

```svg
<svg xmlns="http://www.w3.org/2000/svg"
    xmlns:xlink="http://www.w3.org/1999/xlink"
    width="400px" height="400px" viewBox="0 0 200 200" >
    <title>HSL Color Wheel</title>
    <defs>                                                    ❶
        <circle id="center" r="1.5" fill="black"/>
        <path id="inner" transform="rotate(-15)"
            d="M0,0L15,0A15,15 0 0 1 12.99,7.5 L0,0Z" />   ❷
        <path id="middle" transform="rotate(-15)"
            d="M15,0L28,0A28,28 0 0 1 24.25,14
                L12.99,7.5 A15,15 0 0 0 15,0Z" />
        <path id="outer" transform="rotate(-15)"
            d="M28,0L40,0A40,40 0 0 1 34.64,20
                L24.25,14 A28,28 0 0 0 28,0Z" />
        <circle id="edge" r="39" fill="none"
                stroke="white" stroke-width="2"/>
    </defs>
    <style type="text/css">
        text {
            text-anchor: middle;
            font-size: 8px;
            font-family: sans-serif;
        }
    </style>
    <rect fill="#888" width="100%" height="100%"/>           ❸
    <svg class="wheel" width="100" height="100" x="0" y="0"
        viewBox="-40,-40 80,80">                              ❹
        <use xlink:href="#center"/>
        <use xlink:href="#edge"/>                             ❺
    </svg>
    <svg class="wheel" width="100" height="100" x="100" y="0"
        viewBox="-40,-40 80,80">
        <use xlink:href="#center"/>
        <use xlink:href="#edge"/>
    </svg>
    <svg class="wheel" width="100" height="100" x="0" y="100"
        viewBox="-40,-40 80,80">
        <use xlink:href="#center"/>
        <use xlink:href="#edge"/>
    </svg>
    <svg class="wheel" width="100" height="100" x="100" y="100"
        viewBox="-40,-40 80,80">
        <use xlink:href="#center"/>
        <use xlink:href="#edge"/>
    </svg>
    <script><![CDATA[
        /* script goes here */
```

```
]]> </script>
</svg>
```

❶ All the shapes are predefined to be reused many times. They are encoded to be drawn within an 80×80 centered coordinate system—each complete wheel will be a circle with radius 40.

❷ The wedge-segments are created using path notation and a little bit of trigonometry. Each wedge will be a 30° segment, centered on the *x*-axis. To reduce the trigonometry, the wedges are defined with one edge flat against the *x*-axis and then are rotated back until they are centered over it. This way, the (x,y) coordinates of one end of each arc can be determined as $(r,0)$, where *r* is the radius. The coordinates of the other end are $(r\times\cos(30°)$, $r\times\sin(30°))$, which is equal to $(r\times0.866, r\times0.5)$.

❸ A rectangle filled with 50% gray (#888) provides a background to the image.

❹ Each color wheel is defined by an <svg> element that positions it within the image and creates the correct 80×80 centered coordinate system using its viewBox attribute.

❺ Each <svg> also contains the black center and white edges of the wheel, as these do not need any special calculations.

JavaScript:

```
(function(){
    var svgNS = "http://www.w3.org/2000/svg";
    var xlinkNS = "http://www.w3.org/1999/xlink";

    var wedge = 30; //angle span of each pie piece, in degrees
    var saturation = ["100%", "75%", "50%", "25%"];                    ❶
    var lightness = {outer:"75%", middle:"50%", inner:"25%"};          ❷

    var wheels = document.getElementsByClassName("wheel");             ❸
    var h,s,l,w,p,u;
    for (var i=0, n=wheels.length; i<n; i++){
        w = wheels[i];
        s = saturation[i];                                            ❹
        for (h=0; h < 360; h += wedge ) {
            for (p in lightness){                                     ❺
                l = lightness[p];
                u = document.createElementNS(svgNS, "use" );
                u.setAttributeNS(xlinkNS, "href", "#"+p );
```

```
                u.setAttribute("transform", "rotate("+h+")" );    ❻
                u.style.setProperty("fill", "hsl("+[h,s,l]+")" );  ❼
                w.insertBefore(u, w.firstChild);                   ❽
            }
        }
        var t = document.createElementNS(svgNS, "text" );          ❾
        t.textContent = "s = "+s;
        t.setAttribute("y", "35");
        w.insertBefore(t, null);
    }
})();
```

❶ The saturation values for each wheel are stored in an array,
   ready to be assigned to the individual <svg> elements. Because
   we don't need to do any mathematical calculations on these values, they are stored as strings including the % marker.

❷ Rather than using two separate arrays to hold the lightness values and the id values for the different wedge segments, they are
   paired up using a key-value data object.

❸ The nested <svg> elements are selected by class name.

❹ A for loop cycles through each <svg> and each saturation value
   by index. A nested for loop is then used to cycle through the
   hue values, incrementing them at each cycle by the 30° angle
   span of each wedge.

❺ Finally, a different type of for loop is used to traverse through
   all the data keys in the lightness object. The p variable gets set
   to the key string at each cycle (e.g., "outer", "middle", or
   "inner"). The key can then be used to access the value from the
   object, but it is also used directly to set the xlink:href
   attribute.

❻ The hue value is used to rotate the wedge into place; because the
   wheels use a centered coordinate system, a simple rotation piv-
   ots the path around the center of the wheel. The value of the
   transform attribute is a string representation of the transformation function, rotate(h); the parentheses are part of the string,
   not part of a JavaScript function!

❼ The `fill` is set, as an inline style property, by creating a JavaScript string that contains the CSS `hsl()` function—again, including the parentheses. The comma-separated list of parameters is created by grouping the values into an array; when an array is concatenated to a string, the string equivalent of each value is printed out, separated with commas.

❽ The wedge piece is then added to the `<svg>` *before* the existing first child element, so that it will be drawn underneath the black center and white rim declared in the markup.

❾ The final block of code runs once per `<svg>` and creates the text labels. They are inserted *after* all the other elements ("before" nothing, or `null`) so that the text is visible on top of the color wheel.

The introduction of HSL color functions was intended to make it easier to create sets of matching colors: the same hue in different lightness or saturation values, or the same lightness and saturation but opposite hues. Nonetheless, the HSL model was also chosen because browsers can rapidly convert between HSL and RGB values, and it has its limitations. The hue color wheel does not correspond well with the red-yellow-blue color wheels we know from mixing paint as a child. More importantly, the lightness model doesn't reflect the perceived differences in brightness between equally intense colors of different hues.

For these reasons, and because the history of computer hardware led to certain optimizations being standard in every graphical processor, a more complex color model is used in gradients and color blending.

Mixing and Matching

Your eye's sensitivity to light does not correspond directly with the brightness of the pixels on your computer monitor. You can detect changes between black and dark gray more easily than the equivalent change between white and light gray. With colors, a fully saturated blue light seems much darker than the same intensity of red, and neither is as bright—from your mind's perspective—as the full intensity of the green pixel components.

As a result, mixing equal proportions of red and blue (or blue and green) light doesn't create a color that matches what our brain considers to be halfway in-between. The same is true for nearly every other color combination, and also for shades of gray.

Computer monitors—especially the CRT monitors used when the Web first became popular—add their own distortion to the effective brightness of every color value. Without standardization, the same colors could look very different on different displays.

When blending between colors in computer graphics, most modern computer displays use the sRGB (sometimes called the *standard* RGB) model. It defines functions to convert RGB display colors into a standardized scale that reflects the perceived differences in brightness on an sRGB-compatible computer monitor.

The use of sRGB primarily affects the *blending* of colors. Figure 3-5 compares the results when using the sRGB model to blend colors or shades of gray, versus calculating the intermediary colors as based on simple linear arithmetic (shown in the bottom gradient in each pair).

The sRGB model makes numerous assumptions about the type of equipment and lighting that will be used to view the image. In addition, there is considerable variation from person to person in how colors are perceived—even before you factor in color blindness, a shortage of one or more of the light-sensitive pigments in the eyes. You may not agree that the sRGB color blend is better than the linear model, let alone that it is the best possible blend. But it has become the standard for computer graphics, particularly on the Web.

The sRGB model—and RGB color spaces in general—are less popular in print graphics because they cannot encode all colors that can be created on high-quality printers. The SVG specifications include ways in which alternative color definitions may be used to ensure high-fidelity printed color results. These alternative definitions use color profiles as defined by the International Color Consortium (ICC), a partnership of major digital graphics companies. ICC color profiles for SVG are not implemented in web browsers.

Figure 3-5. Color blending with sRGB color space (top gradient in each pair) versus the linear RGB blending (bottom gradient in each pair), for fully saturated colors and for grayscale

The sRGB color model is used by default for CSS and most of SVG. The SVG specifications define a property, color-interpolation, which could allow authors to switch to the mathematically simpler linear blending of colors (linearRGB mode). This might be preferable if your graphic consists of many very bright, high-saturation colors of contrasting hues. The sRGB blending model can generate unpleasantly dark in-between colors when blending contrasting bright colors, as can be seen in the topmost gradient in Figure 3-5.

None of the major web browsers support linearRGB color blending at the time of writing. Figure 3-5 was generated in the Apache Batik SVG viewer. Even Batik only supports linear blending for gradients, and not for blending layered, partially transparent colors.

The exception to the sRGB dominance is for filter calculations. SVG filters allow you to directly manipulate the RGB color channels, and by default these calculations run in linearRGB mode. There is much better browser support for setting the color-interpolation-filters property to sRGB, to turn *on* sRGB adjustments in filters.

Both of the color interpolation options are style properties that can be set on individual elements or the SVG as a whole, using presentation attributes or CSS rules. For gradients and filters, the property used is the one set on the gradient/filter element, not on the element being painted.

Certain filter operations, as well as SVG masking, use their own explicit means of compensating for the relative brightness of different colors. These operations are based on the *luminance* of colors. Luminance is a measure of brightness, and is distinct from the *lightness* value used in the HSL color functions. Instead, luminance is adjusted based on the fact that a fully saturated green or yellow is perceived as brighter than a fully saturated red, which is nonetheless brighter than a fully saturated blue.

The color-interpolation property *does* affect the conversion from color to luminance for masking in some browsers and is therefore different by default from luminance-based filters.

The luminance adjustments used in these tools have a similar purpose to the sRGB adjustments, but they are not equivalent. sRGB affects the scaling of grays, or of colors with different lightness values. The luminance weighting only affects differences in hue. Furthermore, the luminance factors create a linear scaling of each color channel, while sRGB defines a curved (*gamma*-adjusted) relationship between the color value and perceived intensity.

What does all this matter to you? Mostly, it is a warning. If calculating colors yourself as part of a script, or manipulating them with filters, be aware that simple mathematical averaging of R, G, and B values will create different results from colors created by the browser when blending gradients or combining partially transparent colors. Similarly, changing color hues using filters (luminance-adjusted, and sometimes sRGB-adjusted) will result in different colors than changing the hue value in the hsl() color function.[2]

This section has been mostly theoretical. The visible impact of the way colors are blended comes when working with transparency (the subject of Chapter 4) and with gradients (Chapters 6 through 9).

---

2 Thanks to Noah Blon for bringing my attention to the discrepancies between hsl() color functions and hue-rotate filter operations.

Becoming Transparent

Solid regions of color have their place, but for many graphics, you want to add a little bit of subtlety. Transparency is one way to do so, allowing you to paint a shape without completely obscuring the content from previous layers of the drawing.

Transparency is in some ways another facet of color, and in some ways a distinct and much more complex topic. This is reflected in the different ways you can define transparency, which we'll compare and contrast in this chapter.

One thing is constant when talking about transparency and web design: you don't talk about *transparency*, you talk about *opacity*. The two concepts are direct opposites: when something is fully opaque, it is not at all transparent, and when something has zero opacity, it is fully transparent and therefore invisible.

See-Through Styles

SVG uses three distinct properties to control opacity of basic shapes and text: `opacity`, `fill-opacity`, and `stroke-opacity`. All of these can be set with presentation attributes or with CSS style rules.

CSS Color Module Level 3 extended the `opacity` property to apply to all content. In addition, rather than introduce `*-opacity` properties for every facet of CSS painting, this module introduced new color functions. Partially transparent color can be defined using the `rgba()` and `hsla()` color functions, and then used anywhere in CSS where a color value is needed.

Opacity on the Web is always expressed as a decimal number between 0.0 (invisible) and 1.0 (solid, no transparency). These numbers are also known as *alpha* values, particularly when discussing opacity as an intrinsic part of colors or images. The a in rgba() and hsla() refers to the alpha channel. These functions take four values, instead of the usual three, with the fourth being the alpha value between 0 and 1.

The keyword transparent, which formerly had a special meaning for CSS backgrounds, has been redefined as a named color. Equivalent to rgba(0,0,0,0), it can be used like any other color keyword in browsers that support CSS 3 colors.

The final effect of modifying a graphic's alpha value depends on the method you use. In particular, the overall opacity property works in a significantly different way compared to the other options.

The opacity property applies to the element it is set on—even if that is a <g> group, <svg>, or <use> element—and is not inherited. It takes the final drawn result for that element, including all its child content, and makes it uniformly more transparent.

The opacity value is applied *after* determining the final color at every point where two shapes— or fill and stroke of the same shape—overlap.

Setting opacity to less than 1 creates a stacking context, flattening and containing all child content. In CSS layout, this can significantly affect the position of elements. It has no similar effect in SVG 1.1 content, but in SVG 2 it will affect z-index stacking and will flatten all 3D transformations.

In contrast, when you set stroke-opacity or fill-opacity, or when you use rgba or hsla color functions, the transparent effect is applied at the time each shape is drawn, to that colored section only. The stroke-opacity and fill-opacity properties are both inherited by default.

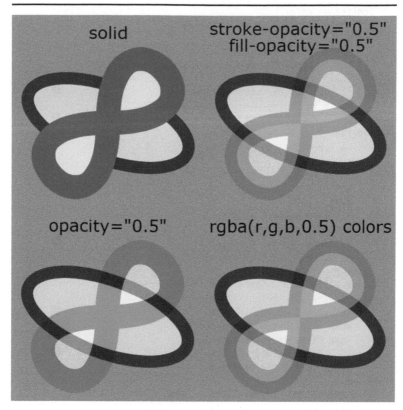

Figure 4-1. A green and yellow shape at full opacity and made partially transparent in three different ways

Figure 4-1 demonstrates the difference, using a figure-8 path with a thick green stroke and a yellow fill, partially overlapping a blue-and-purple ellipse whose opacity does not change. The green and yellow shape is shown at full opacity (top left) and set to half opacity using `stroke-opacity` and `fill-opacity` (top right), `opacity` on a `<use>` element (bottom left), or `rgba` colors for the stroke and fill (bottom right). Example 4-1 gives the code.

Example 4-1. Using different opacity options to control the transparency of your graphics

```
<svg xmlns="http://www.w3.org/2000/svg"
     xmlns:xlink="http://www.w3.org/1999/xlink"
     width="400px" height="400px" viewBox="0 0 200 200"
```

```
  xml:lang="en">
<title>Opacity Adjustments</title>
<defs>
    <ellipse id="background"
             ry="15" rx="35" transform="rotate(20)"
             stroke="purple" fill="lightSkyBlue"
             stroke-width="5" />                        ❶
    <path id="foreground" stroke-width="10"
         d="M0,0C0,-60 60,0 0,0 S 0,60 0,0Z" />         ❷
</defs>
<style type="text/css">
    svg svg {
        overflow: visible;
    }
    text {
        text-anchor: middle;
        font-size: 7px;
        font-family: sans-serif;                        ❸
    }
</style>
<rect fill="#888" width="100%" height="100%"/>
<svg width="100" height="100" x="0" y="0"
    viewBox="-40,-45 80,80">                             ❹
    <use xlink:href="#background"/>
    <use xlink:href="#foreground"
         fill="yellow" stroke="green" />                ❺
    <text y="-35">solid</text>
</svg>
<svg width="100" height="100" x="100" y="0"
    viewBox="-40,-45 80,80">
    <use xlink:href="#background"/>
    <use xlink:href="#foreground"
         fill="yellow" stroke="green"
         fill-opacity="0.5" stroke-opacity="0.5" />     ❻
    <text y="-35" dy="-0.3em"> stroke-opacity="0.5"
        <tspan x="0" dy="1em">fill-opacity="0.5"</tspan>
    </text>
</svg>
<svg width="100" height="100" x="0" y="100"
     viewBox="-40,-45 80,80">
    <use xlink:href="#background"/>
    <use xlink:href="#foreground"
         fill="yellow" stroke="green" opacity="0.5" /> ❼
    <text y="-35">opacity="0.5"</text>
</svg>
<svg width="100" height="100" x="100" y="100"
     viewBox="-40,-45 80,80">
    <use xlink:href="#background"/>
    <use xlink:href="#foreground"
         fill="rgba(100%, 100%, 0%, 0.5)"
         stroke="rgba(0%, 50%, 0%, 0.5)" />
```

```
        <text y="-35">rgba(r,g,b,0.5) colors</text>
    </svg>
</svg>
```

❶ The reused shapes are predefined in a `<defs>` section. The background ellipse has all its painting properties defined as presentation attributes.

❷ The foreground `<path>` has a specified `stroke-width` but will otherwise inherit its painting styles.

❸ A CSS `<style>` block is used to style the text labels and prevent cropping of the nested `<svg>` elements. Note that the 7px `font-size` will be interpreted within the local coordinate system, and so will not create unusually small type.

❹ Each nested `<svg>` re-creates the same local coordinate system in a different quadrant of the main graphic, so that the reused graphics can be positioned in the same way.

❺ The background element is reused as is within each sample, and then the foreground layered on top. In this first example, the foreground is given solid fill and stroke colors.

❻ The following `<svg>` elements position the content in the other quadrants of the graphic, and use different presentation attributes on the foreground `<use>` elements.

❼ For the `opacity` setting, it will apply directly on the `<use>` element as a combined group, instead of inheriting to the reused graphic.

Figure 4-1 also demonstrates some of the concepts we discussed in Chapter 2. The strokes are centered over the edge of each shape. When the stroke is partially transparent (due to `stroke-opacity` or an `rgba` color), this creates a two-toned color effect, with the fill visible under the inside part of the stroke.

Another feature to note is that the overlapping sections of stroke *do not* have a different color tone, compared to areas where the stroke only passes once. Conceptually, we like to think of strokes as if they were made by a marker or paint brush tracing out the lines. If that were true, these double-stroked regions would have twice as intense color, the way it would if you used translucent watercolor paint and passed your brush over the same region twice. However, the computer works by caculating out the total area of the stroke and then applying the coloring evenly, as if it was cut out of a sheet of semi-transparent plastic.

With all these different ways of controlling opacity, what happens when you combine them? The effect is multiplied. For example, the following circle has its fill made partially transparent in two different ways:

```
<circle r="10" fill="hsla(240,100%,75%, 0.5)"
              fill-opacity="0.6">
```

The effect would be exactly the same with the following code, because 0.5×0.6=0.3:

```
<circle r="10" fill="hsl(240,100%,75%)"
              fill-opacity="0.3">
```

It gets a little more complicated with opacity, because the transparency is applied *after* combining the other colors. Nonetheless, an opacity: 0.5 property still causes the alpha value of each pixel in the shape to be cut in half (multiplied by 0.5), after applying the opacity levels from all other properties.

Because the opacity property is applied using a simple mathematical adjustment of each pixel value, it can be efficiently implemented by the graphical processing unit (GPU) of most video cards. Changes in opacity can often be animated quite smoothly as a result, although not all browsers take advantage of this for SVG content.

Partially transparent colors, fill-opacity, and stroke-opacity do not create the same optimization, because they only affect parts of an element. However, if you are *not* animating the opacity, these properties can be more performant because they do not force the creation of a stacking context.

The Net Effect

As mentioned in Chapter 3 ("Mixing and Matching" on page 48), the color created by a partially opaque object is calculated using the sRGB model. According to the specifications, it should be affected by the color-interpolation mode, but sRGB is the default and the only mode supported in most software used to view SVG.

The final color displayed when layers overlap is generated by, first, scaling both colors according to the sRGB model, then taking a weighted average between the background and foreground—where the alpha value is the weight of the foreground—and finally reversing the sRGB scale. This calculation works regardless of whether the background color was created from a single element or from blending multiple partially transparent ones.

This method of blending colors is known as *simple alpha compositing*. In many graphics programs, it is also known as the "normal" blending mode.

Future Focus
Beyond Simple Alpha Blending

Many graphics programs define alternative blending modes that control how the colors from two different layers or objects are combined together.

In SVG 1.1, many of these blending modes are available, but only through filters. A new Compositing and Blending Specification created by the W3C standardizes the definitions of these blending modes for use by CSS and HTML 5 canvas as well. Two of the new CSS properties it introduces can apply to SVG: `mix-blend-mode` and `isolation`.

The `mix-blend-mode` on an element controls how that element is blended into the colors behind it. There are 16 different modes (including the default, `normal`) that define equations for combining the RGBA or HSLA values of the element with the equivalent values for the blended background content.

The `isolation` property on a grouping element or `<use>` element limits how far the blending continues. Child content of an isolated element is blended together, but then that element uses its own blending mode to blend the result into the background. You explicitly isolate an element using `isolation: isolate`, but various other CSS properties will cause isolation, including setting `opacity` other than 1, using filters or masks, setting a blending mode other than `normal` on the group itself, or using 3D transformations. An inline `<svg>` element in HTML will by default be isolated.

At the time of writing, blending modes are supported in the latest versions of Firefox, Chrome, Opera, and Safari. They are not supported yet in many mobile browsers or in Internet Explorer, although they are "under consideration" for Microsoft Edge.

The colors created when using simple alpha blending directly correspond to colors in an sRGB gradient between the background color and the solid color of the object. The alpha value determines the distance along the gradient. If alpha is zero, and the object is completely transparent, the initial value of the gradient is used—in other words, the background color. If alpha is 0.5, the midpoint of the gradient is used. If alpha is 1 (the object is completely opaque), the displayed color is the same as the end point of the gradient—the foreground object's own color.

Figure 4-2 demonstrates this relationship by comparing a smooth gradient from red (#F00) to blue (#00F) with the result of layering blue squares overtop of a solid red rectangle, where the squares vary in their fill-opacity values.

It may appear to you as if the squares in Figure 4-2 were also filled with gradients, transitioning in the opposite direction. This is a well-recognized optical illusion. Your eyes and brain enhance the contrast between colors on either side of an edge. When a solid-colored element has different contrasting colors on each side—or a gradient on one side—the contrast enhancement is perceived as a gradient.

To confirm that you really are looking at a solid color, use pieces of paper (all the same color) to cover up the adjacent sections of the figure, until you only see a single, solid-color square.

Example 4-2 presents the code used to generate Figure 4-2.

Example 4-2. Using opacity to create blended colors that match gradients

```
<svg xmlns="http://www.w3.org/2000/svg"
     xmlns:xlink="http://www.w3.org/1999/xlink"
     width="400px" height="200px" viewBox="0 0 400 200"
     xml:lang="en">
    <title>Blending with opacity and gradients</title>
```

Figure 4-2. Blending colors with gradients and with opacity; the squares consist of a solid red rectangle underneath blue squares with fill-opacity of 0, 0.25, 0.5, 0.75, and 1

```
<defs>
    <linearGradient id="gradient">
        <stop offset="0" stop-color="#F00"/>
        <stop offset="1" stop-color="#00F"/>
    </linearGradient>
    <rect id="square" width="100" height="100" y="100"/>
</defs>

<rect fill="url(#gradient)" width="400" height="100"/>
<rect fill="#F00" width="400" height="100" y="100"/>
<g fill="#00F">
    <use xlink:href="#square" x="-50" fill-opacity="0" />
    <use xlink:href="#square" x="50" fill-opacity="0.25" />
    <use xlink:href="#square" x="150" fill-opacity="0.5" />
    <use xlink:href="#square" x="250" fill-opacity="0.75" />
    <use xlink:href="#square" x="350" fill-opacity="1" />
</g>
</svg>
```

Chapter 6 will introduce the `<linearGradient>` and `<stop>` elements used in Example 4-2 and describe how they can be adjusted to create different gradient effects. But first, Chapter 5 will explore what it means in SVG to fill one element with a URL reference to another.

Serving Paint

When the fill or stroke is more complicated than a single color (transparent or otherwise), SVG uses a concept called a *paint server* to describe how the graphic is rendered.

The paint servers are defined using their own SVG elements. Those elements—gradients and patterns—do not directly create any visible graphics. They are only used through the fill and stroke properties of shapes and text. However, by using XML markup to define the paint server, it can be infinitely variable: any SVG graphics can be used to generate an SVG pattern, including other patterns!

In contrast, when using CSS to style HTML content, all the information about how to paint an element must be contained within the CSS style rules. In CSS 2.1, the only way to create patterns was to reference external image files. Since then, CSS has introduced many graphical effects that were previously only possible with SVG, such as gradients and improved image positioning. Although the end result may look similar, the all-CSS syntax for these properties is quite different from their SVG equivalent. Throughout the rest of the book, the two approaches will be compared in "CSS Versus SVG" sidebars.

This chapter introduces the basic paint server model, and then demonstrates how it can be used in the simplest case, to serve up a single color of paint.

Paint and Wallpaper

A key feature of all SVG paint servers is that they generate a rectangular region of graphical content. This can be limiting at times, but it allows for underlying performance optimizations.

An SVG paint server doesn't need to know anything about the shape it is told to fill—it just slops on paint indiscriminately all over the wall. The shape itself acts as a mask or stencil that blocks off which parts of the paint actually reach the drawing, in the same way that a wall painter covers (*masks*) floorboards, ceilings, light fixtures, etc., so that only the wall gets painted.

Another way of thinking about paint servers—particularly when talking about gradients and patterns—is to picture the paint content as a large sheet of wallpaper. The shape is cut out from that sheet, as imagined in Figure 5-1.

Figure 5-1. A filled shape can be thought of as a shape cut out of a rectangular sheet of patterned paper

The computer doesn't use paper and scissors, of course; instead, as it rasterizes (scans across) the shape, for every point that is "inside" the filled region, the computer looks up the corresponding (x,y) point from the paint server. A paint server can therefore be any object that can assign a specific color value to each (x,y) value.

In theory, the "paint" could be anything: a single color, one or more gradients, repeating patterns, bitmap graphics, text, even other SVG files. In practice, SVG 1.1 has two types of paint servers, gradients and repeating patterns. However, those core elements can be used to create all of the options just mentioned, as the rest of the book will demonstrate.

Identifying Your Assets

The name "server" suggests an external source for multiple resources. Theoretically, you can create a separate asset file containing all your paint servers and reference it from the `fill` or `stroke` property, but this currently has poor browser support. More generally, the name *paint server* refers to the fact that each gradient or pattern object can serve paint (rendering instructions) to multiple SVG shapes.

 At the time of writing, external paint servers are only supported in Firefox and in pre-Blink versions of Opera that use the Presto rendering engine.

In order to use a paint server, you reference the paint server element using URL syntax, wrapped in the CSS `url()` functional notation. Because of the browser support limitation, this URL is nearly always an internal reference like `url(#myReference)`. The hash mark (#) indicates that what follows is a target toward a specific element; the fact that there is nothing *before* the hash mark indicates that the browser should look for that element in the current document. Specifically, it should look for an element with an `id` attribute that matches the target fragment (i.e., `<pattern id="myReference">`).

Thus, referencing a paint server with an ID of `"customBlue"` as a fill could look something like:

```
<rect fill="url(#customBlue)" width="100" height="100"/>
```

Because `fill` is a presentation attribute, you could also use a `<style>` block elsewhere in the document to set the value:

```
rect {
    fill: url(#customBlue);
}
```

The preceding rule would set all rectangles in the document to use that paint server, provided that the style wasn't overridden by more specific CSS rules.

Relative URLs in *external* stylesheets are always relative to the CSS file location, not the location of the document using those styles. This includes local URL fragments like `#customBlue`, which will never match anything if specified in an external CSS file. In combination with the lack of support for external paint servers, this unfortunately means that you cannot effectively use external stylesheets to set paint server references.

 Relative URLs are also affected by the `xml:base` attribute or the HTML `<base>` element; using either can cause your paint server references to fail.

In theory (or if you only need to support Firefox), if you had a set of colors that are predefined in a file called *brand.svg*, you could provide the relative path to that resource, then use the target fragment to point to the specific element:

```
<rect fill="url(brand.svg#customBlue)"
    width="100" height="100"/>
```

Or you could even provide the absolute URI to that same resource—assuming the external file could be securely accessed from your web domain:

```
<rect fill="url(//example.com/assets/brand.svg#customBlue)"
    width="100" height="100"/>
```

The lack of support for this option is unfortunate, because the server concept can be thought of as being just another form of asset library, a way of storing commonly used colors, gradients, patterns, masks, and other resources in a single file. For now, if you have paint servers that are used by multiple SVGs, you need to incorporate them directly in each document, either by using some preprocessing on your server or by using AJAX techniques to import them with client-side JavaScript.

Because numerous things might interfere with the ability to load an external resource—even separate from browser support—the SVG `fill` and `stroke` properties allow you to specify a fallback color value. The color is given after the `url()` reference, separated by whitespace, like the following:

```
rect {
    fill: url(brandColors.svg#customBlue) mediumBlue;
}
```

Or, using presentation attributes and hex color syntax:

```
<rect fill="url(brandColors.svg#customBlue) #0000CD"
      width="100" height="100"/>
```

If the referenced paint server cannot be loaded, the rectangles will be painted with the specified solid blue color.

Future Focus
Layered Fill Paint and Fallbacks

SVG 2 introduces layered fills or layered strokes, similar to how CSS box layout supports layered background images.

As with multiple background images, the multiple paint options will be specified using a comma-separated list of layers from top to bottom. A fallback color will still be allowed, at the end of the list, separated by whitespace.

Unlike with the CSS **background** shorthand—which sets both the list of **background-image** values and the single **background-color** value—that final color would not normally be drawn underneath the other layers.

A sample declaration would look something like the following:

```
.typeA {
    fill: url(#pattern1), url(#gradient) mediumBlue;
}
.typeB {
    fill: url(#pattern2), url(#gradient) darkSeaGreen;
}
```

If the paint servers are loaded correctly, the **typeA** and **typeB** graphics would be distinguished by different patterns layered overtop of the same gradient. If the paint servers could not be found (perhaps your AJAX script did not run successfully), then the two classes would be drawn with different solid colors.

If you *did* want a solid color to be drawn underneath a pattern or gradient, you would separate the color into its own layer using a comma:

```
.typeA {
    fill: url(#pattern), mediumBlue;
}
.typeB {
    fill: url(#pattern), darkSeaGreen;
}
```

In this case, both classes of graphics use the same pattern (which maybe adds a textured effect), but layered over different solid colors.

The Solid Gradient

Oftentimes, especially when working with commercial uses of color, a designer will give that color a specific name. The same color may show up in many graphics related to the brand: different versions of the company logo, heading text, product labels, and so on. Rather than having to keep a list of RGB values for each color, it is much easier to define them once, give them a name, and then use that name in the content. This also makes it much easier if you decide to change one of the colors later on in the design process!

An SVG paint server is ideally suited for this task. It can be referenced by ID in the `fill` or `stroke` properties of multiple graphics, but the actual color value is only specified once and can be easily updated (or animated, as we'll show in Chapter 14).

The original SVG specifications did not explicitly include a solid color paint server, but all browsers allow you to use a gradient with a single, un-changing color to this effect. Example 5-1 demonstrates this strategy; it uses `<linearGradient>` elements to define four named colors that are used in the branding strategy for the fictional company ACME. The colors are then used to draw a company logo, which is shown in Figure 5-2.

Example 5-1. Defining named colors for consistent branding using single-color gradients

```
<svg xmlns="http://www.w3.org/2000/svg"
    xmlns:xlink="http://www.w3.org/1999/xlink"
    xml:lang="en"
    width="100mm" height="50mm">                    ❶
    <title>ACME Logo</title>
    <defs>
        <linearGradient id="AcmeRed">                ❷
            <stop stop-color="#FF4022" />
        </linearGradient>
        <linearGradient id="AcmeMaroon">
            <stop stop-color="#80201C" />
        </linearGradient>
        <linearGradient id="AcmeGold">
            <stop stop-color="#FFFC32" />
```

Figure 5-2. ACME Logo using named colors

```
    </linearGradient>
    <linearGradient id="AcmeWhiteGold">
        <stop stop-color="#FFFCE0" />
    </linearGradient>
    <symbol id="AcmeLogo" viewBox="0,-40 160,80" >      ❸
        <path d="M0,0 L40,-40 L40,-20 L160,-20
                 L160,20 L40,20 L40,40z"
              fill="url(#AcmeRed)"/>                      ❹
        <path d="M16,-10 L35,-29 L35,-15 L155,-15 L155,-10 z"
              fill="url(#AcmeGold)"/>
        <path d="M13,-7 L16,-10 L155,-10 L155,-7 z"
              fill="url(#AcmeMaroon)"/>
        <text x="40" y="15"
              style="font-family:Arial; font-weight:bold;
                     font-size:20pt;"
              fill="url(#AcmeWhiteGold)">ACME</text>
    </symbol>
    </defs>
    <use xlink:href="#AcmeLogo" />                        ❺
</svg>
```

❶   The SVG does not have a `viewBox`; scaling is controlled by the
    `<symbol>` element that contains the logo. However, default
    `width` and `height` values ensure that the image has the correct
    intrinsic aspect ratio and a reasonable default size when embed-
    ded in other web pages.

❷   The company has four brand colors, AcmeRed, AcmeMaroon,
    AcmeGold, and AcmeWhiteGold. Each color is defined as a

paint-server using a `<linearGradient>` with a single `<stop>` element.

❸ The logo itself is defined inside a `<symbol>` element for easy reuse in other graphics. The `viewBox` creates a coordinate system that is centered on the vertical axis.

❹ Each shape within the symbol uses one of the predefined paint servers to set the `fill` color.

❺ The logo is drawn within the SVG with a `<use>` element. The `<use>` element does not have any positioning or sizing attributes, so the reused `<symbol>` will scale to fill the entire SVG area.

Examining the gradients more closely, each consists of two elements, `<linearGradient>` and `<stop>`:

```
<linearGradient id="AcmeRed">
    <stop stop-color="#FF4022" />
</linearGradient>
```

The `<linearGradient>` defines the paint server, and gives it the `id` value that will be used to reference it. This gradient element is also a container for the `<stop>` element that defines the color. For a normal gradient, there would be multiple stops defining the initial, final, and intermediary colors.

The color is specified using the `stop-color` presentation attribute. There is also a `stop-opacity` presentation attribute, similar to `fill-opacity` or `stroke-opacity`; by default, colors are fully opaque.

 Although Example 5-1 works as intended in every web browser tested, it fails in Apache Batik, which is more strict on syntax. To make it work, the `<stop>` elements also require an `offset` attribute, which we'll discuss in "Gradiated Gradients" on page 75.

Because the colors are defined in a single location, they can be changed easily and consistently, or animated uniformly. Because `stop-color` is a presentation attribute, you don't even need to edit the XML to change the color; you can override it with CSS rules.

Figure 5-3. ACME Logo using named colors, converted to mono-chrome

As a result, you can use conditional CSS rules to change the color. A stylesheet with media queries can be used to assign print colors for high-quality printers, or for grayscale printing. Because the color is used by reference in the rest of the graphic, the stylesheet does not need to identify all the elements that use each color, nor does it need to distinguish between `fill` and `stroke` values.

 Although `stop-color` is a presentation attribute, it is not inherited by default. It must be explicitly set on the `<stop>` element, either directly or by using the `inherit` keyword.

Example 5-2 gives a sample set of print styles. For color printing, it redefines the colors using HSL notation, which can then be mapped to the full color gamut used on the print device. For monochrome printing, it assigns each color to a shade of gray that will create stronger contrast than if the colors were converted to gray automatically. The grayscale version is shown in Figure 5-3.

Example 5-2. Redefining named colors for print graphics

```
@media print AND (color) {
    #AcmeRed stop        { stop-color: hsl(10, 100%, 60%); }
    #AcmeMaroon stop     { stop-color: hsl( 0,  65%, 30%); }
    #AcmeGold stop       { stop-color: hsl(60, 100%, 60%); }
    #AcmeWhiteGold stop  { stop-color: hsl(55, 100%, 90%); }
```

```
}
@media print AND (monochrome) {
    #AcmeRed stop        { stop-color: #555; }
    #AcmeMaroon stop     { stop-color: #222; }
    #AcmeGold stop       { stop-color: #DDD; }
    #AcmeWhiteGold stop { stop-color: #FFF; }
}
```

 Although most browsers correctly apply CSS print styles when printing a web page, they do not always apply monochrome styles when the user chooses to print in black and white on a color printer.

Using paint servers to name nonstandard colors in this way has the additional advantage that it makes your code easier for others to read. By using meaningful id values, the color and purpose of each element becomes apparent to any programmer who has to adapt your work in the future.

Future Focus
The <solidcolor> Paint Server

Named color paint servers have many benefits. However, using a single-color gradient to create a named color is a bit of a hack; it certainly was not the original purpose of these elements.

SVG 2 therefore uses the <solidcolor> element to create a single-color paint server with no hackery. It uses the solid-color and solid-opacity presentation attributes to set the color value.

Using <solidcolor> elements, the four brand colors from Example 5-1 could be defined as follows:

```
<solidcolor id="AcmeRed"        solid-color="#FF4022" />
<solidcolor id="AcmeMaroon"     solid-color="#80201C" />
<solidcolor id="AcmeGold"       solid-color="#FFFC32" />
<solidcolor id="AcmeWhiteGold" solid-color="#FFFCE0" />
```

This not only reduces the amount of markup, it also makes the purpose of your code more readily apparent.

The <solidColor> element (note the capital C!) was included in the SVG Tiny 1.2 specification, so it is supported in some graphics programs; you would

---

need to explicitly set the **version="1.2"** attribute on the root **<svg>** element. (In contrast, web browsers ignore **version** and use the latest spec for all SVG content.) The latest draft SVG 2 specification changes the capitalization to make the element more HTML-friendly, which unfortunately breaks compatibility in case-sensitive XML viewers.

At the time of writing, neither **<solidColor>** nor **<solidcolor>** are supported in the stable version of any major web browser. However, an implementation is under development in Firefox.

CHAPTER 6

Simple Gradients

Vector graphics are often thought of as "line drawings," with sharp edges and consistent blocks of color. That clean, minimalist style can often be just what your design needs. But a complete graphics language should also have the option to create soft edges and color transitions. Gradients are the simplest way to create these effects in SVG.

Gradients consist of smooth transitions from one color or opacity state to another. SVG currently supports two types of gradients: linear gradients, where each color in the transition is stretched out along parallel lines, and radial gradients, where each color makes a circular shape.

This chapter introduces the basic structure of the SVG gradient elements, and the different color transitions they can create. The SVG syntax will be contrasted with the CSS syntax to create similar effects. For now, the examples will use the default orientation and scale of each gradient, and will use them to fill simple rectangles. The following chapters will explore the full flexibility of SVG gradients.

Gradiated Gradients

The single-color gradients from Example 5-1 demonstrated the bare-minimum markup for a gradient. However, they didn't use any of the features that create a gradiated result. For that, we'll need at least two color stops so that a color transition can be displayed.

The basic structure of a two-color linear gradient is as follows:

```
<linearGradient id="red-blue">
    <stop stop-color="red" offset="0"/>
    <stop stop-color="lightSkyBlue" offset="1"/>
</linearGradient>
```

The two <stop> elements define the colors that should be blended together to create the gradient; the result is displayed in Figure 6-1, used to fill a rectangle. Each <stop> has a new attribute, offset, that positions that color along the distance of the gradient. The offset value is expressed either as a number between 0.0 and 1.0 or as a percentage; here, the very beginning of the gradient is pure red and the very end is light blue.

Figure 6-1. Gradient with two stop colors

When you have more than two color stops, the spacing between the offsets controls the rate of change in the color, as shown in Figure 6-2, which uses the following asymmetrical gradient:

```
<linearGradient id="red-blue-2">
    <stop stop-color="red" offset="0"/>
    <stop stop-color="lightSkyBlue" offset="0.3"/>
    <stop stop-color="red" offset="1"/>
</linearGradient>
```

Figure 6-2. Gradient with three stops at uneven offsets

If the first offset is greater than zero, or the last offset is less than 1, there will be blocks of solid color on either side of the gradiated section, as in the following gradient, displayed in Figure 6-3:

```
<linearGradient id="red-blue-3">
    <stop stop-color="red" offset="0.3"/>
    <stop stop-color="lightSkyBlue" offset="0.7"/>
</linearGradient>
```

Figure 6-3. Gradient with two stops, offset from the edges

This is effectively what happens when you only have one <stop>, as in the solid-colored gradients (Example 5-1): the offset on both sides is filled in with the same solid color.

 Offsets outside the range of 0 to 1 (or 0% to 100%) will be clamped to that interval.

The order of XML elements matters, and <stop> elements must be given in order from start to end of the gradient. If you specify an offset that is less than the offset for a previous stop, it will be adjusted to exactly match the previous maximum offset.

If consecutive stops have the same offset, you can create a sharp edge or stripe, as in the following code used to draw Figure 6-4:

```
<linearGradient id="red-blue-4">
    <stop stop-color="red" offset="0.3"/>
    <stop stop-color="lightSkyBlue" offset="0.3"/>
    <stop stop-color="lightSkyBlue" offset="0.7"/>
    <stop stop-color="red" offset="0.7"/>
</linearGradient>
```

Figure 6-4. Stripes created using a gradient

Transparency Gradients

The previous examples are all fully opaque color gradients, but we mentioned that gradients can control opacity as well. One way would be to use rgba() and hsla() semitransparent color values for stop-color. However, SVG has an easier solution, which allows opacity to be manipulated independently of color.

The opacity of each gradient stop is controlled by the stop-opacity property. As with all the opacity properties, the value is a number between 0 and 1. As with stop-color, the value is not inherited by default.

Using stop-opacity, you can create a gradient with a single color transitioning from opaque to transparent, or you can transition both color and opacity, as in the following gradient:

```
<linearGradient id="red-blue-5">
  <stop stop-color="red"         stop-opacity="0" offset="0"/>
  <stop stop-color="lightSkyBlue" stop-opacity="1" offset="1"/>
</linearGradient>
```

This semitransparent gradient is displayed in Figure 6-5 as a filled rectangle superimposed over top of the text "Gradients…". On the far left, the color is pure red, but it is completely transparent. As the gradient progresses to the right, it both changes color and becomes more opaque, obscuring the text more and more.

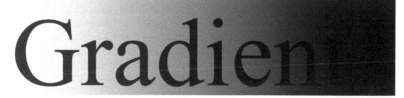

Figure 6-5. Semitransparent colored gradient

The only required attribute here is `offset`; `stop-color` automatically defaults to black and `stop-opacity` to 1 (100% opaque, or no transparency). We've been using the defaults to skip the opacity value in most of the colored gradients, but you could also skip the color, as in this gradient which transitions from transparent black to opaque black:

```
<linearGradient id="brightness">
    <stop offset="0" stop-opacity="0"/>
    <stop offset="1" />
</linearGradient>
```

This gradient is displayed in Figure 6-6, again using text drawn behind the gradient-filled rectangle to emphasize the opacity change.

Figure 6-6. Single-color opacity gradient

Controlling the Color Transition

More complex gradients can be created with more stops. For instance, the following will create a rainbow gradient, cycling through fully saturated colors from magenta to blue to cyan to green, yellow, red, and back to magenta again:

```
<linearGradient id="rainbow">
    <stop stop-color="#F0F" offset="0"/>
```

```
    <stop stop-color="#00F" offset="0.1667"/>
    <stop stop-color="#0FF" offset="0.3333"/>
    <stop stop-color="#0F0" offset="0.5"/>
    <stop stop-color="#FF0" offset="0.6667"/>
    <stop stop-color="#F00" offset="0.8333"/>
    <stop stop-color="#F0F" offset="1"/>
</linearGradient>
```

The resulting rainbow is shown in Figure 6-7.

Figure 6-7. Rainbow gradient using seven stops

The color stops were specifically chosen so that at least one color channel would remain maximized at all times, maintaining the fully saturated effect. The following snippet defines the exact same gradient, using HSL notation for the colors and percentages for the offsets:

```
<linearGradient id="rainbow">
    <stop stop-color="hsl(300, 100%, 50%)" offset="0%"/>
    <stop stop-color="hsl(240, 100%, 50%)" offset="16.67%"/>
    <stop stop-color="hsl(180, 100%, 50%)" offset="33.33%"/>
    <stop stop-color="hsl(120, 100%, 50%)" offset="50%"/>
    <stop stop-color="hsl( 60, 100%, 50%)" offset="66.67%"/>
    <stop stop-color="hsl(  0, 100%, 50%)" offset="83.33%"/>
    <stop stop-color="hsl(-60, 100%, 50%)" offset="100%"/>
</linearGradient>
```

 The color magenta—also known as fuchsia—is defined using both a hue of 300° (the start of the gradient) and a hue of –60° (the end of the gradient). Just as these are the same angle on a circle, they are the same hue on the color wheel.

Although the colors can be specified using HSL values, the colors are blended in straight lines through RGB color space, not by circling around the HSL color wheel. As mentioned in "Mixing and Matching" on page 48, the intermediary colors are affected by the

Figure 6-8. Rainbow gradients using red, blue, and green stops (top), and using magenta, cyan, and yellow stops (bottom)

sRGB model's weighting of color brightness. Once adjusted to the sRGB model, each channel (red, green, and blue) is then increased or decreased independently.

If we had not specified both primary and secondary colors, the midpoint between magenta (#F0F) and cyan (#0FF) would not normally be fully saturated blue (#00F). Instead, it would be a much lighter blue, with both the red and green channels partially lit. If you were to blend pure red (#F00) with saturated blue (#00F), the result would be a dark purple—with both color channels halfway between fully lit and off—not a fully saturated magenta.

Figure 6-8 compares the deep, muddy blends generated from the primary colors with the much lighter, spring-toned gradient from the secondary colors. The complete code for the figure is presented in Example 6-1.

Example 6-1. Comparing two multicolored gradients

```
<svg xmlns="http://www.w3.org/2000/svg"
    xmlns:xlink="http://www.w3.org/1999/xlink"
    width="4in" height="2in">
    <title xml:lang="en">Dark and Light Rainbow Gradients</title>
    <linearGradient id="primary">                          ❶
        <stop stop-color="#F00" offset="0"/>
        <stop stop-color="#00F" offset="0.3333"/>
        <stop stop-color="#0F0" offset="0.6667"/>
        <stop stop-color="#F00" offset="1"/>              ❷
```

```
    </linearGradient>
    <linearGradient id="secondary">
        <stop stop-color="#F0F" offset="0"/>
        <stop stop-color="#0FF" offset="0.3333"/>
        <stop stop-color="#FF0" offset="0.6667"/>
        <stop stop-color="#F0F" offset="1"/>
    </linearGradient>
    <rect width="85.714%" height="1in" x="0" y="0"
        fill="url(#primary)" />
    <rect width="85.714%" height="1in" x="14.286%" y="1in"
        fill="url(#secondary)" />                              ❸
</svg>
```

❶   Although the <linearGradient> elements *could* be contained within a <defs> block, it is not necessary—a gradient is never drawn directly regardless.

❷   Each of these gradients uses three colors, but four stops, in order to cycle back to the starting color at the end.

❸   The two rectangles are each six-sevenths of the figure wide (85.714%), offset by one-seventh (14.286%) of the width of the figure (one-sixth of the rectangle width), in order to align the parts of the gradient with approximately the same hue. Note that the hues do not perfectly align because of the adjustments from the sRGB model; for example, halfway between magenta and cyan, the color is still slightly purplish.

As Figure 6-8 demonstrates, the markup to define paint servers can sometimes be longer than the markup to define the shapes being painted. For better organization, the reusable content is usually placed at the top of the file, and is often grouped together within a <defs> (definitions) element. Alternatively, if a gradient is only being used once, you may wish to define it immediately before the shape it will be used with.

 For optimal browser support, always define your gradients earlier in the document than the elements that use them. Many versions of Safari will not correctly apply content defined later in the file.

CSS Versus SVG
Defining Gradients with CSS Functions

Gradients were introduced to CSS 3 with the Image Values and Replaced Content Module; the specification is a W3C candidate recommendation and CSS gradients are supported in all the latest web browsers. Support for older browsers can be extended by duplicating your style declarations with older, experimental prefixed syntax; there is no support in Internet Explorer versions prior to 10, or in the Opera Mini browser.

Although the final appearance of CSS and SVG gradients are much the same, there are fundamental differences in the way they are defined and used. In addition, there are more easy-to-overlook differences in the details, which we'll highlight over the course of the next few chapters.

The most obvious difference is in the way they are defined: SVG gradients are created with XML markup elements, while CSS gradients are created using functional notation within a stylesheet.

A simple linear gradient is defined in CSS with the `linear-gradient` function, the parameters of which are a comma-separated list of color stop values. Each stop consists of the color value and then the offset value, separated by white-space, as follows:

```
background: linear-gradient(red 0%, lightSkyBlue 100%);
background: linear-gradient(#F0F 0%, #0FF 33.33%,
                           #FF0 66.67%, #F0F 100%);
```

The default direction of a CSS linear gradient is from top to bottom, in contrast to the default for SVG which is left to right. (We'll show how you can change the orientation of both types of gradients in Chapter 7.)

If the offset values are omitted, the stops are distributed evenly from 0% to 100%. The following declarations are therefore equivalent to the previous gradients:

```
background: linear-gradient(red, lightSkyBlue);
background: linear-gradient(#F0F, #0FF, #FF0, #F0F);
```

If you specify some—but not all—of the offsets, then the unspecified values will be distributed evenly between the fixed points.

You cannot specify CSS gradient offsets using decimal numbers in place of percentages, but you *can* specify them using lengths with units or `calc()` functions. For example, the following CSS creates a background gradient that fades from black to white over the padding region and then stays plain white for the height of the element, no matter how tall that is:

```
padding: 1em;
background: linear-gradient(black, white 1em,
                      white calc(100% - 1em), black);
```

You can also use offsets greater than 100% or less than zero, and the colors will be adjusted as if the visible gradient was part of a larger one.

There is no direct way to set a **stop-opacity** value with CSS gradients, but you can use the **rgba()** and **hsla()** color functions to define semitransparent colors.

A more subtle difference between CSS and SVG gradients is that CSS does not treat paint servers as a unique resource type; instead, CSS gradients are defined as a standalone vector image with no fixed dimensions or aspect ratio.

CSS gradient functions are therefore used in place of **url()** references to image files, primarily within **background-image** lists (or the **background** shorthand). They can also be used within **list-style-image** or **border-image** properties, although browser support for these properties lagged behind support for background gradients.

CSS gradients cannot currently be used to replace a paint server reference in the **fill** or **stroke** property of SVG elements, although this will almost certainly change in SVG 2.

CHAPTER 7

Gradients in All Shapes and Sizes

So far, we've discussed how to create gradients, and how to position color and opacity stops in between the beginning (left) and end (right) of the gradient. Now, if all of your graphical needs involved gradients that went from left to right, then you'd be set. However, it's likely that you might want gradients that go from top to bottom, or perhaps at a 60° angle, or otherwise transformed.

This chapter discusses the two ways in which you can control the position of a linear gradient, and also how you can control its scale. We're going to assume you're already comfortable with basic SVG shape elements (particularly <line>), coordinate systems, and transformations. There are a number of tricky little distinctions to be aware of, and once again there are details that differ between SVG and CSS, so we'll be highlighting those as well.

One thing we can't do much about is the significant quality differences between web browsers when it comes to how smoothly gradients are rendered. Particularly when using sharp color transitions, be sure to test your code to see if the results are acceptable.

The Gradient Vector

The first approach to positioning a gradient uses x1, y1, x2, and y2 attributes to position the start and end of the gradient, similar to drawing a line. By default, x2 is 100% and the other attributes are 0. If you drew a line with these attributes, it would go from left to right across the top of the drawing:

```
<line x1="0" y1="0" x2="100%" y2="0" />
```

In contrast, if you wanted a diagonal line from the top left to the bottom right, you would use the following:

```
<line x1="0" y1="0" x2="100%" y2="100%" />
```

What do the same attributes mean for a linear gradient? The line they define is known as the *gradient vector*. Stop offsets—and the blended values in between them—are measured according to the distance along that line. The colors are then extended infinitely to either side of the line. So for the following gradient, the blue stop is in the top left corner (the point defined by x1 and y1), while the green stop is in the bottom right corner (defined by x2 and y2):

```
<linearGradient id="blue-green"
                x1="0" y1="0" x2="100%" y2="100%" >
    <stop stop-color="blue" offset="0"/>
    <stop stop-color="darkSeaGreen" offset="1"/>
</linearGradient>
```

You can of course take advantage of the default values for the attributes, and write the same gradient using only the following attributes:

```
<linearGradient id="blue-green" y2="100%" >
```

Figure 7-1 shows rectangles filled with linear gradients using all possible combinations of 0% and 100% for the gradient vector attributes, except for the combinations that would make the start and end points the same. Each column starts the vector in a different corner—defined by the (*x1,y1*) values—and then each row uses a different end point.

 If the start and end points of the gradient vector are the same, the shape will be filled with a solid color. *Which* solid color, however, is currently dependent on the browser. The SVG specifications say that the entire area should be painted with the color of the *last* gradient stop, but at the time of writing, Blink and WebKit browsers and Internet Explorer use the *first* gradient stop.

Example 7-1 presents part of the code used to draw Figure 7-1. The code makes use of a convenient shorthand for gradients: if you use the xlink:href attribute of one gradient to reference another, the new gradient is built by starting from the old one and then changing

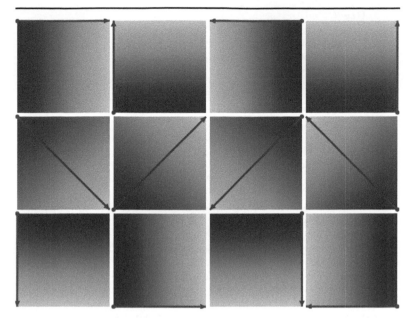

Figure 7-1. Gradients defined with different gradient vectors

it to match any new attributes. If the new gradient does not have any `<stop>` elements—as in the example—the stops from the referenced gradient are used.

The `xlink:href` value is a URL, but according to the SVG 1.1 specifications should point to an element in the same document. Firefox, however, supports links to gradients defined in external files.

The example then redraws each gradient vector as a line overtop the gradient; line markers are used to draw arrows at the end of the line so you can tell which way it is pointing.

Example 7-1. Using attributes to position the gradient vector

```
<svg xmlns="http://www.w3.org/2000/svg"
    xmlns:xlink="http://www.w3.org/1999/xlink"
    width="400px" height="300px" viewBox="0 0 400 300">
  <title>Same Gradient, Different Vectors</title>
  <style type="text/css">
```

```
        line {
            stroke: darkMagenta;                    ❶
            stroke-width: 2;
            marker-start: url(#start);
            marker-end: url(#end);
        }
        marker {
            fill: darkMagenta;
            stroke: none;                            ❷
        }
        svg {
            overflow: visible;
        }
    </style>
    <defs>
      <linearGradient id="blue-green" >            ❸
          <stop stop-color="blue" offset="0"/>
          <stop stop-color="darkSeaGreen" offset="1"/>
      </linearGradient>
      <marker id="start" viewBox="-2 -2 4 4">       ❹
        <circle r="1.5"/>
      </marker>
      <marker id="end" viewBox="-4 -2 4 4" orient="auto">
        <polygon points="-4,-2 0,0 -4,2"/>
      </marker>
    </defs>

    <g transform="translate(2,2)">                   ❺
      <svg width="1in" height="1in">                 ❻
        <linearGradient id="blue-green-1" xlink:href="#blue-green"/>
        <rect width="100%" height="100%" fill="url(#blue-green-1)"/>
        <line x1="0" y1="0" x2="100%" y2="0"/>       ❼
      </svg>

      <svg width="1in" height="1in" x="0" y="100">
        <linearGradient id="blue-green-2" xlink:href="#blue-green"
                        x2="100%" y2="100%"/>        ❽
        <rect width="100%" height="100%" fill="url(#blue-green-2)"/>
        <line x1="0" y1="0" x2="100%" y2="100%"/>
      </svg>

      <!-- 9 more samples omitted for length -->    ❾

      <svg width="1in" height="1in" x="300" y="200">
        <linearGradient id="blue-green-12" xlink:href="#blue-green"
                        x1="100%" y1="100%" x2="0" y2="100%"/>  ❿
        <rect width="100%" height="100%" fill="url(#blue-green-12)"/>
        <line x1="100%" y1="100%" x2="0" y2="100%"/>
      </svg>
    </g>
</svg>
```

❶ The stroke property must be set in order for a <line> to be visible; the two marker properties create the arrow effect.

❷ The markers are filled to match the color of the line stroke; the stroke is explicitly set to none to deal with an Internet Explorer bug, where markers inherit styles from the lines they mark.

❸ The first linear gradient is never used directly; instead, it defines the gradient stops for all the other gradients.

❹ The <marker> elements draw the arrowhead and the pivot point for the vectors.

❺ Each swatch is drawn as a 1-inch square (96px); to give a little padding, the swatches are positioned at 100px intervals, starting at a 2px offset from the top left.

❻ Each <linearGradient> uses the xlink:href attribute to duplicate the stops from the master gradient; the blue-green-1 gradient uses the default positioning attributes to create a left-to-right gradient.

❼ The <line> explicitly declares the same positioning attributes to display the vector.

❽ For the second (and subsequent) swatches, the gradient vector must be defined using explicit values for some or all of the positioning attributes.

❾ You should be able to figure out the rest of the code from the arrows displayed in Figure 7-1; it's much too repetitive to print it all in the book. If you wanted to go for bonus points, you could write JavaScript to generate all the elements instead of repeating the markup.

❿ For the final gradient, all of the positioning attributes are set explicitly to create a gradient vector the runs from right-to-left across the bottom of the rectangle. Note, however, that the final gradient looks exactly the same as the one with a vector from right-to-left across the *top* of the rectangle.

All of the gradient samples in Figure 7-1 extend across the entire square, from one corner to another. This is not required. If the vector does not cover the entire shape, the solid color will (by default) be extended on either side. This effect is similar to that created by offsetting the first and last stop away from the start and end of the gradient vector.

Changing the gradient vector length and changing the offsets have different effects when using repeating gradients, which we'll discuss in Chapter 8.

The start and end points of the gradient vector can also extend *outside* the 0% to 100% range; unlike with stop offsets, there is no clamping. However, at this point you may be asking "100% of what?"

The Object Bounding Box

In Example 7-1, we used nested <svg> elements to create local coordinate systems in which each rectangle—and therefore each gradient—took up 100% height and width. This meant that we could use percentages for the coordinates of the <line> elements and have them directly match the percentages used for the gradient vector.

In general, however, the shape that you are filling with the gradient will not take up the entire coordinate system. So it's important to understand that the values used in the gradient vector attributes are *not*, by default, measured in the local coordinate system that is used when drawing a <line>. Instead, they are defined in a new coordinate system based on the *object bounding box* of the shape being filled.

What's an object bounding box? For a rectangle like the ones used in Example 7-1 it's, well, the rectangle. Specifically, the geometric area of the rectangle itself, without any strokes. For any other shape, it's the tightest rectangle that can enclose that shape within its (possibly transformed) coordinate system. Again, the bounding box does not include any strokes or markers.

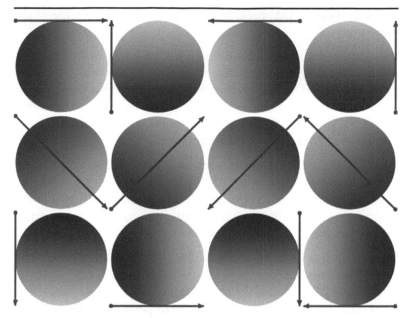

Figure 7-2. Gradients defined with different gradient vectors, used to fill circles

 If the shape has a height or width of zero after excluding strokes or markers, the bounding box will be empty and the gradient will be treated as if it was in error (the fallback color will be used). This can be a problem when stroking straight lines; we'll discuss workarounds in Chapter 13.

For non-rectangular shapes, the gradient vector might start and end outside the shape even if the vector start and end points are all within the 0% to 100% range. Figure 7-2 shows what happens if you replace all the rectangles from Example 7-1 with circles of the form:

```
<circle cx="50%" cy="50%" r="50%" fill="url(#gradient-id)"/>
```

Each circle fills up its local coordinate system as much as it can, but it doesn't reach to the corners. The gradient definitions haven't changed, so the gradient vectors *do* reach to the corners. The result for the diagonal vectors is that the stop colors at the start and end of the gradient are clipped out. To revisit our paint server analogies, the painted effect is scaled to fit the entire object bounding box and only later is the masking tape removed to reveal the shape underneath.

As mentioned, the object bounding box is an entire new coordinate system. Not only are percentages scaled to fit the box, but so are basic user units. One unit in the horizontal direction equals 100% of the bounding box width, and one unit in the vertical direction equals 100% of the height. In other words, you can use decimals between 0 and 1 in place of the percentages.

You can even use lengths with units, but—as with every other form of scaling in SVG—the length units scale with the user units. A 1px length equals 1 user unit equals 100% of the width or height under this new coordinate system. Every other length unit would equal many times the width or height of the shape.

Because units scale to match the width and height of the bounding box, a horizontal unit may no longer match a vertical unit. They did in Example 7-1, because the shapes being filled were square. As a result, the diagonal gradient vectors were perfect 45° lines. It also means that lines *perpendicular* to (i.e., at right angles to) the gradient vector were perfect 45° lines in the opposite direction, the same angle as a diagonal between the opposite corners.

This is important, because these perpendicular lines equate to parts of the gradient that have the same color. The stop color values are extended on either side of the gradient vector following perpendicular lines. When the gradient vector connects opposite corners of the box on a diagonal, the perpendicular line to the midpoint of the gradient—equivalent to a stop offset of 50%—stretches along the diagonal between the other corners of the box. Example 7-2 constructs a gradient with a sharp color transition at a 50% offset to emphasize this relationship.

Example 7-2. Creating a diagonal stripe from a diagonal gradient

```
<svg xmlns="http://www.w3.org/2000/svg"
    xmlns:xlink="http://www.w3.org/1999/xlink"
    width="100%" height="100%">
    <title xml:lang="en">Stretched Object Bounding Box gradients
    </title>
    <style type='text/css'>
    </style>
    <linearGradient id="diagonal" y2="100%">
        <stop offset="0" stop-color="white"/>
```

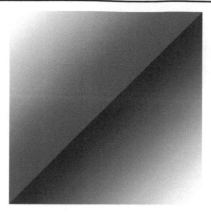

Figure 7-3. A diagonal gradient with a sharp transition at 50% offset, drawn in a square

```
    <stop offset="0.5" stop-color="red"/>
    <stop offset="0.5" stop-color="blue"/>
    <stop offset="1" stop-color="white"/>
  </linearGradient>
  <rect height="100%" width="100%" fill="url(#diagonal)"/>
</svg>
```

In Example 7-2, both the SVG as a whole and the gradient-filled rectangle are set to fill 100% of the width and height of the browser window or image area the SVG is drawn into. Figure 7-3 shows how it looks when drawn into a square region. The gradient vector is the 45° diagonal from the top left to bottom right, and the stripe at the 50% gradient offset makes a perfect diagonal from the top right to the bottom left.

If the shape (or more to the point, the object bounding box) that you're filling is *not* a perfect square, what happens? A diagonal is no longer a 45° angle. However, thanks to the stretched effect of the object bounding box coordinate system, the midpoint of the gradient still follows a diagonal line between the opposite corners, as shown in Figure 7-4.

The lines of equal color are no longer perpendicular to the gradient vector in the normal sense of the word—or at least, not in the outside coordinate system. In the stretched coordinate system, they have the same mathematical relationship between x and y coordinates as perpendicular lines normally have. In mathematics, this

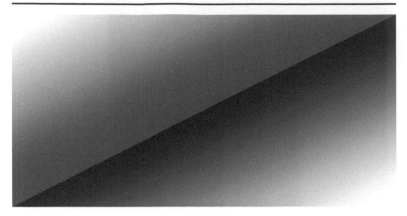

Figure 7-4. A diagonal gradient with a sharp transition at 50% offset, drawn in an oblong rectangle

"officially perpendicular" line is actually called a *normal* vector, but mathematicians have strange ideas about what is normal.

Object bounding box coordinate systems therefore create a non-uniform scale, similar to a two-parameter `scale(sx,sy)` transformation or a `preserveAspectRatio="none"` setting.

Drawing Outside the Box

If you were reading carefully, you would have noticed those sneaky little words "by default" not that long ago. Object bounding box units are the *default* for defining a gradient vector, but they aren't the only option. You can use the `gradientUnits` attribute on the `<linearGradient>` element to change things up.

Setting `gradientUnits` to the keyword `userSpaceOnUse` makes the browser interpret your x1, y1, x2, and y2 attributes within the coordinate system used to draw the shape that is being filled.

 If you wanted to explicitly set the default behavior, the other value for `gradientUnits` is `objectBoundingBox`.

Figure 7-5. A user-space diagonal gradient with a sharp transition at 50% offset, drawn in an oblong rectangle that completely fills the coordinate system

Figure 7-5 shows the result of modifying Example 7-2 to change the `gradientUnits` value:

```
<linearGradient id="diagonal" y2="100%"
                gradientUnits="userSpaceOnUse">
```

Because the rectangle completely fills the coordinate system, the gradient vector still goes from the top left corner of the rectangle to the bottom right. However, because the coordinate system itself has not been distorted, the 50% stop is drawn at a real-world right angle to this diagonal, and no longer connects the other corners.

Avoiding distorted coordinates is only one reason why you might use `userSpaceOnUse`. With `userSpaceOnUse` units, you can create a single gradient that continues from one shape to another. This is demonstrated in Example 7-3, with the results shown in Figure 7-6.

Example 7-3. Using userSpaceOnUse gradient units to fill multiple shapes

```
<svg xmlns="http://www.w3.org/2000/svg"
     xmlns:xlink="http://www.w3.org/1999/xlink"
     width="400px" height="300px" viewBox="0 0 400 300">
    <title xml:lang="en">Tropical Sunset User-Space Gradient</title>
    <linearGradient id="sunset" gradientUnits="userSpaceOnUse"
                    y1="1em" x2="0" y2="250px">                    ❶
        <stop stop-color="midnightBlue" offset="0"/>
        <stop stop-color="deepSkyBlue" offset="0.25"/>
```

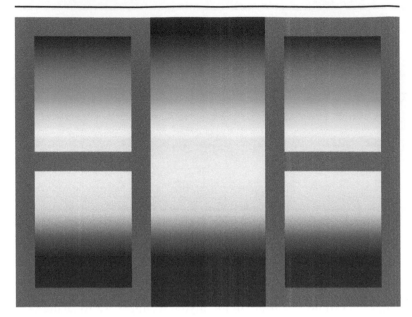

Figure 7-6. Gradients that continue across multiple shapes

```
        <stop stop-color="yellow" offset="0.5"/>
        <stop stop-color="lightPink" offset="0.8"/>
        <stop stop-color="darkMagenta" offset="0.99"/>
        <stop stop-color="#046" offset="0.99"/>              ❷
    </linearGradient>

    <rect height="100%" width="100%" fill="dimGray" />       ❸

    <g fill="url(#sunset)">                                  ❹
        <rect x="20" y="20" width="100" height="120" />
        <rect x="280" y="20" width="100" height="120" />
        <rect x="20" y="160" width="100" height="120" />
        <rect x="280" y="160" width="100" height="120" />
    </g>
    <rect x="140" y="0" width="120" height="300"
        fill="url(#sunset)" />                               ❺
</svg>
```

❶ The userSpaceOnUse value for gradientUnits allows us to use
   lengths such as 1em or 250px to position the gradient vector.
   The x1 attribute isn't specified, so defaults to 0, while the x2
   attribute (100% by default) is reset to 0 to create a straight vertical gradient.

❷ The final two gradient stops have the same offset value, creating a sharp stripe for the line between the sunset sky and the still water; all points in the gradient beyond the end of the gradient vector will be painted with the dark blue-green color #046.

❸ A gray rectangle fills the entire SVG, behind the elements that will be filled with the gradient.

❹ As always, you can specify a fill value on a grouping element, and it will be inherited by the child shapes. However, the gradient is still calculated for each shape individually; if they used an objectBoundingBox gradient, each shape would have a gradient based on its own bounding box, not on the group.

❺ To confirm that the continuous nature of the gradient has nothing to do with the group, the central rectangle is drawn separately. It is the full height of the SVG so you can see the entire gradient, including the solid-colored parts beyond the ends of the gradient vector.

 The initial code for Example 7-3 placed the final, sharp gradient transition (between the sky and the sea) at offset="1". According to the specifications, when multiple stops have the same offset, the final color value should be used for that point, and any padded colors beyond. However, Blink and WebKit browsers ignored the final stop with that offset value and filled in the remaining space with dark magenta.

For consistent results between browsers, avoid using sharp transitions at 0% or 100% offset.

The image in Figure 7-6 *could* have been drawn by filling the background with a single continuous gradient, and then creating complex paths to re-create the shapes of the patio doors opening onto that tropical sunset. Instead, the gray door frames are actually the only places where the backdrop is visible, and the windows and opening are actually rectangles drawn on top. They appear continuous because they are all filled with the same continuous gradient. However, keep in mind that the "user space" is still not an absolute coordinate system—it is affected by any transformations or nested coordinate systems that apply to the shape being filled.

 Although all browsers apply transformations to user-space paint servers, nested coordinate systems are more buggy. WebKit, Blink, and Internet Explorer use the parent SVG of the *gradient*, not the shape, to convert percentages to user units.

CSS Versus SVG
Positioning CSS Gradients with Keywords

The default direction for a CSS linear gradient is top to bottom, as mentioned in Chapter 6. You can, of course, change this default. The syntax is, of course, completely different from SVG. The syntax is also rather different from earlier experimental CSS gradients; to maximize support for earlier browsers, you may want to use a CSS preprocessor or script that will re-create your gradients in the older syntaxes.

You specify the direction of a CSS gradient by adding an extra parameter to the function, before the list of color stops. To create gradients that fit neatly from side to side, or corner to corner, you use keywords: first the keyword **to** and then one of **left**, **right**, **top**, or **bottom** for sides, or a combination of those keywords (like **top right**) for corners. The keyword describes the end-point of the gradient (where the gradient is going *to*); the start point is the opposite side or corner.

When using the corner notation, the angle of the gradient transition is adjusted so that the 50% point of the gradient connects up the other corners. Although the implementation instructions in the specifications are different, the effect is the same as a corner-to-corner SVG gradient in object bounding box units.

Example 7-4 directly compares the SVG diagonal gradient from Example 7-2 (as an embedded image) with a similar CSS gradient (on the body of the web page). The CSS gradient is **to bottom left**, meaning that it is *from* the top right. Figure 7-7 shows the result, including the inset SVG gradient.

Example 7-4. Creating a diagonal striped gradient in CSS

```
<!DOCTYPE html>
<html xml:lang="en">
<head>
    <meta charset="utf-8" />
    <title>Positioning CSS gradients using keywords</title>
    <style type='text/css'>
    html, body {
        height: 100%;
        margin: 0; padding: 0;
    }
    body {
        background: linear-gradient(to bottom left,
                         white, red 50%, blue 50%, white);
    }
    img {
        position: absolute;
        width: 50%; height: 50%;
        left: 25%; top: 25%;
    }
    </style>
</head>
<body>
    <img src="gradient-vector-diagonals.svg">
</body>
</html>
```

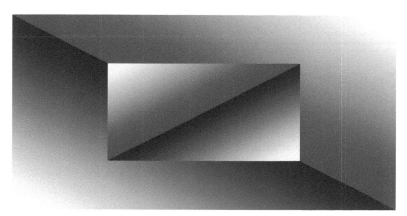

Figure 7-7. A CSS gradient as a background to an SVG gradient

The screenshots for these and other CSS gradients are from Firefox. At the time of writing, Blink browsers perform very poorly when rendering sharp transitions along diagonal lines in CSS gradients, particularly on large backgrounds like this; the diagonal line is very jagged. The problem is reduced, though not eliminated, on SVG gradients.

For smaller images, acceptable results can often be achieved by separating the stop offsets by a percentage point or two, creating a forced anti-aliasing effect. On a full-page gradient like this, that only created jagged purple lines.

You cannot control the length of the gradient vector in CSS; a linear gradient is always adjusted to just fit within the image area, from corner to corner. To create blocks of solid content on either end, or to extend the gradient beyond the box, you can adjust the offsets of the first and last stop. As mentioned in the discussion of SVG gradients, the difference between adjusting the gradient vector length and adjusting the offsets is only important for repeating gradients.

Gradients in CSS always create rectangular images, so there is no object bounding box complication; however, if you use border radius or clipping to reduce the amount of the image visible, this will clip off the corners of the gradient similar to circles and other shapes in SVG.

There is no direct equivalent in CSS to a user-space gradient definition. For background images, you can achieve a similar effect with `background-attachment: fixed`.

Gradients, Transformed

We mentioned at the start of the chapter that there were two ways to control the direction of a linear gradient in SVG. The second approach uses the `gradientTransform` attribute.

The value of the `gradientTransform` attribute is a list of the same transformation functions you can use to manipulate the position and orientation of shapes:

- `translate(`*tx,ty*`)` to shift without distorting

- scale(s) or scale(sx,sy) to zoom in or out, stretch, or flip into a mirror image

- rotate(a) or rotate(a,cx,cy) to rotate, around the origin or the specified centerpoint

- skewX(a) or skewY(a) to tilt one axis or the other

Any number of these functions can be listed in series.

Future Focus
Using CSS Rules to Transform Gradients

The CSS Transforms Module makes `gradientTransform` a presentation attribute that maps to the new `transform` CSS style property. Although it is not yet supported in browsers, in the future, you will be able to set `transform` styles on the gradient element and they would have the same effect as a `gradientTransform` attribute.

The syntax of CSS transformations are slightly different from that used in SVG: length and angle values require units in CSS, where in SVG 1.1 they are always specified as numbers. The new module introduces new shorthand transformation functions, such as `translateY` and `scaleX`. It also deprecates the three-value rotate function (which cannot be used in CSS rules), replacing it with a separate `transform-origin` property, which would affect gradient transformations.

The CSS Transforms Module also introduces three-dimensional transformation functions. These will not apply to paint servers and would invalidate the transformation list entirely.

The effects you can create by transforming a linear gradient are similar to the effects you create by manipulating the gradient vector. For any given graphic, one or the other may be easier to calculate.

 You can combine transformations with positioning attributes. Just as when transforming shapes, the positioning attributes are calculated in the transformed coordinate system.

What does it mean to transform a gradient? It means that the wall-paper created by the paint server is transformed, *before* cutting out the shape being filled. In contrast, when you transform a shape that is filled with a gradient, *both* the shape and the gradient are transformed.

Figure 7-8 compares the two effects, using transformed and un-transformed gradients in transformed and un-transformed shapes. Example 7-5 provides the code.

Example 7-5. Transforming shapes and gradients

```svg
<svg xmlns="http://www.w3.org/2000/svg"
    xmlns:xlink="http://www.w3.org/1999/xlink"
    width="400" height="500" viewBox="0,0 400,500">
    <title xml:lang="en">Transforming shapes, gradients, or both
    </title>

    <linearGradient id="stripe" x2="0" y2="100%">          ❶
        <stop offset="0" stop-color="yellow"/>
        <stop offset="0.1" stop-color="gold"/>
        <stop offset="0.5" stop-color="tomato"/>
        <stop offset="0.5" stop-color="blueViolet"/>
        <stop offset="0.9" stop-color="indigo"/>
        <stop offset="1" stop-color="midnightblue"/>
    </linearGradient>
    <linearGradient id="stripe-transformed" xlink:href="#stripe"
                    gradientTransform="skewY(25)" />       ❷

    <g fill="url(#stripe)" >                               ❸
        <rect height="190" width="190" x="5" y="5" />
        <rect height="190" width="190" x="5" y="5"
            transform="translate(200,0) skewY(25)"/>       ❹
    </g>
    <g transform="translate(0,200)"
       fill="url(#stripe-transformed)">
        <rect height="190" width="190" x="5" y="5" />      ❺
        <rect height="190" width="190" x="5" y="5"
            transform="translate(200,0) skewY(25)"/>       ❻
    </g>
</svg>
```

❶ The basic gradient is oriented top to bottom, as defined by the positioning attributes: the start point is the default (0,0) and the end point is (0,100%).

Figure 7-8. Skewed gradients and skewed squares: the untransformed gradients (top) and the skewed gradients (bottom)

❷ The second gradient uses xlink:href to duplicate the same pattern of color stops; the gradientTransform attribute applies a skew transformation to the pattern.

❸ The first two <rect> elements are grouped together to apply the fill value; each will be filled with the un-transformed gradient.

❹ The second square is translated horizontally into the top right of the graphic and then skewed. However, the gradient used to fill it was not skewed separately, so the color stops still align exactly with the top and bottom edges of the square.

❺ The squares on the bottom row use the transformed gradients. On the left, the square itself has not been skewed, only the gradient.

❻ The final square is both skewed itself and filled with the skewed gradient; the effect on the final gradient angle is therefore compounded.

The transformation on the shape maintains the relationship between the gradient colors and the edges of the shape: squares in the same row of Figure 7-8 have the same colors in the corners, regardless of whether or not the shape as a whole is skewed. In contrast, when the gradient is transformed, it moves separately from the shape, changing which parts of the gradient are visible. The deep midnight-blue color is almost completely cut off, while large sections of solid yellow are visible.

There is no direct way to transform a shape but *not* the paint server content used to fill it. Even userSpaceOnUse gradients will reflect the coordinate system transformations on the shape using the gradient.

 If you want un-transformed paint server content inside a transformed shape, you can use a clipping path to apply the transformed shape boundaries to a larger, untransformed rectangle filled with the paint.

Skewing, clearly, is one way gradient transformations can be used to create a diagonal gradient. Rotating is another. Example 7-6 creates rainbow gradients rotated at 45° angle-intervals, and then uses these to fill ellipses arranged around the edges and corners of the SVG. Figure 7-9 shows the result.

Example 7-6. Transforming gradients using rotations

```
<svg xmlns="http://www.w3.org/2000/svg"
     xmlns:xlink="http://www.w3.org/1999/xlink"
     width="400" height="300" viewBox="-200,-150 400,300"> ❶
```

```
<title xml:lang="en">Rotated Gradients</title>
<defs>
    <linearGradient id="rainbow" >
        <stop stop-color="darkViolet" offset="0"/>
        <stop stop-color="blue" offset="0.143"/>       ❷
        <stop stop-color="cyan" offset="0.286"/>
        <stop stop-color="limeGreen" offset="0.429"/>
        <stop stop-color="yellow" offset="0.572"/>
        <stop stop-color="orange" offset="0.715"/>
        <stop stop-color="red" offset="0.857"/>
        <stop stop-color="maroon" offset="1"/>
    </linearGradient>
    <linearGradient id="rainbow45" xlink:href="#rainbow"
                    gradientTransform="rotate(45)"/>   ❸
    <linearGradient id="rainbow90" xlink:href="#rainbow"
                    gradientTransform="rotate(90)"/>
    <linearGradient id="rainbow135" xlink:href="#rainbow"
                    gradientTransform="rotate(135)"/>
    <linearGradient id="rainbow180" xlink:href="#rainbow"
                    gradientTransform="rotate(180)"/>
    <linearGradient id="rainbow225" xlink:href="#rainbow"
                    gradientTransform="rotate(225)"/>
    <linearGradient id="rainbow270" xlink:href="#rainbow"
                    gradientTransform="rotate(270)"/>
    <linearGradient id="rainbow315" xlink:href="#rainbow"
                    gradientTransform="rotate(315)"/>
</defs>

<ellipse rx="60" ry="40" cx="130" cy="0"
        fill="url(#rainbow)"/>                          ❹
<ellipse rx="60" ry="40" cx="130" cy="100"
        fill="url(#rainbow45)"/>
<ellipse rx="60" ry="40" cx="0" cy="100"
        fill="url(#rainbow90)"/>
<ellipse rx="60" ry="40" cx="-130" cy="100"
        fill="url(#rainbow135)"/>
<ellipse rx="60" ry="40" cx="-130" cy="0"
        fill="url(#rainbow180)"/>
<ellipse rx="60" ry="40" cx="-130" cy="-100"
        fill="url(#rainbow225)"/>
<ellipse rx="60" ry="40" cx="0" cy="-100"
        fill="url(#rainbow270)"/>
<ellipse rx="60" ry="40" cx="130" cy="-100"
        fill="url(#rainbow315)"/>
</svg>
```

❶ The SVG uses a centered coordinate system.

❷ The rainbow gradient has eight stops, so the offsets are multiples of $1/_7$ (0.143).

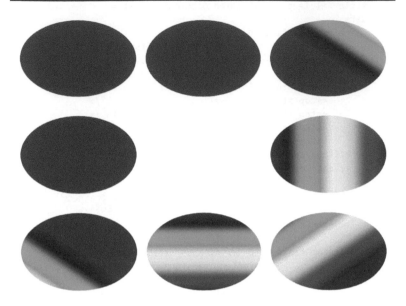

Figure 7-9. Ellipses filled with rotated gradients

❸ Again, the almost-identical gradients are created by using
xlink:href to link the original gradient, and then adding the
new attributes: in this case, the gradientTransform.

❹ The original gradient is arranged in the default left-to-right orientation; the ellipse filled with that gradient is positioned on the
right edge of the SVG. The remaining ellipses are positioned in
a clockwise manner around the SVG, to match the increasing
clockwise rotation in the gradient transform angle.

Wait—why are some of the shapes filled with solid violet instead of a
gradient? Because, while the ellipse may have been arranged around
the center of the SVG coordinate system, the *gradients* are rotated
around the center of *their* coordinate system: the object bounding
box coordinates for each shape. As with all SVG coordinate systems,
the default origin is the top left corner—and for gradients, there's no
viewBox attribute to allow you to change that.

The gradient vector (initially pointing left to right along the top of
each shape's bounding box) is rotated around the origin of each box
(the top left corner). Rotating the vector by 90° (as in the bottom

center ellipse) will shift it so that the gradient changes from top to bottom. However, rotate any further and the vector is pointing outside of the shape's bounding box. Most or all of the shape is in the region before the start of the gradient, and is therefore painted solid with the color of the first gradient stop (the aforementioned darkViolet).

To effectively use rotational transformations of linear gradients in object bounding box space, you'll need additional manipulations. Some options:

- Use translations within the gradientTransform attribute to reposition the gradient into the shape.
- Use the three-value rotate(a, 0.5, 0.5) function to rotate around the coordinate system's center point (or use transform-origin if using CSS rules).
- Change the vector's positioning attributes so that it will be on the correct side of the origin *after* the rotation.

There are further complications. Although you've transformed the gradient's direction, a rotation does not change its length; the stop offsets will still be judged relative to the horizontal length of the vector. Because of the distorted object bounding box coordinates, the default length of a horizontal gradient (1 horizontal unit) will still fill the box vertically (1 vertical unit) after a 90° rotation. However, it won't match the diagonal length (1.141 stretched units) after a 45° rotation, so a 50% offset will *not* neatly connect the other corners of the box.

In other words, the gradient stretches and shrinks as it rotates, but not quite the way you might expect.

If you were to use userSpaceOnUse units for the gradient, it would be rotated around the origin of the entire SVG's coordinate system—which in this case, is centered in the middle of the image. Figure 7-10 shows this effect; the only change in the code, relative to Example 7-6, is in the attributes for the main gradient element:

```
<linearGradient id="rainbow" gradientUnits="userSpaceOnUse"
                x1="20%" x2="50%">
```

The change in x1 and x2 values is required because the percentages will now be calculated relative to the SVG's width instead of the width of each shape. These new attributes only need to be set once;

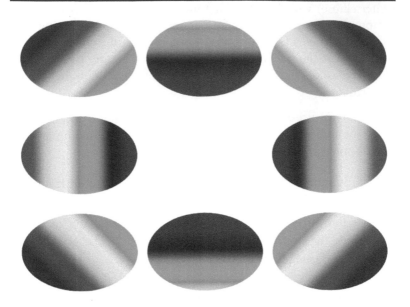

Figure 7-10. Ellipses filled with gradients rotated in the user space

they are automatically duplicated to all the other gradients that reference this one.

If you look closely, there is another difference between Figures 7-9 and 7-10. To make it easier to see, Figure 7-11 extracts the bottom-right ellipse from each figure—the one with a gradient transform of rotate(45). The ellipse on the left uses the object bounding box gradient, while the ellipse on the right uses user space coordinates. The angles aren't the same. With the object bounding box gradient, 45° looks more like 60°.

The reason is that the transformation angles are calculated in the stretched coordinate system created by the object bounding box. If the bounding rectangle is roughly square, the final angle will match the angle you specify. If not—as with these ellipses—the angles will be squished or stretched accordingly. A 45° angle in object bounding box space always matches the diagonal of the box, but it won't necessarily match the same angle in any other coordinate system.

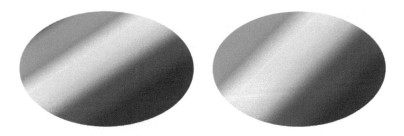

Figure 7-11. Comparing gradients rotated (left) in object bounding box space and (right) the user coordinate space

Positioning CSS Gradients with Angles

CSS gradients can also be positioned using rotational angles, although the result is somewhat different than in SVG.

You specify an angle—with units—as the first parameter to the `linear-gradient` function, as an alternative to using directional keywords. Because the default direction is top to bottom, the angles are calculated relative to a vertical vector pointing down; a `-90deg` setting is required to create the SVG default of a gradient pointing to the right.

Example 7-7 is an adaptation of Example 7-4; instead of comparing a CSS gradient with an SVG gradient, it compares two CSS gradients. The gradient on the `<body>` is angled using the `to` corner syntax, while the gradient on the inset `<div>` element is angled using degrees. The final web page is displayed in Figure 7-12.

Example 7-7. Using angles instead of keywords to control CSS gradients

```
<!DOCTYPE html>
<html lang="en">
<head>
    <meta charset="utf-8" />
    <title>Angling CSS gradients versus using corners</title>

    <style type='text/css'>
    html, body {
        height: 100%;
        margin: 0; padding: 0;
```

```
    }
    body {
        background: linear-gradient(to bottom left,
                        white, red 50%, blue 50%, white);
    }
    div {
        background: linear-gradient(-45deg,
                        white, red 50%, blue 50%, white);
        position: absolute;
        width: 50%; height: 50%;
        left: 25%; top: 25%;
    }
    </style>
</head>
<body>
    <div></div>
</body>
</html>
```

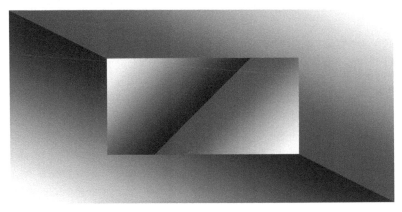

Figure 7-12. A fixed-angle gradient on top of a corner-to-corner CSS gradient

The gradient that is specified using an angle is drawn with *exactly* that angle, even though it means that the 50% stop no longer lines up with the bottom left and top right corners of the element. The length and position of the gradient vector, however, is automatically adjusted so that the gradient still starts and ends on the top left and bottom right corners. Again, the only way to create a CSS gradient that *doesn't* start and end in the corners is to adjust the offsets of individual color stops.

CHAPTER 8

And Repeat

As we manipulated the gradient vector and the gradient transform in Chapter 7, we pointed out a few times how areas beyond the end of the gradient vector are filled in with solid color. We've also mentioned how this is only the *default* behavior.

This chapter examines the alternative: repeating gradients that continue to transition for as long as required to fill the shape. Again, there are both SVG and CSS ways of achieving this, and we'll compare the two.

With all the features of linear gradients now introduced, the chapter concludes with some examples of one of the more common—but, unfortunately, more problematic—uses of SVG gradients: to style re-usable SVG icons within an HTML page. There are a number of web browser bugs you'll need to avoid to get everything working as intended.

How to Spread Your Gradient

The appearance of a gradient beyond the ends of the gradient vector is set by the spreadMethod attribute on the <linearGradient> element. It controls how the gradient *spreads* out toward infinity.

The default value for this attribute is pad. With it, everything before the start of the vector is padded with the first stop-color, while everything beyond the end point is padded with the last stop-color. The examples we've seen so far have all used the padding behavior by default, but Example 8-1 does so explicitly; the x1 and x2 attributes limit the gradient to the middle 10% of the object bounding box, but the rest of the shape will be padded in blue and pink. The resulting gradient is shown in Figure 8-1.

Figure 8-1. A narrow gradient padded with solid colors

Example 8-1. Using padded gradients to fill a shape

```
<svg xmlns="http://www.w3.org/2000/svg"
     width="4in" height="1in">
    <title xml:lang="en">Padded Gradient</title>
    <linearGradient id="divider" spreadMethod="pad"
                    x1="45%" x2="55%" >                    ❶
        <stop stop-color="lightSteelBlue" offset="0%"/>
        <stop stop-color="darkRed" offset="50%"/>
        <stop stop-color="salmon" offset="100%"/>          ❷
    </linearGradient>
    <rect width="100%" height="100%" fill="url(#divider)" />
</svg>
```

❶ You don't really need to specify `spreadMethod`, because `pad` is the default value; it is included here for emphasis.

❷ Note that the stop offsets are a percentage of the gradient vector length, not of the object bounding box or user space.

The other options for `spreadMethod` are `repeat` and `reflect`. Both of these settings cause the gradient to be repeated as many times as necessary to fill the shape.

WebKit (Safari browser and older Chrome) does not support the `repeat` and `reflect` values of `spreadMethod`. Firefox temporarily dropped support for repeated and reflected gradients when changing underlying code; they were reintroduced in 2014 with version 32. Where not supported, all gradients are rendered with padded colors.

If the repeated effect is essential to your graphic, you have two workarounds:

- Manually repeat the gradient stops (and adjust the size of the gradient vector) as many times as required to fill your shape.
- Use a `<pattern>` element (as described in Chapter 10) to create repeating gradient tiles.

Reflections on Infinite Gradients

The `reflect` method reverses the order of stops on each repeat cycle. This creates a smooth transition at the start and end points, alternating between the specified colors without any sharp discontinuities. The colors alternate in peaks and troughs.

Taking the same code from Example 8-1 and adding the `spreadMethod="reflect"` attribute results in Figure 8-2.

Figure 8-2. A narrow gradient reflected on either side

Although the central gradient is the same as in Figure 8-1, the visual effect is quite different when that gradient region is repeated and reflected, creating an appearance of metallic tubes of alternating colors. Note that the repetitions happen in both directions, before and after the gradient vector you specify.

The effect of a reflected gradient is strongly influenced by the length of the gradient vector and the level of contrast in the colors. Example 8-2 creates a more subtle, wave-like reflected gradient, shown in Figure 8-3.

Figure 8-3. A reflected three-color gradient

Example 8-2. Using reflected gradients to create a smooth repeating pattern

```
<svg xmlns="http://www.w3.org/2000/svg"
     width="4in" height="1in">
    <title xml:lang="en">Reflecting Gradient</title>
    <linearGradient id="waves" spreadMethod="reflect"
                    x2="10%" y2="10%">
        <stop stop-color="darkGreen" offset="0"/>
        <stop stop-color="mediumSeaGreen" offset="50%"/>
        <stop stop-color="skyBlue" offset="100%"/>
    </linearGradient>
    <rect width="100%" height="100%" fill="url(#waves)" />
</svg>
```

The gradient vector runs from the top left corner (default x1 and y1 values) to the point 10% along the diagonal. This is the distance for a single, uni-directional cycle of the gradient. The resulting shape therefore has five pairs (10 cycles total) of alternating gradients, green to blue and back again, along the diagonal.

Repeating Without Reflecting

Reflected gradients create smooth effects, shifting to one color and then back to the other. In contrast, when spreadMethod is repeat, the gradient stops repeat in the same order from beginning to end.

Unless the start and end colors are identical, this will result in a discontinuity in the gradient.

The sharp difference can be shown by once again adapting the code from Example 8-1, to now use `spreadMethod="repeat"`. The result is Figure 8-4.

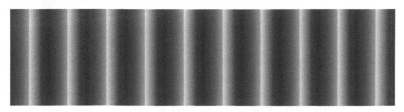

Figure 8-4. A narrow gradient repeated on either side

A "sharp" difference, indeed—the edges of each gradient cycle now create sharp lines, as if you're looking at the creases of an accordion, each side lit differently.

Repeated gradients are useful when creating striped effects. Example 8-3 takes advantage of them to create a striped wallpaper effect, as shown in Figure 8-5.

Figure 8-5. Striped wallpaper created with a repeating gradient

Example 8-3. Using repeating gradients to create a striped pattern

```
<svg xmlns="http://www.w3.org/2000/svg"
     width="4in" height="1in">
    <title xml:lang="en">Repeating Gradient</title>
    <linearGradient id="wallpaper" spreadMethod="repeat"
                    gradientUnits="userSpaceOnUse"
                    x1="5px" x2="45px">                      ❶
        <stop stop-color="indigo" offset="50%"/>            ❷
        <stop stop-color="deepSkyBlue" offset="50%"/>
        <stop stop-color="lightSkyBlue" offset="90%"/>      ❸
```

```
    </linearGradient>
    <rect width="100%" height="100%" fill="url(#wallpaper)" />
</svg>
```

❶ The gradient is sized using user-space units, so the width of each gradient cycle can be specified in absolute units instead of as a percentage of the referencing shape. The gradient vector is horizontal (y1 and y2 are left as the default 0), and each cycle will be 40px wide—the difference between the x1 and x2 values.

❷ The first stop is positioned halfway into the cycle (50% offset); the space between the start of each repeat cycle and the offset will continue to be padded with that first stop color. In other words, the first half of each repeat will be a solid stripe in indigo.

❸ After a sharp transition to blue at 50% offset, there is a subtle gradient to a lighter blue at 90% offset; the remainder of the repeat cycle will be filled in with the light blue.

Example 8-3 also demonstrates something we mentioned in Chapter 7: off-setting stops from the start or end of the gradient vector is not the same (in repeated or reflected gradients) as changing the length of the vector. The color is padded in between the <stop> and the end of the vector; the repetition applies to the vector itself.

CSS Versus SVG
Repeating CSS Gradients

The `repeating-linear-gradient()` function is used to create repeating linear gradients in CSS. The parameters are the exact same as for a regular linear gradient: a direction parameter (as keywords or an angle) followed by a list of color stops.

 Repeating CSS gradients were adopted later than regular gradients in many browsers. However, they are now supported in the latest versions of all the major browsers, including Safari (which does not support repeating SVG gradients).

The repeated section *exactly* matches the distance between the first and last stop. To see the repeats, you need to explicitly set offsets for at least one of these stops; otherwise, a single cycle will fill up the entire CSS layout box.

To create a block of solid color in between repeats, you would need to provide two stops with the same color. For example, to create the vertical blue and indigo wallpaper stripes, the code would be as follows:

```
background: repeating-linear-gradient(to right,
            indigo 5px, indigo 25px,
            deepSkyBlue 25px,
            lightSkyBlue 41px, lightSkyBlue 45px);
```

The repeating block is still 40px wide, the difference between the first and last stop. The in-between stops have also been converted to **px** values. If we had used percentage values, they would be calculated relative to the CSS layout box, not the gradient repeat distance; a 50% offset would be much larger than the 45px final offset, throwing off the scale completely.

There is no shorthand to create a reflecting gradient in CSS. To create a reflected pattern, you duplicate the stops yourself to create a complete repeating block, as in the following code:

```
background: repeating-linear-gradient(to bottom right,
            darkGreen, mediumSeaGreen 5%,
            skyBlue 10%,
            mediumSeaGreen 15%, darkGreen 20%);
```

In this case, the offset of the first stop is 0 by default; the repeating pattern is therefore 20% of the length of the diagonal, the same as a back-and-forth cycle in Example 8-2.

For horizontal and vertical gradients in CSS backgrounds, you can also create repeating gradients by using **background-size** to define a background image just large enough for one repeat, and tiling it with the **background-repeat** property to fill the element.

The tiled approach approach has two conveniences compared to **repeating-linear-gradient**. You can use percentages for distance along the gradient, independent of the repeat size, and you do not have to explicitly include extra stops for solid colors at the start and end of the repeat. For example, you could create the wallpaper effect with the following shorthand style rule:

```
background: linear-gradient(to right,
            indigo 50%,
            deepSkyBlue 50%,
```

```
                  lightSkyBlue 90%)
           5px 0/40px 100% repeat-x;
```

If you wanted to change the width or offset of the stripes, you would now only have to adjust one value (the `40px 100% background-size` value for total width, or the `5px 0 background-position` value for the offset), instead of having to adjust each stop offset.

With a little trigonometry, you can also repeat diagonal gradients this way, by carefully figuring out the correct `background-size` to create a repeating tile; however, rounding effects may create visible edges between tiles.

Using (and Reusing) Gradients in HTML

The gradient examples so far have used the gradients to fill simple shapes within an SVG file; most have simply filled a rectangle the full size of the graphic. The use case for a simple SVG gradient backdrop is dwindling, however, with widespread support for CSS gradients. At the same time, the use cases for other SVG graphics have been increasing with improved browser support. This includes inline SVG code, markup within the HTML file that is styled with the main document's stylesheets.

Gradients can be used with icons, charts, or other SVG code within an HTML page. For the most part, it works the same as in a stand-alone SVG document, but there are a few complications, most of which can be traced to browser bugs.

For a single large SVG (e.g., a data visualization), all the SVG code, including gradient definitions, is usually included together.

For an SVG icon system, in contrast, the icons are usually defined once and then reused with <use> elements. This keeps your web page organized and allows the main inline markup to be clear and concise. In the simplest form, each icon instance can be written with only slightly more markup than an embedded image:

```
<svg class="icon"><use xlink:href="#star" /></svg>
```

Elsewhere in the same document, a <symbol> element with id="star" would define the actual graphic that will scale to fit the size you assign (in CSS) to an <svg> element of class icon.

Depending on the use, you may need to include a title tooltip, accessible name, and fallback text:

```
<svg class="icon" role="img" aria-labelledby="icon-0001">
    <use xlink:href="#star">
        <title>Tooltip</title>
        <desc id="icon-0001">Alternative Text</desc>
    </use>
</svg>
```

The `<title>` content will be used as a tooltip in modern browsers. The `<desc>` content will be used as the accessible name (because of the `aria-labelledby` attribute) and will also be visible in older browsers that do not support SVG.

The original graphics in each `<symbol>` generally have minimal style rules assigned, so that they can inherit the styles set on the `<use>` instances, including interactive styles such as hover or focus effects. Those styles can include `fill` or `stroke` references to a gradient element. However, as previously mentioned in Chapter 5, URL parsing rules and poor support for external SVG resources prevent those styles from being assigned in an external stylesheet.

 In all browsers except Firefox, paint servers must be in the same document as the graphics; style rules therefore also must be defined in that document, not an external stylesheet.

Theoretically, an external stylesheet could be used with `url()` references that link back to the main document. In practice, this contradicts the main purpose of having an external stylesheet that you can reuse for many documents.

Because they cannot be collected in an external asset file, the gradients themselves are normally collected with the icon definitions in their own `<svg>` element that does not draw anything to the screen. (They must be inside an `<svg>` element to be correctly parsed as SVG content.)

As mentioned when we introduced user-space gradients, all browsers except Firefox use the parent <svg> of the gradient element to scale userSpaceOnUse gradients, instead of the coordinate system for the shape being painted. User-space gradients therefore break when using a separate definitions SVG.

For optimal browser support and easy to maintain markup, this SVG is usually placed at the top of the HTML <body>.

Older WebKit browsers will not correctly locate symbols and other reusable content defined later in the document than the elements that reuse them.

Ideally, you would place that definitions SVG inside your HTML <head> with other non-displayed content. At the very least, you would use display: none to ensure that extra SVG did not affect your web page. Unfortunately, neither approach can be used in practice.

All browsers tested do not render gradients (or patterns) when an ancestor element of the gradient has display set to none, despite very clear statements in the SVG specifications that display should not have an effect. This is the most frustrating example of cross-browser *consistency* in SVG.

As a result, you need to use alternative CSS to ensure that the definitions SVG does not affect your web page, and ARIA attributes to ensure that assitive technologies do not process it. Furthermore, to avoid problems if the CSS takes too long to load, you will want to also use SVG attributes to collapse the size of the definitions element. Finally, because Internet Explorer implements the never-finalized SVG 1.2 proposal for keyboard control of SVG, you need to use the focusable attribute to explicitly tell it that the SVG should not receive keyboard focus.

Figure 8-6. Gradient-filled and stroked icons in an HTML page

 In Internet Explorer, all `<svg>` elements in HTML are keyboard-focusable by default, and are only removed from the tab index with `focusable="false"`. In the latest versions of WebKit/Blink browsers, `<svg>` elements are *not* keyboard focusable by default, but can be made so by setting the `tabindex` attribute to a positive integer. Firefox has not yet implemented either form of focus control.

With all those warnings out of the way, what does it look like to use gradients for SVG icons in an HTML file? Example 8-4 presents the core markup and styles for a web page that uses SVG as icons in the navigation menu. Different-colored gradients are used to distinguish the current site from navigation options, and to indicate hover/focus states; Figure 8-6 show the appearance when the first navigation link is focused.

Example 8-4. Using gradients within SVG icons in an HTML page

HTML MARKUP:

```
<!DOCTYPE html>
<html lang="en">
<head>
    <meta charset="utf-8" />
    <title>Re-using Symbols with Gradients</title>
    <style type='text/css'>
        /* styles must be included in the same document */
    </style>
</head>
<body>
    <svg class="defs-only" aria-hidden="true" focusable="false"
         width="0" height="0">                                        ❶
        <linearGradient id="silver-shine" spreadMethod="repeat"
                        gradientTransform="rotate(40) scale(0.8)" >
            <stop offset="0" stop-color="gray" />
            <stop offset="0.35" stop-color="silver" />
            <stop offset="1" stop-color="gray" />
        </linearGradient>
        <linearGradient id="gold-shine"
                        xlink:href="#silver-shine" >                  ❷
            <stop offset="0" stop-color="gold" />
            <stop offset="0.35" stop-color="lightYellow" />
            <stop offset="1" stop-color="gold" />
        </linearGradient>
        <symbol id="home" viewBox="0 0 200 200">                      ❸
            <path d="M30,180 V80 H10 L100,10 190,80 H170 V180
                     H90 V100 H60 V180 H30 Z
                     M110,100 H150 V140 H110 Z"
                  fill-rule="evenodd" />
        </symbol>
        <symbol id="star" viewBox="10 10 170 150">
            <path d="M100,10 L150,140 20,50 180,50 50,140 Z" />
        </symbol>
        <symbol id="magnify" viewBox="0 0 200 200">
            <path d="M10,170 L70,110 A60,60 0 1,1 90,130 L30,190Z
                     M85,104 A44,44 0 1,1 96,116 Z"
                  fill-rule="evenodd" />
            <path d="M85,104 A44,44 0 1,1 96,116 Z" fill-opacity="0.7" />
        </symbol>
    </svg>
    <a class="skip-nav" href="#main">Skip to Main Content</a>
    <header>
        <h1>Gradients Gone Wild</h1>
        <nav>
            <ul>
                <li><a href="/">HOME
                        <svg class="nav-icon" role="presentation">
```

```
                    <use xlink:href="#home" />              ④
                </svg>
            </a>
        </li>
        <li><a href="/favorites">Favorites
                <svg class="nav-icon" role="presentation">
                    <use xlink:href="#star" />
                </svg>
            </a>
        </li>
        <li><a title="(You are here)">Search          ⑤
                <svg class="nav-icon" role="presentation">
                    <use xlink:href="#magnify" />
                </svg>
            </a>
        </li>
    </ul>
</nav>
</header>
<main id="main">
    <h1>Search the Site</h1>
    <form>
        <input type="search" name="q"
            aria-label="Enter Search Terms"/>
        <button type="submit" aria-label="Search">
            <svg>
                <use xlink:href="#magnify" />          ⑥
                GO
            </svg>
        </button>
    </form>
</main>
</body>
</html>
```

❶ The initial <svg> contains the definitions of reusable content. In
    addition to the defs-only class that triggers CSS hiding, it has
    an aria-hidden="true" attribute and width and height set to 0
    in the markup, as well as focusable="false" so that Internet
    Explorer does not give it keyboard focus.

❷ The two gradients use the same geometry, so the spreadMethod
    and gradientTransform attributes are copied from one to the
    other with an xlink:href reference. The colors are different,
    however, and the <stop> elements included in the second gradi-
    ent completely replace those from the first.

❸   There are three <symbol> elements defining the icons, each with a viewBox attribute so they will scale to fit the context in which they are used.

❹   In the main web page markup, each navigation icon is its own <svg> nested within the <a> element within the navigation list. A single <use> element references the symbol; with no positioning attributes on the <use> element, the reused symbol stretches to fit the size set on the <svg>.

❺   The current page will be represented in the navigation list by an anchor element (<a>) that does not have an href attribute, and is therefore not a valid hyperlink.

❻   The markup for the button icon is similar to that for the navigation; the difference in appearance stems from the different inherited styles and scale of the SVG. In modern browsers, there is no visible text for the button, so an aria-label attribute is added for an accessible name. The plain-text content ("GO") within the SVG provides a fallback for old browsers.

RELEVANT CSS STYLES:

```
svg.defs-only {
    display: block;
    position: absolute;
    height: 0; width: 0;
    overflow: hidden;                    ❶
}
svg.nav-icon  {
    display: block;
    width: 3em;
    height: 3em;
    margin: auto;
    fill: url(#silver-shine);            ❷
}
a:not(:link) > .nav-icon {
    fill: url(#gold-shine);              ❸
}
nav a:link:focus, nav a:link:hover {
    stroke: url(#gold-shine);
    stroke-width: 10px;                  ❹
}
input, button {
    display: inline-block;
    height: 2em;
```

```
    padding: 0 0.5em;
}
input[type="search"] {
    width: calc(100% - 5em);
}
button {
    display: inline-block;
    width: 3em;
    vertical-align: top;
    color: inherit;
}
button svg {
    height: 100%;
    width: 100%;
    fill: currentColor;                    ❺
}
```

❶ The defs-only class complements the attributes in the markup, to ensure that the definitions-only <svg> element does not affect the layout or visual appearance in any way.

❷ The <svg> elements used as navigation icons have a fixed height and width. A fill setting referencing one of the gradients is set on the SVG; it will be inherited by the <use> element and then by the reused symbol.

❸ The :link pseudoclass is used to distinguish between <a> elements with and without valid hyperlinks. When the class does *not* match, the SVG within is restyled to use the brighter gold gradient, to emphasize that this is the active page.

❹ For the other icons, a gold stroke is added to indicate interactivity when the user hovers or focuses the link. To prove that they can be, the styles are set on the <a> element directly. They will still be inherited by the SVG and its content, because none of the SVG elements set an alternative stroke style. Nonetheless, the 10px stroke width will be applied in the final coordinate system of the stroked graphics, which in this case is the coordinate system defined within each symbol.

❺ Because the styles are all inherited when used, they can be changed when the graphics are used in a different context on the same page. The search icon used within a form button will be styled using the current text color inherited from the <button>.

Because the SVG markup definitions and styles would be the same in every page on the web site, it would normally be compiled using some form of server-side processing. Alternatively, if the SVG code was extensive, and if most users visit multiple pages on the website, a client-side AJAX script could be used, allowing the SVG asset file to be cached on the browser.

 Many popular SVG icon systems only use AJAX to import SVG symbols if external file references for <use> elements are not supported. WebKit and Blink browsers currently support these external symbol references, but not gradients and other paint servers. Ensure your script has specific rules for importing gradients and patterns if required.

Because the main graphical definitions are contained in a separate block of markup, it is easy to dynamically generate new instances of each icon, or switch those instances to use different gradients.

Example 8-5 uses the same gradients as Example 8-4, and one of the same icons, to dynamically generate a star-rating graphic based on a data attribute included in the HTML code. The gradient and symbol definitions are static markup, but the <use> instances are generated as required based on the data.

Because each SVG now contains multiple copies of each icon, a viewBox on the <svg> and positioning attributes on the <use> elements are required to scale everything correctly. In addition, ARIA attributes are used to convey the rating scale to assistive technologies, using the markup for a read-only range slider in a form. The visual appearance of each rating—how many stars are highlighted in the graphic—is derived directly from the aria-valuenow attribute, using CSS rules based on the nth-of-type selector. Figure 8-7 shows the final web page.

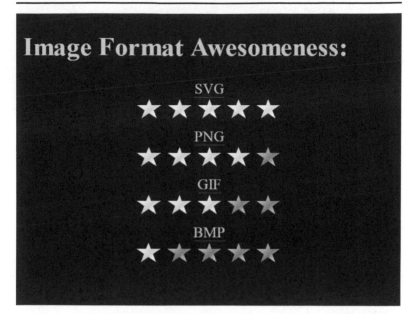

Figure 8-7. Dynamically generated SVG star-rating icons with gradient effects

Example 8-5. Using gradients with dynamically inserted SVG icons

HTML Markup:

```
<!DOCTYPE html>
<html lang="en">
<head>
    <meta charset="utf-8" />
    <title>Reusing Symbols with Gradients</title>
    <style type='text/css'>
        /* styles must be in the same document */
    </style>
</head>
<body>
    <svg class="defs-only" aria-hidden="true" focusable="false"
        width="0" height="0">                                    ❶
        <linearGradient id="silver-shine" spreadMethod="repeat"
                        gradientTransform="rotate(40) scale(0.8)" >
            <stop offset="0" stop-color="gray" />
            <stop offset="0.35" stop-color="silver" />
            <stop offset="1" stop-color="gray" />
        </linearGradient>
        <linearGradient id="gold-shine" xlink:href="#silver-shine">
            <stop offset="0" stop-color="gold" />
```

```
            <stop offset="0.35" stop-color="lightYellow" />
            <stop offset="1" stop-color="gold" />
        </linearGradient>
        <symbol id="star" viewBox="0 0 200 200">
            <path d="M100,10 L150,140 20,50 180,50 50,140 Z" />
        </symbol>
    </svg>
    <h1>Image Format Awesomeness:</h1>
    <ol>
        <li id="svg" data-rating="5">                              ❷
            <abbr title="Scalable Vector Graphics">SVG</abbr>
        </li>
        <li id="png" data-rating="4">
            <abbr title="Portable Network Graphics">PNG</abbr>
        </li>
        <li id="gif" data-rating="3">
            <abbr title="Graphics Interchange Format">GIF</abbr>
        </li>
        <li id="bmp" data-rating="1">
            <abbr title="Bitmap (Windows)">BMP</abbr>
        </li>
    </ol>
    <script>
        /* script could be loaded as a separate file */
    </script>
</body>
</html>
```

❶   The graphics definitions are the same as for Example 8-4, except that only one `<symbol>` is required.

❷   The main web page markup does not initially have any SVG content; instead, each item in the list is distinguished by the `data-rating` attribute.

CSS STYLES:

```
html {
    background-color: #222;
    color: lightSkyBlue;
}
svg.defs-only {
    display: block;
    position: absolute;
    height: 0; width: 0;
    overflow: hidden;                          ❶
}
ol {
    padding: 0;
}
```

```
li {
    display: block;
    text-align: center;
    list-style: none;
    font-size: larger;
}
svg.star-rating  {
    display: block;
    margin: auto;
    width: 10em;
    max-width: 100%;
    height: auto;
    max-height: 2em;                         ❷
}
.star {
    fill: url(#silver-shine);                ❸
}
[aria-valuenow="1"] .star:nth-of-type(-n+1),
[aria-valuenow="2"] .star:nth-of-type(-n+2),
[aria-valuenow="3"] .star:nth-of-type(-n+3),
[aria-valuenow="4"] .star:nth-of-type(-n+4),
[aria-valuenow="5"] .star:nth-of-type(-n+5)
{
    fill: url(#gold-shine);                  ❹
}
[data-rating]:not(.initialized)::after {
    display: block;
    color: darkgoldenrod;
    text-shadow: black 1px 1px 1px,
                 gold 0 0 3px;
    content: attr(data-rating);             ❺
}
```

❶ The same svg.defs-only styles from Example 8-4 are used to hide the element containing all the graphics definitions.

❷ The SVG elements that will contain the star-ratings are given a fixed width that will scale down if required; a max-height setting ensures a reasonable height in browsers that do not support auto-scaling of SVG proportions based on the viewBox.

❸ The star icons are by default set to use the silver-gray gradient.

❹ The correct number of stars are turned gold using a series of selectors tied to the aria-valuenow attribute. For example, the :nth-of-type(-n+3) selects the first three <use> icons in the group; these are the only icons for which a positive integer value of n will match the index of that element.

❺ If the script does not run—and the SVG stars are therefore not generated—a CSS pseudo-element will print the value of the data-rating attribute to the screen.

JavaScript:

```
(function(){
    var ns = {svg:"http://www.w3.org/2000/svg",
              xlink:"http://www.w3.org/1999/xlink"};
    var maxRating = 5;
    var index = 0;

    var ratings = document.querySelectorAll("[data-rating]");     ❶
    for (var i=0, n=ratings.length; i<n; i++){
        var r = ratings[i];
        //add an `id` value if it doesn't exist
        r.id = r.id || "rating-" + (index++);

        //parse the rating
        var value = parseInt(r.getAttribute("data-rating"),10);

        //create and insert an SVG to represent the rating
        var s = document.createElementNS(ns.svg, "svg");          ❷
        s.setAttribute("viewBox", "0 0 " + maxRating + " 1");
        s.setAttribute("class", "star-rating");
        s.setAttribute("role", "slider");
        s.setAttribute("aria-labelledby", r.id);
        s.setAttribute("aria-valuemin", 0);
        s.setAttribute("aria-valuemax", maxRating);
        s.setAttribute("aria-valuenow", value);
        s.setAttribute("aria-readonly", true);

        //create a group and give it a tooltip title
        var g = document.createElementNS(ns.svg, "g");
        s.insertBefore(g, null);
        var t = document.createElementNS(ns.svg, "title");
        t.textContent = value + " out of " + maxRating;           ❸
        g.insertBefore(t, g.firstChild);

        //create and insert the stars into the group
        for (var j=0; j<maxRating; j++) {
            var u = document.createElementNS(ns.svg, "use");
            u.setAttribute("class", "star");
            u.setAttributeNS(ns.xlink, "href", "#star");
            u.setAttribute("width", "1");
            u.setAttribute("x", j);
            g.insertBefore(u, null);                              ❹
```

```
        }
        r.insertBefore(s, null);
        r.classList.add("initialized");                    ❺
    }
})();
```

❶ The script selects all elements with the data-rating attribute, and then loops through them. Each one is assigned an arbitrary id if one does not already exist; these will be needed for the ARIA references.

❷ An SVG element is created and customized with viewBox, class, and ARIA attributes, incorporating the rating value parsed from the data attribute as well as the maximum rating stored as a constant in the script.

❸ A <title> element is used to translate the rating into tooltip text. Because many browsers do not display tooltips for a <title> element that is a direct child of <svg>, an extra group (<g>) element is created to hold the title and the star icons.

❹ The star icons themselves (<use> elements) are all identical except for the x attribute which spaces them out across the SVG's width. The icons are added to the <g>.

❺ The entire graphic is inserted at the end of the element that had the data-rating attribute. That element is then updated with the initialized class, to turn off the fallback CSS.

The dynamically generated content for each SVG is the same except for the aria-valuenow and aria-labelledby attributes and the <title> content. Written as markup, it would look like the following:

```
<svg viewBox="0 0 5 1"
    role="slider" aria-labelledby="png"
    aria-valuemin="0" aria-valuemax="5"
    aria-valuenow="4" aria-readonly="true">
    <g>
        <title>4 out of 5</title>
        <use class="star" xlink:href="#star" width="1"/>
        <use class="star" xlink:href="#star" width="1" x="1"/>
        <use class="star" xlink:href="#star" width="1" x="2"/>
        <use class="star" xlink:href="#star" width="1" x="3"/>
```

```
    <use class="star" xlink:href="#star" width="1" x="4"/>
  </g>
</svg>
```

This structure lends itself well to JavaScript libraries that use markup templates to generate dynamic content. However, be sure to confirm that the templating tool you are using properly recognizes SVG elements and assigns them to the SVG namespace; otherwise, you may end up generating a dynamic DOM with all the correct tag names and attributes, but no SVG graphics.

CHAPTER 9

Radial Gradients

Linear gradients, as we have seen, are defined by the coordinates of a line (the gradient vector). The color stops are positions along this line. Each color value is then extended to infinity in a straight line on either side. By adjusting the stops and manipulating the vector, linear gradients can create many effects. But they aren't the only gradient option in SVG.

A *radial* gradient is one in which color changes radiate outward from a central point. These gradients can create the appearance of a glowing light, or can be used to represent the shading on spheres and similar rounded structures.

In its simplest form, a radial gradient is defined by a circle, with the colors changing from the circle's center to its edge. This is the default behavior for SVG's `<radialGradient>` element. As usual, the default behavior is not the only option, and you can create a number of effects with SVG radial gradients—including effects you cannot yet create with CSS gradients.

This chapter looks at all the possibilities, skimming through the areas where radial gradients are similar to linear gradients and focusing on the differences. The final section looks at the big picture, showing how you can combine many different gradients to create a complex scene.

Radial Gradient Basics

Radial gradients are similar to linear gradients in structure, at least in the markup. As with `<linearGradient>`, a `<radialGradient>` is a container for `<stop>` elements, each of which have an `offset` attribute with values between 0 and 1 (or 0% and 100%). The value at each stop is still specified with `stop-color` and `stop-opacity` styles or presentation attributes.

The difference is in how those stop offsets are mapped to the two-dimensional space being filled.

For radial gradients, the offset is a proportion of the distance between the starting point and the ending circle. You can modify both the position of the starting point (known as the *focal point*) and the size and position of the ending circle.

By default—when a `<radialGradient>` does not have any positioning attributes—the ending circle is the largest circle that will fill the object bounding box, and the focal point is its center.

Example 9-1 adapts four of the basic red-blue gradients that were used to introduce stops and offsets in Chapter 6; the stops are the same, except now they are inside `<radialGradient>` elements.

 If the radial gradients used in Example 9-1 were in the same file as their linear counterparts, we could have used `xlink:href` to copy the stops, even though they are different gradient types.

The gradients in Example 9-1 are used to fill circles, with the result shown in Figure 9-1.

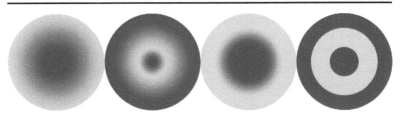

Figure 9-1. Radial gradients with various stop patterns

Example 9-1. Creating radial gradients to fill circles

```svg
<svg xmlns="http://www.w3.org/2000/svg"
    width="4in" height="1in">
    <title xml:lang="en">Radial Gradients</title>
    <radialGradient id="red-blue">
        <stop stop-color="red" offset="0"/>
        <stop stop-color="lightSkyBlue" offset="1"/>
    </radialGradient>
    <radialGradient id="red-blue-2">
        <stop stop-color="red" offset="0"/>
        <stop stop-color="lightSkyBlue" offset="0.3"/>
        <stop stop-color="red" offset="1"/>
    </radialGradient>
    <radialGradient id="red-blue-3">
        <stop stop-color="red" offset="0.3"/>
        <stop stop-color="lightSkyBlue" offset="0.7"/>
    </radialGradient>
    <radialGradient id="red-blue-4">
        <stop stop-color="red" offset="0.3"/>
        <stop stop-color="lightSkyBlue" offset="0.3"/>
        <stop stop-color="lightSkyBlue" offset="0.7"/>
        <stop stop-color="red" offset="0.7"/>
    </radialGradient>
    <circle r="0.5in" cy="50%" cx="12.5%" fill="url(#red-blue)" />
    <circle r="0.5in" cy="50%" cx="37.5%" fill="url(#red-blue-2)" />
    <circle r="0.5in" cy="50%" cx="62.5%" fill="url(#red-blue-3)" />
    <circle r="0.5in" cy="50%" cx="87.5%" fill="url(#red-blue-4)" />
</svg>
```

Instead of the color stops being drawn as parallel lines, they are drawn as concentric circles. When the color transitions are sharp, as in the last sample, this creates a bull's-eye effect.

Filling the Box

When filling a circle with a radial gradient, the ending circle of the gradient—the largest circle that will fill the object bounding box—is the circle itself. The gradient therefore fits the shape perfectly. In cases where it doesn't, the extra space is filled according to the spreadMethod property, which means that, by default, they are padded with the final stop color.

Figure 9-2 shows the gradients from Example 9-1 used to fill 1-inch-square rectangles.

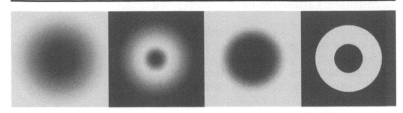

Figure 9-2. Squares filled with radial gradients

Radial gradients also neatly fill `<ellipse>` elements, as demonstrated in Figure 9-3; each stop now represents a concentric ellipse.

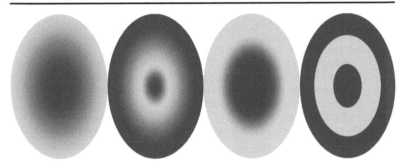

Figure 9-3. Ellipses filled with radial gradients

The same elliptical pattern is also seen when the gradients fill rectangles that are the same size as the ellipse's bounding box, as shown in Figure 9-4.

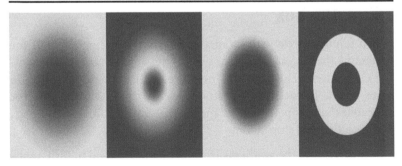

Figure 9-4. Non-square rectangles filled with radial gradients

Again, the results in Figures 9-3 and 9-4 use the exact same gradients that were defined in Example 9-1; there are no attributes on the gradient elements that indicate an elliptical pattern should be used. Instead, the elliptical pattern is a direct result of the stretched coordinate system created by object bounding box units. The stop patterns are still mathematically "circles," in that each point with that stop's color is the same distance from the center point—but only when you measure it in the stretched coordinates.

The only way to create a radial SVG gradient that always follows a perfect circular shape, regardless of the bounding box dimensions, is to use `gradientUnits="userSpaceOnUse"`. You will then need to use other properties to size and position the gradient to match the shape it will fill.

When filling squares or rectangles, the 100% stop offset is positioned around the (possibly stretched) circle that just touches each side. In the figures, however, the solid-color padding camouflages this boundary. The `spreadMethod` attribute can again be used to change the padding effect, and again the other options are `repeat` and `reflect`.

As mentioned in Chapter 8, WebKit browsers do not support repeating or reflecting gradients at the time of writing. Older versions of other browsers (pre-2014 Firefox and pre-2013 Chrome) will also pad the gradient irrespective of the `spreadMethod`.

When you repeat or reflect a radial gradient, you do not end up with a dotted pattern of repeating circles. Instead, the color pattern along each ray—radiating outward from the central point—is extended, repeating or reflecting, until it reaches the edge of the shape. This dramatically changes the look of the corners when a radial gradient is used to fill a rectangle. The different options are used in Example 9-2; the effects are shown in Figure 9-5.

Figure 9-5. Radial gradients with different spread methods: pad (left), repeat (center), and reflect (right)

Example 9-2. Changing the corner effect using spreadMethod

```
<svg xmlns="http://www.w3.org/2000/svg"
     xmlns:xlink="http://www.w3.org/1999/xlink"
     width="4in" height="1in">
    <title xml:lang="en">Repeating Radial Gradients</title>
    <radialGradient id="red-blue" spreadMethod="pad">
        <stop stop-color="red" offset="0"/>
        <stop stop-color="lightSkyBlue" offset="1"/>
    </radialGradient>
    <radialGradient id="repeat" spreadMethod="repeat"
                    xlink:href="#red-blue" />
    <radialGradient id="reflect" spreadMethod="reflect"
                    xlink:href="#red-blue" />

    <rect height="1in" width="32%" x="0" fill="url(#red-blue)" />
    <rect height="1in" width="32%" x="34%" fill="url(#repeat)" />
    <rect height="1in" width="32%" x="68%" fill="url(#reflect)" />
</svg>
```

With a repeating gradient, the color switches instantaneously along the edge of the circle/ellipse, to restart at the first color stop. With a reflected gradient, the edge is shown as a peak before the color shifts back. To really see these effects, however, we will first need to create a radial gradient where the gradient circle doesn't fill up the entire bounding box.

CSS Versus SVG
Radial Gradients in CSS

CSS also has radial gradients, defined using the `radial-gradient` function. As with linear gradients, the syntax and options are similar but not identical to SVG gradients.

One important feature of CSS radial gradients—not currently supported in SVG—is the ability to select between circular and elliptical gradient shapes. The optional first parameter to the **radial-gradient** function is a description of the final shape. It can include the keyword **circle** to force the gradient to follow a perfect circle, regardless of the aspect ratio of the image being generated, or the keyword **ellipse** to stretch to fit the box.

A perfect circle inside a non-square box cannot just touch all sides of the box. The shape parameter therefore also contains sizing information, which can be used for both circles and ellipses. The simplest way to specify the size is to use one of the four sizing keywords: **closest-side**, **farthest-side**, **closest-corner**, or **farthest-corner**.

The information about the ending shape and size of the gradient is followed by a comma and then a comma-separated list of color stops. For example, the following background style rule produces the gradient in Figure 9-6:

```
background: radial-gradient(circle closest-side,
                           red, lightSkyBlue);
```

Figure 9-6. Circular CSS gradient

The default shape is **ellipse** and the default size is **farthest-corner**, so the following gradients are all equivalent:

```
background: radial-gradient(red, lightSkyBlue);
background: radial-gradient(ellipse,
                           red 0%, lightSkyBlue);
background: radial-gradient(farthest-corner,
                           red, lightSkyBlue 100%);
background: radial-gradient(farthest-corner ellipse,
                           red 0%, lightSkyBlue 100%);
```

Using **farthest-corner** means that there are no empty corners to pad, but it also means that the final color stop will only be visible *in* the corners, as shown in Figure 9-7:

Figure 9-7. Elliptical CSS gradient

The positions of individual color stops can be defined using lengths with units or as percentages. When percentages are used, they are a percentage of the circle/ellipse radius. When lengths are used for elliptical gradients, they are measured along the horizontal radius of the ellipse. If an offset is not specified, the colors are distributed evenly in the space available.

As with linear gradients, CSS has a separate `repeating-radial-gradient` function. The parameters are the same as for the normal radial gradient; the size of each cycle of the gradient will be calculated from the difference between the first and last offset.

 When the first offset is non-zero, Blink and WebKit browsers currently fill in the center of the circle with that solid color. Firefox and Internet Explorer repeat the gradient inward as well as out, following the specification's generic instructions (for all types of gradients) to repeat the cycle "in both directions."

Again, to create a reflected gradient, you must make the gradient circle twice as large and then double the color stops yourself.

Scaling the Circle

You know by now that the default position and size of a linear gradient can be changed with attributes on the gradient element. The same is true for radial gradients. Just as the positioning attributes for `<linearGradient>` looked much like the attributes for a `<line>`, so the positioning attributes for a `<radialGradient>` look much like those of a `<circle>`.

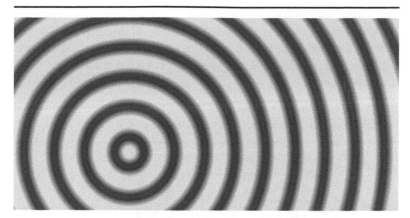

Figure 9-8. A reflecting radial gradient with a fixed circle size

The attributes cx, cy, and r on a <radialGradient> define the size and position of the 100% offset circle. They are all equal to 50% by default, which creates a circle centered in the coordinate system and filling its full width and height. The focal point (the point with the 0% offset color) by default shifts to match the (cx,cy) point.

Example 9-3 modifies these attributes to create a small circular gradient off-center in userSpaceOnUse coordinate system. This provides enough space, between the edge of the gradient circle and the edge of the shape, that a reflect spread method can create a nice ripple effect, like the waves from a raindrop in a puddle, as shown in Figure 9-8.

Example 9-3. Controlling the size and position of a radial gradient

```
<svg xmlns="http://www.w3.org/2000/svg"
     width="4in" height="2in">
    <title xml:lang="en">Repeating Radial Ripples</title>
    <radialGradient id="raindrop" spreadMethod="reflect"
                    gradientUnits="userSpaceOnUse"
                    cx="30%" cy="70%" r="15px">
        <stop stop-color="lightSteelBlue" offset="0.4"/>
        <stop stop-color="darkSlateGray" offset="0.8"/>
        <stop stop-color="darkSlateBlue" offset="1"/>
    </radialGradient>
    <rect height="100%" width="100%" fill="url(#raindrop)" />
</svg>
```

The radius of the base circle is 15px, so for every 15px distance, the gradient cycles through the list of stops—in one direction or the other. The dark rings in the figure are spaced 30px apart, the distance required to cycle through the reflected gradient in both directions.

In contrast, with `spreadMethod="repeat"`, you see the individual repetitions (and 15px spacing) more clearly, as shown in Figure 9-9.

Figure 9-9. A repeating radial gradient with a fixed circle size

Controlling the Size and Position of CSS Radial Gradients

You can control the size and position of the gradient circle in CSS by adding more information to the first parameter of the `radial-gradient` or `repeating-radial-gradient` function.

The full syntax for that first parameter is given as follows:

```
[ <ending-shape> || <size> ]? [ at <position> ]?
```

Translated into English that means: optionally, the shape and/or the size, in either order, optionally followed by the keyword **at** and the position.

The shape is one of the keywords **circle** or **ellipse**. The *size* can be given as a closest/farthest-side/corner keyword or it can be given as explicit radius lengths. Circles have one radius length, ellipses have two: horizontal radius first, then vertical radius. The shape keyword is not required when you use lengths for the size, because it can be determined from the number of length values.

For elliptical gradients, the two radius values can also be specified as percentages of the image width and height, respectively. You cannot currently specify the size of a *circular* CSS gradient using percentages. Future versions of CSS gradients may adopt SVG's method of calculating circular radius percentages proportional to the diagonal length; this is now used in the CSS Shapes Module for circles.

The position of a CSS radial gradient is equivalent to the **cx** and **cy** attributes for SVG. It may be given as lengths or percentages, or as a combination of the keywords used for specifying CSS background position. The keyword **at** must be included in order to distinguish position information from sizing information. The default position is **at center**, or **at 50% 50%**.

When positioning a gradient at a side or corner (e.g., **at right top**), the distance to the **closest-side** or **closest-corner** may be zero, collapsing circular gradients into a point and elliptical gradients into linear gradients.

With all that information—and remembering that CSS does not have *reflected* gradients, only simple repeating ones—the ripples in a puddle gradient from Example 9-3 can be re-created in CSS with the following code:

```
background: repeating-radial-gradient(
            30px at 30% 70%,
            lightSteelBlue 0%, lightSteelBlue 20%,
            darkSlateGray 40%, darkSlateBlue 50%,
            darkSlateGray 60%,
            lightSteelBlue 80%, lightSteelBlue 100%);
```

The circle's radius has been doubled (from 15px to 30px) to make room for both reflections of the gradient; similarly, the percentage offsets have been cut in half (so that 100% in the SVG gradient becomes 50% of the CSS gradient cycle) and the stops have been duplicated to fill in the rest of the cycle. Unlike with repeating linear gradients, you do not have to worry about percentage offsets upsetting your gradient scale—they are always percentages of the shape radius you specify.

Adjusting the Focus

There are two other positioning attributes for a radial gradient: fx and fy. These are the coordinates of the focal point of the gradient. While the gradient circle describes the position of the 100% offset stop, the focal point describes the position of the 0% stop.

The gradients we've seen have used the default focal point, which coincides with the circle's center; the default value of fx is the value of cx and the default for fy is the value of cy. Any other values create an asymmetrical gradient.

What does it mean to have a focal point other than the center of the circle? It means that the length of the gradient cycle will be different in every direction. Every ray radiating out from that point will pass through all the stop colors by the time it reaches the edge of the circle.

 The focal point should be *inside* the gradient circle; if it isn't, according to SVG 1.1, it would be shifted to exactly meet the nearest edge of the circle. SVG 2 proposes a different behavior, based on what is currently used in HTML canvas gradient functions. In other words, don't expect a consistent appearance cross-browser if the focal point is outside the circle!

What does it *look* like to have a focal point other than the center of the circle? The effect is to compress the gradient in one direction while expanding it in the other. It's probably easiest just to show you.

Example 9-4 constructs a grid of gradients, shifting the focal point to left and right of center using fx, and shifting the center of the gradient circle up and down using cy. The resulting combinations are shown in Figure 9-10.

The example uses a spreadMethod of reflect to show how the repeat distance in any given direction matches the original distance between the focal point and the circle's edge. It also just looks really cool!

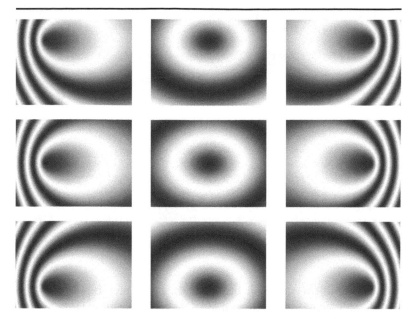

Figure 9-10. Comparison of changes in the center of radial gradients (rows) and changes in the focal point position (columns)

Example 9-4. Controlling the size and position of a radial gradient

```
<svg xmlns="http://www.w3.org/2000/svg"
    xmlns:xlink="http://www.w3.org/1999/xlink"
    width="4in" height="3in">
    <title xml:lang="en">Focus Point Versus Center Point</title>
    <defs>
        <radialGradient id="center" spreadMethod="reflect"
                        r="30%">                                    ❶
            <stop stop-color="darkRed" offset="0"/>
            <stop stop-color="lightYellow" offset="1"/>
        </radialGradient>
        <radialGradient id="left" xlink:href="#center"
                        fx="25%"/>                                  ❷
        <radialGradient id="right" xlink:href="#center"
                        fx="75%"/>

        <radialGradient id="left-up" xlink:href="#left"
                        cy="25%"/>                                  ❸
        <radialGradient id="left-down" xlink:href="#left"
                        cy="75%"/>
        <radialGradient id="center-up" xlink:href="#center"
                        cy="25%"/>
        <radialGradient id="center-down" xlink:href="#center"
```

```
                              cy="75%"/>
      <radialGradient id="right-up" xlink:href="#right"
                              cy="25%"/>
      <radialGradient id="right-down" xlink:href="#right"
                              cy="75%"/>

      <rect id="r" width="30%" height="30%" />              ❹
   </defs>

   <use xlink:href="#r" x="0%"  y="0%"  fill="url(#left-up)"/>
   <use xlink:href="#r" x="35%" y="0%"  fill="url(#center-up)"/>
   <use xlink:href="#r" x="70%" y="0%"  fill="url(#right-up)"/>
   <use xlink:href="#r" x="0%"  y="35%" fill="url(#left)"/>
   <use xlink:href="#r" x="35%" y="35%" fill="url(#center)"/>
   <use xlink:href="#r" x="70%" y="35%" fill="url(#right)"/>
   <use xlink:href="#r" x="0%"  y="70%" fill="url(#left-down)"/>
   <use xlink:href="#r" x="35%" y="70%" fill="url(#center-down)"/>
   <use xlink:href="#r" x="70%" y="70%" fill="url(#right-down)"/>
</svg>
```

❶ The gradient that will be used for the center block uses the default, centered, circle and focal point. The radius is set at 30% of the object bounding box, to leave room for the repeat effects.

❷ The other gradients for the center row are created by adjusting the fx to left or right of center, after duplicating the color stops and radius from the first gradient using xlink:href.

❸ The remaining gradients duplicate the color stops, radius, and focal point from one of the previous gradients, and then adjust the cy value.

❹ Because there will be nine rectangles with the same width and height, a predefined shape is created and then duplicated with <use> elements.

As you can see, changing the center point of the gradient circle has the effect of translating the entire gradient pattern. Changing the focal point, in contrast, significantly changes the overall pattern of the gradient, particularly in the repeats.

If you changed the center point *without* changing the focal point, that would change the look of the gradient considerably, of course. In Example 9-4, the fy vertical position of the gradient isn't set, so it automatically adjusts to match the change in cy.

Future Focus
Widening the Focus Beyond a Point

SVG 2 adds a new `fr` attribute to radial gradients. It would define a circle around the focus point that would represent the 0% offset for the gradient. A similar parameter is already available in HTML canvas drawing functions.

When the focal point is the center of the main circle, the resulting gradient is the same as having a non-zero first stop offset, except that the extra spacing would not be included in the repeat cycles. For asymmetrical gradients, the geometry would be distinct from anything that can currently be generated in SVG.

Transforming Radial Gradients

The `gradientTransform` attribute applies to `<radialGradient>`, and functions in the same way that it does for linear gradients—it changes the underlying coordinate system of the gradient, translating, rotating, scaling, or skewing not only the center point but the entire gradient.

Once again, you have to watch out for the effects of the stretched object bounding box coordinate system. No matter how you rotate an `objectBoundingBox` radial gradient, it will always be stretched out along the longer axis of the shape.

You can, however, create an ellipse stretched along a different axis by using a skew transformation. Example 9-5 uses the same skew transformation on three versions of a gradient which differ according to their focal point, as shown in Figure 9-11.

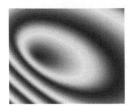

Figure 9-11. Skewed radial gradients, with different focal points

Example 9-5. Skewing radial gradients

```
<svg xmlns="http://www.w3.org/2000/svg"
    xmlns:xlink="http://www.w3.org/1999/xlink"
    width="4in" height="1in">
  <title xml:lang="en">Skewed Radial Gradients</title>
  <defs>
    <radialGradient id="center" spreadMethod="repeat" r="40%"
        gradientTransform="translate(-0.3,0) skewX(30)">    ❶
      <stop stop-color="indigo" offset="0"/>
      <stop stop-color="lightPink" offset="0.5"/>
      <stop stop-color="lightSkyBlue" offset="0.7"/>
      <stop stop-color="indigo" offset="1"/>              ❷
    </radialGradient>
    <radialGradient id="left" xlink:href="#center"
                    fx="25%"/>
    <radialGradient id="right" xlink:href="#center"
                    fx="75%"/>                              ❸

    <rect id="r" width="30%" height="100%" />
  </defs>

  <use xlink:href="#r" x="0%"  y="0%" fill="url(#left)"/>
  <use xlink:href="#r" x="35%" y="0%" fill="url(#center)"/>
  <use xlink:href="#r" x="70%" y="0%" fill="url(#right)"/>
</svg>
```

❶ The skewX(30) transformation will shift points on the gradient
   to the right to an increasing amount as the *y*-position increases.

❷ The gradient uses the repeat spread method, so the order of
   stops will not alternate. However, the first and last stop have the
   same color, avoiding a sharp transition.

❸ As in Example 9-4, the alternative gradients are created by shifting the focal point left and right.

The `gradientTransform` used in Example 9-5 also includes a horizontal translation to reposition the center of the gradient, which will also be affected by the skew.

Transformations on a `<radialGradient>` are calculated relative to the origin (top-left corner) of the coordinate system, not the center of the gradient.

Skews and off-center focal points allow radial gradients to go beyond perfect geometric symmetry and provide a sense of three-dimensionality. They are therefore one way in which gradients can be used as part of realistic drawings.

Grand Gradients

To create nuanced representations of real objects, you need to factor in the variation in color created by light and shadow. SVG includes filter functions expressly intended to simulate lighting effects, but these add extra processing time. If you can use gradients to achieve the same effect, it will often be much more efficient—particularly if you are going to animate the image later.

Figure 9-12 compares the two effects. One shape uses an asymmetrical radial gradient to simulate a yellow light shining on a red ball, the other uses lighting filters to achieve a similar effect. The gradient does not create quite the same three-dimensional curve as the filter, but it is close. The complete code is presented in Example 9-6.

Example 9-6. Creating lighting effects with gradients or filters

```
<svg xmlns="http://www.w3.org/2000/svg"
     width="4in" height="2in" >
    <title xml:lang="en">Simulated Lighting Versus
                    Lighting Filters</title>

    <radialGradient id="faux-lighting"
                    cx="45%" cy="45%" r="60%"
                    fx="30%" fy="30%" >                    ❶
        <stop offset="0.1" stop-color="lightYellow" />
        <stop offset="0.9" stop-color="darkRed" />       ❷
    </radialGradient>
    <circle cx="25%" cy="50%" r="0.9in"
            fill="url(#faux-lighting)"/>                  ❸
```

Figure 9-12. A spotlit ball, approximated with gradients (left) or calcu-lated with lighting filters (right)

```
<filter id="yellow-glow" primitiveUnits="objectBoundingBox">
    <feGaussianBlur in="SourceAlpha" stdDeviation="0.3" />
    <feComposite in2="SourceAlpha" operator="in" />        ❹
    <feSpecularLighting surfaceScale="0.1"
                    specularConstant="1"
                    specularExponent="20"
                    lighting-color="lightYellow"
                    result="highlight">
        <fePointLight x="0.35" y="0.35" z="0.7"/>          ❺
    </feSpecularLighting>
    <feComposite in="SourceGraphic" in2="highlight"
                operator="arithmetic"
                k1="0" k2="1" k3="0.9" k4="0" />
        <feComposite in2="SourceAlpha" operator="in" />    ❻
</filter>
<circle cx="75%" cy="50%" r="0.9in"
        fill="darkRed" filter="url(#yellow-glow)" />       ❼
</svg>
```

❶ The `<radialGradient>` defines a circle that is slightly larger than the bounding box, and off-center towards the upper left. The focal point is shifted even further to the upper left. This side of the shape will therefore be more strongly influenced by the initial color stops, while the bottom right will be dominated by the final color stop.

❷ The stops are offset slightly from the start and end of the gradient rays, creating a small circle of solid light yellow around the focal point and revealing the final red at the far edge of the gradient circle.

❸ The effect is applied simply as the `fill` property of the first circle.

❹ The filter starts by generating a blurred version of the alpha channel of the shape, then clipping it to the original shape edges. This creates a layer whose alpha value decreases as it gets closer to the shape's edges.

❺ The lighting filter uses the alpha channel from the previous step as a *bump map* to define the three-dimensional shape of an object. It then calculates the amount of light that would be added to the shape, using the various attributes to define the reflectiveness of the shape and using the `<fePointLight>` element to define the position and pattern of incident light. The `lighting-color` property specifies the same light yellow color for the light.

❻ The final steps combine the lighting effect with the underlying colored graphic, again clipping it so the light is only visible on the parts of the shape that were originally opaque.

❼ The second circle is filled in solid with `darkRed`, and then has the lighting glow applied via the `filter` property.

One strong justification for using gradients instead of lighting filters, currently, is cross-browser consistency. The lighting filters are inconsistenly implemented between browsers, if they are implemented at all.

 WebKit does not currently implement the lighting effect filters; these filter elements return a transparent layer. Given the way the layers are combined in Example 9-6, this results in the original flat red circle being displayed; for other filter combinations, the graphic could disappear completely.

Even in browsers that support filter lighting effects, the exact implementations vary considerably. Figure 9-12 showed the result in Fire-

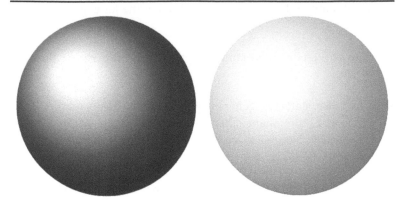

Figure 9-13. A different browser's rendering of the spotlit ball, with gradients (left) and with filters (right)

fox; Figure 9-13 is the same code rendered by Chrome, with a much stronger washed-out effect of the light. Internet Explorer generates an image in-between the two.

The other reason to opt for gradients over filters is performance, for two reasons. First, the lighting-filter is a many-step computation while gradient generation is a single function. Second, filters are calculated on the rendered, rasterized image, and therefore need to be recalculated any time the underlying shape changes or moves.

CSS Versus SVG
Mimicking a Focal Point with CSS Radial Gradients

There is currently no way in CSS to adjust the focal point of the gradient. In some cases—for non-repeating gradients—you can mimic the effect of an asymmetrical focal point by using layered background images. The focal point color is drawn as a color-to-transparent gradient or gradients, overtop of another gradient representing the ending shape.

Using this approach, Example 9-7 re-creates the spotlit red ball with CSS gradients. Figure 9-14 shows the result beside the original SVG gradient version.

Figure 9-14. Generating a focal point gradient effect, with a single SVG gradient (left) and with layered CSS gradients (right)

Example 9-7. Simulating off-center radial lighting with layered CSS gradients

```
<!DOCTYPE html>
<html lang="en">
<head>
    <meta charset="utf-8" />
    <title>CSS and SVG Simulated Lighting Gradients</title>
    <style type='text/css'>
    html, body {
        height: 2in;
        width: 4in;
        margin: 0; padding: 0;
        text-align: center;                              ❶
    }
    svg, div.sphere {
        height: 1.8in;
        width: 1.8in;
        display: block;
        float: left;
        margin: 0.1in;
    }
    div.sphere {
        border-radius: 50%;
        background:
            radial-gradient(ellipse 40% 40% at 32% 32%,
                lightYellow 15%,
                rgba(100%, 100%, 88%, 0.5) 40%,
```

```
                    transparent),
            radial-gradient(ellipse 55% 55% at 40% 40%,
                rgba(100%, 100%, 88%, 0.4) 20%,
                transparent),
            radial-gradient(ellipse 60% 60% at 45% 45%,
                rgb(100%,55%,45%), darkRed 90%);          ❷
    }
    </style>
</head>
<body>
    <svg>
        <radialGradient id="faux-lighting"
                        cx="45%" cy="45%" r="60%"
                        fx="30%" fy="30%" >
            <stop offset="0.1" stop-color="lightYellow" />
            <stop offset="0.9" stop-color="darkRed" />
        </radialGradient>
        <circle cx="50%" cy="50%" r="50%"
            fill="url(#faux-lighting)"/>              ❸
    </svg>
    <div class="sphere"></div>                          ❹
</body>
</html>
```

❶ The first two CSS rules layout the overall web page to match the SVG layout from Example 9-6, including the (not usually recommended) absolute dimensions for the entire page.

❷ The gradient effect is applied as layered background images, with three separate **radial-gradient** functions combining to create the shift from the focal point to the ending circle. The in-between stops use a partially transparent version of the **lightYellow** color, created with the **rgba** color function.

❸ The SVG gradient is included for comparison as inline SVG code.

❹ The HTML markup for the CSS gradient is a single **<div>** element to display the background content.

For optimal results on all browsers, the `transparent` keyword used in Example 9-7 should be replaced with another `rgba` function that matches the light yellow highlight color. Some older versions of Firefox will shift colors toward black when transitioning to the `transparent` keyword (which is officially transparent black). The specifications now provide explicit guidance that avoids this problem.

There are currently proposals to add focal point parameters (including a focal radius) to CSS gradients to make this effect easier, but the exact syntax has not yet been finalized.

SVG gradients are a deceptively simple topic. There may only be two types of gradients, linear and radial, but there are numerous possible variations to create different effect. Using all these variations, gradients can add considerable nuance and detail to simple vector shapes.

Gradients are a major part of the SVG developer's toolkit, and they can be used to create remarkably complex and sophisticated images. In most cases, these images do not consist of a single, geometrically exact gradient, but rather multiple, overlapping elements with partially transparent gradients.

A good exercise is to consider something like a theatrical stage, complete with red velvet side and top curtains and a stage with a spotlight. As a graphic, it's handy for highlighting a given object—a picture, slide, video or block of text—and because it is SVG, the curtains can even be directly manipulated to open and close.

When curtain fabric folds in and out, it is caught by the available light to show areas of brightness and shadow, which can be represented well with a shaded red gradient. One of us (Amelia) had previously created a poor approximation of this scene using simple rectangles filled with repeating gradients. The version displayed in Figure 9-15 was created by Kurt, carefully shading the curtains by positioning the stops in the gradients to match the curves in the paths.

The image is made up of three distinct layers.

Figure 9-15. A curtain-draped stage, built from SVG gradients

At the back, covering the full width, is the stage, which is simply a rectangle the width of the graphic starting about 350 units from the top, with multiple gradient overlays on it to create the appearance of a spotlight on a brown wooden floor. The lip of the stage is actually part of one of the gradients, and illustrates how you can use such gradients to "draw" hard boundaries. The light, in turn, is mostly transparent, with the opacity increasing toward the center and the focal point offset to create the effect of a spotlight hitting the stage at an angle. This is a soft spotlight, where the edges are not clearly delineated but instead appear to spill over into the surrounding darkness.

The next layer consists of the left and right side curtains, which use the same core path shape and a reasonably complex red/maroon pattern that corresponds to highlights and shadows in the folds themselves. The right curtain is the same as the left curtain, but flipped and translated to align with the right side of the screen. Each side curtain has a shadow curtain behind it, created from the same path but displaced slightly, and with an opacity of 50%.

Finally, the top curtain overlays the other curtains, and like the side curtains features a very elaborate linear gradient with 40 stops, determined primarily by trial and error. It also has an offset shadow.

The complete code for the image is presented as Example 9-8.

Example 9-8. Using complex and layered gradients to create a stage

```
<svg xmlns="http://www.w3.org/2000/svg"
    xmlns:xlink="http://www.w3.org/1999/xlink"
    width="100%" height="100%" viewBox="0 0 1000 650"
    id="curtains" >                                          ❶
    <title xml:lang="en">Stage Curtains</title>
    <style type="text/css">
        .curtain-shadow {
            fill: black;
            fill-opacity: 0.5;                               ❷
        }
        .side-curtain {
            fill: url(#side-curtain-gradient);
        }
        .ceiling-curtain {
            fill: url(#ceiling-curtain-gradient);
        }
    </style>
    <defs>                                                   ❸
        <path id="curtain" transform="scale(0.55)"
            d="m 0.319,0 0.252,1000 c 0,0 -2.761,40 44.129,30
46.9,-10 38.6,-20 46.9,-10 8.3,0 27.4,10 47.4,0 19,-21 63,10 63,10
0,0 11,10 44,0 33,-10 58,0 58,0 0,0 19,40 52,20 33,-30 34,-30
34,-30 L 390,-0.53 z"/>
        <path id="ceiling-curtain" transform="scale(1,0.5)"
            d="m 0,0 1000,0 0,180 c 0,0 -26,17 -49,9 -22,-9
-48,-32 -57,-18 -8,15 -31,3 -54,-5 -23,-9 -20,45 -49,23 -28,-23
-11,11 -34,0 -23,-12 -23,-32 -46,-18 -22,15 -17,-8 -37,-8 -20,0
-25,23 -54,11 -29,-11 -43,-25 -49,-3 -5,23 -5,23 -28,0 -23,-22
-46,6 -46,6 0,0 -28,12 -43,-3 -14,-14 -54,-8 -54,6 0,14 -23,20
-31,3 -9,-17 8,26 -29,8 -37,-17 -11,-34 -40,-17 -29,17 -49,-3
-63,-5 -14,-3 -14,37 -28,25 -15,-11 -9,-14 -32,-17 -23,-3 -28,37
-46,23 C 114,186 120,157 106,169 91.4,180 85.7,214 74.3,203
62.9,191 60,171 48.6,177 37.1,183 25.7,203 25.7,203 L 2.86,177
C 0,171 0,0 0,0 z"/>
        <linearGradient id="side-curtain-gradient">    ❹
            <stop stop-color="#800000" offset="0"/>
            <stop stop-color="#c00000" offset="0.08"/>
            <stop stop-color="#e00000" offset=".15"/>
            <stop stop-color="#800000" offset="0.24"/>
            <stop stop-color="#400000" offset="0.26"/>
            <stop stop-color="#600000" offset="0.28"/>
            <stop stop-color="#800000" offset="0.30"/>
            <stop stop-color="#c00000" offset="0.33"/>
            <stop stop-color="#800000" offset="0.41"/>
            <stop stop-color="#c00000" offset="0.56"/>
            <stop stop-color="#800000" offset="0.75"/>
```

```
        <stop stop-color="#400000" offset="0.82"/>
        <stop stop-color="#800000" offset="0.89"/>
        <stop stop-color="#C00000" offset="0.94"/>
        <stop stop-color="#800000" offset="1"/>
    </linearGradient>
    <linearGradient id="ceiling-curtain-gradient">
        <stop stop-color="#400000" offset="0"/>
        <stop stop-color="#700000" offset="0.013"/>
        <stop stop-color="#800000" offset="0.013"/>
        <stop stop-color="#C00000" offset="0.03"/>
        <stop stop-color="#D00000" offset="0.04"/>
        <stop stop-color="#C00000" offset="0.05"/>
        <stop stop-color="#600000" offset="0.065"/>
        <stop stop-color="#B00000" offset="0.078"/>
        <stop stop-color="#D00000" offset="0.09"/>
        <stop stop-color="#800000" offset="0.12"/>
        <stop stop-color="#A00000" offset="0.135"/>
        <stop stop-color="#D00000" offset="0.145"/>
        <stop stop-color="#C00000" offset="0.16"/>
        <stop stop-color="#600000" offset="0.19"/>
        <stop stop-color="#D00000" offset="0.21"/>
        <stop stop-color="#800000" offset="0.24"/>
        <stop stop-color="#C00000" offset="0.28"/>
        <stop stop-color="#600000" offset="0.32"/>
        <stop stop-color="#800000" offset="0.33"/>
        <stop stop-color="#C00000" offset="0.34"/>
        <stop stop-color="#800000" offset="0.37"/>
        <stop stop-color="#D00000" offset="0.39"/>
        <stop stop-color="#800000" offset="0.42"/>
        <stop stop-color="#E00000" offset="0.46"/>
        <stop stop-color="#A00000" offset="0.51"/>
        <stop stop-color="#D00000" offset="0.55"/>
        <stop stop-color="#800000" offset="0.57"/>
        <stop stop-color="#D00000" offset="0.61"/>
        <stop stop-color="#800000" offset="0.67"/>
        <stop stop-color="#D00000" offset="0.69"/>
        <stop stop-color="#800000" offset="0.71"/>
        <stop stop-color="#C00000" offset="0.74"/>
        <stop stop-color="#D00000" offset="0.76"/>
        <stop stop-color="#800000" offset="0.78"/>
        <stop stop-color="#C00000" offset="0.80"/>
        <stop stop-color="#E00000" offset="0.83"/>
        <stop stop-color="#800000" offset="0.86"/>
        <stop stop-color="#C00000" offset="0.88"/>
        <stop stop-color="#E00000" offset="0.91"/>
        <stop stop-color="#800000" offset="0.94"/>
        <stop stop-color="#C00000" offset="1"/>
    </linearGradient>
    <linearGradient id="stageGradient" x2="0" y2="1">  ❺
        <stop stop-color="#100800" offset="0"/>
        <stop stop-color="saddleBrown" offset="0.97"/>
```

```
            <stop stop-color="#A06020" offset="0.97"/>
            <stop stop-color="saddleBrown" offset="1"/>
        </linearGradient>
        <linearGradient id="shadowGradient" x2="0" y2="1"> ❻
            <stop stop-opacity="0.6" offset="0" />
            <stop stop-opacity="0" offset="0.97"/>
        </linearGradient>
        <radialGradient id="spotlightGradient" cy="0.9" fy="0.6">
            <stop stop-color="#FFFFFF" offset="0"
                  stop-opacity="0.4"/>
            <stop stop-color="#FFFFFF" offset="0.35"
                  stop-opacity="0.1"/>
            <stop stop-color="#000000" offset="1"
                  stop-opacity="0"/>                          ❼
        </radialGradient>

        <rect id="stage" width="1000" height="330" y="260" />
    </defs>

    <rect id="background" width="100%" height="100%"
          fill="black"/>

    <g id="stage-illuminated">                               ❽
        <use xlink:href="#stage" fill="url(#stageGradient)"/>
        <use xlink:href="#stage" fill="url(#shadowGradient)"/>
        <use xlink:href="#stage" fill="url(#spotlightGradient)"/>
    </g>

    <g id="side-curtain-left" >                              ❾
        <use xlink:href="#curtain" class="curtain-shadow"
             x="-1" y="3"/>
        <use xlink:href="#curtain" class="side-curtain"/>
    </g>
    <g id="side-curtain-right"
       transform="translate(1000,0) scale(-1,1)">            ❿
        <use xlink:href="#side-curtain-left"/>
    </g>
    <g id="ceiling-curtain">                                 ⓫
        <use xlink:href="#ceiling-curtain" class="curtain-shadow"
             x="5" y="5" />
        <use xlink:href="#ceiling-curtain"
             class="ceiling-curtain"/>
    </g>
</svg>
```

❶ An id on the <svg> element makes the entire scene available for
reuse within another graphic (although you would have to
import the markup into the other file to get all the styles to work
correctly in web browsers).

❷ The `fill` values for the curtains are set using CSS rules. In particular, the shadows for the curtains are created simply by substituting the gradient fills with half-transparent black.

❸ There are two complex path elements, one for the side curtains and one for the fringe across the ceiling. Neither has any styling attributes set directly; they will be styled when they are duplicated with `<use>` elements.

❹ The first two `<linearGradient>` objects for the curtains have been carefully designed to match the corresponding `<path>` elements. Many SVG graphics editors have visual tools that can make this easier, although some fussing is inevitable.

❺ The remaining gradients are used for the stage; the first one fills in the color of the wood from top to bottom, including a sharp transition near the bottom to draw the edge of the stage.

❻ The `shadowGradient` uses the default black `stop-color`, adjusting `stop-opacity` instead to create an extra layer of dark shading from the back to front of the stage (top to bottom of the rectangle). Applying this as a separate layer makes it easier to later adjust the brightness separately from the color hue.

❼ The `<radialGradient>` that creates the spotlight will also be layered on top of the stage, so it also makes use of the `stop-opacity` property to allow the other layers to show through.

❽ After drawing a solid black backdrop, the stage is drawn using the same rectangle three times, to layer together the three different gradients. This is, of course, a perfect example of why layered fills are an eagerly anticipated feature of SVG 2—they would allow the stage to be drawn as a single shape filled with all three gradients stacked together.

❾ The left curtain is drawn by layering two versions of the curtain shape together, one with the shadow styles and one with the main curtain styles.

❿ The right curtain is drawn by duplicating and transforming the left curtain.

⓫ Finally, the ceiling curtain is drawn using the same layered approach.

Although Example 9-8 contains a lot of code compared to most of the examples in the book, it is still relatively small for an image file: 7KB as editable text, 1.4KB when compressed with gzip. In comparison, a PNG version of the same image, large enough to fill most desktop displays, is over 80KB in size.

Future Focus
Mesh Gradients for Flexible Color Transitions

Although the stage-and-curtains example is elegant, it is also conveniently well suited for SVG gradients. The folds of hanging curtains are nicely parallel and so can be effectively matched to a linear gradient. In general, this is not always true. The colors and shadows of objects transition in all sorts of directions, not only as parallel lines or ellipses. Currently, to re-create any sort of complex shading pattern, you must layer together many different partially transparent gradients.

SVG 2 introduces a means of describing complex two-dimensional color transitions, using what are known as *mesh gradients*. The mesh is a grid of intersecting paths that may be straight or curved. Gradient color stops are then assigned to the intersection points of these paths, and the colors in each *patch* of the gradient (a region bound by four curves) is interpolated from them. Although mesh gradients are probably not something you would be coding by hand, Adobe Illustrator and Inkscape already support the creation of gradient meshes, and the SVG proposal is designed to be compatible.

Mesh gradients are too complex to be a likely candidate for CSS gradient functions. However, the CSS Image Values and Replaced Content Module Level 4 introduces a more manageable new gradient function, `conic-gradient()`, and its variant, `repeating-conic-gradient()`.

A conic gradient is one in which colors change as you move in a circle around a center point; each color is then extended as far as required along a straight line radiating out from the center point. This is in contrast to a radial gradient, in which the colors change as they radiate away from the focal point, and stay the same in each concentric circle. The stops in a conic gradient are defined not by a fixed distance, but by a fixed angle.

The proposed CSS syntax would use the **at** keyword to optionally describe the position of the center point (by default, the center of the image) using the same syntax as for radial gradients. The list of stops would then follow, with offsets described either using angle units or as percentages of the full circle. The zero-angle would be the vertical line pointing up from the center point. Angles outside of the range 0°–360° would be cropped off. As with the other CSS gradients, color stops without specified offsets would be distributed evenly.

Some valid conic gradient syntaxes include:

```
/* a hue color wheel */
conic-gradient(red,yellow,lime,cyan,blue,magenta,red);

/* oscillating orange rays */
repeating-conic-gradient(at top left,
            tomato, gold 10deg);

/* checkerboard */
conic-gradient(black 0 25%, white 25% 50%,
            black 50% 75%, white 75% 100%);
```

The final example makes use of another shorthand introduced by the Level 4 specification, which will apply to all CSS gradient functions. When a gradient includes a region of solid color, instead of having to define two consecutive stops with the same color value, you could instead list two offsets for a single color value.

Conic gradients are not directly supported in any browsers at the time of writing. Lea Verou, a member of the CSS working group, has created a JavaScript polyfill that uses HTML canvas to convert conic-gradient declarations into static images.

Because CSS gradient functions will be directly usable in SVG 2, there are currently no plans to create dedicated SVG conic-gradient elements. However, the same effect (or a close approximation, anyway) could also be created using the mesh gradient structure.

CHAPTER 10

Tiles and Textures

While introducing paint servers in Chapter 5, we mentioned that there were a number of different sources you might wish to use to paint a shape: a single color, one or more gradients, repeating patterns, bitmap graphics, text, even other SVG files. So far, we have described how to use a solid color or a single gradient. All the remaining possibilites will use a single paint server element: `<pattern>`.

An SVG pattern defines a block of SVG graphics that will be used as a paint server for other shapes. Any SVG content can be used, including images, text, and shapes filled with gradients. A pattern is repeated in a rectangular (or *transformed* rectangular) tiled layout. You can, however, make one tile the full size of the shape to create a non-repeating fill; that opens so many possibilities it will be discussed separately, in Chapter 11.

There are a number of options for sizing both the tiles and the pattern content. This make many different designs possible—but others remain difficult. This chapter tries to emphasize both what can and what can't be done, and offers some workaround suggestions for the more frustrating situations. We also compare SVG patterns with a type of repeating pattern most web designers are familiar with: repeating CSS background images.

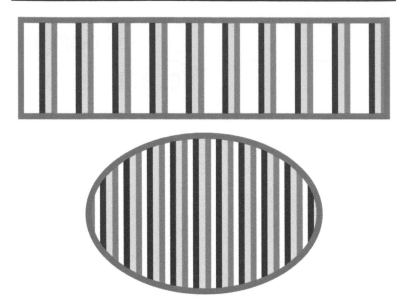

Figure 10-1. Shapes filled with a simple repeating stripes pattern

Building a Building Block

In many ways, the `<pattern>` element is similar to the gradient elements introduced in previous chapters. The attributes on the element itself define the shape and size of the pattern *tile* (repeating unit). The child content of the `<pattern>` makes up the graphics that are drawn to the screen.

The attributes on `<linearGradient>` and `<radialGradient>` matched those of a `<line>` and `<circle>`. The geometrical attributes on a `<pattern>` are like those of a `<rect>` or `<image>`: x, y, width, and height. All are zero by default, and as usual, a width or height of zero prevents the content from being drawn.

To understand how patterns work, it's usually best to see one in action. Example 10-1 presents the code for a simple striped pattern, and then uses it to fill two shapes. Figure 10-1 shows the result.

Example 10-1. Filling shapes with a simple repeating stripes pattern

```
<svg xmlns="http://www.w3.org/2000/svg"
     xmlns:xlink="http://www.w3.org/1999/xlink"
```

```
    width="4in" height="3in" >
<title xml:lang="en">Striped Pattern</title>
<style type="text/css">
    svg {
        stroke-width: 6px;
    }
</style>
<pattern id="stripes" x="5%" width="10%" height="100%">
    <line x1="3" x2="3" y2="100%" stroke="maroon" />
    <line x1="9" x2="9" y2="100%" stroke="gold" />
    <line x1="15" x2="15" y2="100%" stroke="tomato" />
</pattern>

<g stroke="royalBlue" fill="url(#stripes)">
    <rect x="0.1in" y="0.1in" width="3.8in" height="1in" />
    <ellipse cx="50%" cy="2.1in" rx="1.2in" ry="0.8in" />
</g>
</svg>
```

The pattern itself is declared with the following code:

```
<pattern id="stripes" x="5%" width="10%" height="100%">
```

The id attribute, as with other paint servers, is required so that the pattern can be used. The width and height attributes define the size of each repeating tile. The tiles are arranged starting from the point defined by the x horizontal offset and y vertical offset (here left as the default 0). The (x,y) point defines the position of the top left corner of the reference tile; additional tiles are then placed above, below, left, and right for as many repeats as required to fill the shape.

But how are width, height, x, and y measured? Look at Figure 10-1 again, paying attention to the differences between the two shapes. The stripes are the same width in both shapes, but are much closer together in the ellipse. The width is clearly not an absolute value.

By default, the attributes that control the size of the pattern tile are calculated in objectBoundingBox units. Each tile extends the full height (100%) of the bounding box, but only 10% of its width. No matter how wide the shape is, there will be exactly 10 sets of stripes spaced out across it.

As you might have guessed from your experience with gradients, the default object bounding box dimensions for tiles can be changed to userSpaceOnUse.

The relevant attribute is called `patternUnits`, and "Stretching to Fit" on page 171 will examine the effects of changing it.

The x and y offsets are also measured relative to the bounding box. For Example 10-1, the 5% horizontal offset is half of the 10% tile width. This positions the first complete stripe shifted over that distance from the top left corner of the bounding box. However, the pattern still repeats in all directions: in the ellipse, you can just see the edge of another stripe on the left side, because the stripes extend farther across the tile width than the 5% offset.

The stripes themselves, therefore, are *not* scaled proportionate to the object bounding box. By default, the contents of a pattern are measured in the `userSpaceOnUse` coordinate system (i.e., the coordinate system in effect for the shape being filled). The origin of that coordinate system, however, is translated to the top left corner of each pattern tile.

This scaling of the pattern graphics is controlled by a `patternContentUnits` attribute on the `<pattern>` element. `userSpaceOnUse` is the default; and the alternative option is `objectBoundingBox`.

The stripes—the three `<line>` elements—are much longer than they need to be, extending to 100% of the full height of the SVG. According to the SVG 1.1 specifications, the pattern should use the value of 100% in effect for the shape being filled. However, as mentioned in Chapter 7, user space units are not consistently implemented by browsers when the shape is nested in a different SVG from the paint server.

For many pattern designs, it is necessary to over-size the graphics to be sure that the entire tile is filled, no matter the size of the shape. A pattern element has `overflow: hidden` set by default, which causes the graphics will be clipped to the tile.

Visible `overflow` is intentionally left undefined for patterns in SVG 1.1 and 2, in response to inconsistent implementations in SVG 1. This means that each browser can handle it however they choose. Changing this setting is therefore not recommended.

A more practical example of using pattern tiles that scale with the bounding box, but stripes that don't, is given in Example 10-2. It uses a pattern to divide a rectangle into a fixed number of equal pieces, each one outlined with a thin grid line. This type of overlay grid is a common tool in image editing software; it is shown here within a super-simplified web application, overlaid on top of a photograph.

To demonstrate the scaling effect of the pattern tiles, a thumbnail version of the photo is also included with its own grid; the grid squares are smaller on the thumbnail, but the grid lines stay the same thickness. In both cases, the lines are actually drawn much larger than required, and trimmed to fit with hidden overflow. The complete page is shown in Figure 10-2.

Example 10-2. A resizable grid pattern within a photo-editing application

HTML Markup & JavaScript:

```
<!DOCTYPE html>
<html>
<head>
    <meta charset="utf-8" />
    <title>Photo Grid Overlay</title>
    <style type='text/css'>
        /* styles must be in the same document */
    </style>
</head>
<body>
    <fieldset id="grid-options"
            role="radiogroup" aria-controls="graphics">         ❶
        <legend>Show Grid:</legend>
        <label>
            <input type="radio" name="grid" value="none" checked>
            None</label>
        <label><input type="radio" name="grid" value="grid4">
            2&times;2</label>
        <label><input type="radio" name="grid" value="grid9">
```

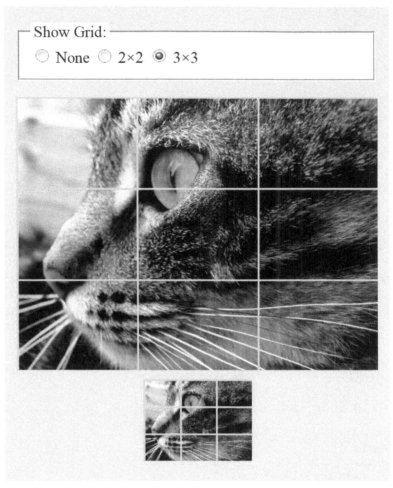

Figure 10-2. The same 3×3 pattern grid filling rectangles of different sizes

```
            3&times;3</label>
    </fieldset>

<svg id="graphics" viewBox="0 0 400 400">
    <title>Photo View</title>
    <pattern id="grid4" width="50%" height="50%" >        ❷
        <g stroke="gold" stroke-width="4px">
            <line x2="100%" />                            ❸
            <line y2="100%" />
        </g>
```

```
        </pattern>
        <pattern id="grid9" xlink:href="#grid4"
                width="33.33333%" height="33.33333%" />   ❹

        <g>
            <title>Full image</title>
            <image width="400" height="300"
                   xlink:href="cat.jpeg" />
            <rect width="400" height="300" class="grid" />   ❺
        </g>
        <g transform="translate(140,310)">
            <title>Thumbnail</title>
            <image width="120" height="90"
                   xlink:href="cat.jpeg" />
            <rect width="120" height="90" class="grid" />
        </g>
    </svg>
    <script>
        document.getElementById("grid-options")
            .addEventListener("change", updateGrid);   ❻

        function updateGrid(e) {
            var svg = document.getElementById("graphics"),
                radio = e.target;
            if (radio.checked) {
                svg.setAttribute("class", radio.value);   ❼
            }
        }
    </script>
</body>
</html>
```

❶ The initial HTML markup sets up a small form field with
    options for turning on the grid.

❷ The inline SVG code defines the `<pattern>` elements. The pat-
    terns use the default `patternUnits` setting: `width` and `height` of
    the pattern tiles are percentages of the bounding box.

❸ The content, however, is drawn in the user space coordinate sys-
    tem. It consists of two lines (grouped together to apply common
    styles), each of which starts at the origin and extends in either
    the horizontal or vertical direction, up to the width or height of
    the SVG—which will usually be beyond the pattern tile edge.

❹ The second pattern is written shorthand, using an `xlink:href`
    reference to the first pattern, but then overriding the `width` and

height attributes. Just as with gradients, the `xlink:href` attribute allows one `<pattern>` element to become the template for another.

❺ The rest of the SVG code describes the visible content: `<image>` elements with matching `<rect>` elements to contain the grid.

❻ The short JavaScript snippet listens for changes to the radio-button selection.

❼ A simple function responds by changing the class on the `<svg>` element, which will trigger appropriate CSS changes. For this simple demo, the `setAttribute` method is used to cancel out previous class settings and apply new ones in a single step. For a more complex application, you would probably need to be more careful about not affecting other classes.

CSS STYLES:

```
body {
    padding: 0.5em 0.25em;
    background-color: lightGray;
}
fieldset {
    display: block;
    background-color: white;
    margin-bottom: 1em;              ❶
}
legend {
    background-color: inherit;
    border-radius: 0.25em;
    padding: 0 0.2em;
}
svg {
    width: 100%;
    min-height: 300px;
    max-height: 100vh;              ❷
    shape-rendering: crispEdges;
}
.grid {
    fill: none;
    pointer-events: none;          ❸
}
.grid4 .grid {
    fill: url(#grid4);             ❹
}
.grid9 .grid {
```

```
    fill: url(#grid9);
}
```

❶ The first few CSS rules control the overall layout of the web
page and form elements.

❷ The `<svg>` element is given minimum and maximum height
values, but in the latest browsers it will auto-size according to
the aspect ratio set in the `viewBox` attribute. The `shape-rendering: crispEdges` setting turns off anti-aliasing of vector
graphics, which otherwise could make the grid lines appear
blurred.

❸ The rectangles with class `grid` will by default have no fill.
Thanks to the `pointer-events` setting, they will not be interactive, whether filled or not.

❹ When the `grid4` or `grid9` classes are set on a parent element,
the grid rectangle is set to be filled with the appropriate pattern,
identified with a matching `id`.

The end result is functional, but it is not ideal. The grid lines use a
4px stroke width, but half of that width is always cropped off,
because they are centered over the edge of the pattern tiles. This
means that the grid lines are visible on the top and left sides of the
rectangle, but not on the bottom right. The intersections therefore
don't quite match the geometric halves or thirds of the photograph's
width or height.

There is no simple way to fix this with SVG patterns. When using
object bounding box units for the tile *size*, you cannot offset the tile
by a fixed number of pixels to compensate for the imbalance,
because x and y are also interpreted in bounding box units. And
because the grid lines are drawn in user-space units, there is no way
to position additional lines on the opposite sides of each tile.

Stretching to Fit

There are very few pattern designs that work well with the default of
`objectBoundingBox` units for the pattern tile and `userSpaceOnUse`
units for the content. For patterns other than thin stripes or grids,
you usually *want* the graphics to scale to match the pattern tile.

In other words, you want both attributes, `patternUnits` and `patternContentUnits`, to have the same value, either `objectBoundingBox` or `userSpaceOnUse`.

 Due to the mismatched defaults, you normally only need to declare one or the other, not both. Either set `patternUnits = "userSpaceOnUse"` or else set `patternContentUnits = "objectBoundingBox"`.

When both the pattern tile and its contents scale relative to the object bounding box, you create a pattern that adjusts to fit the shape being filled. There are always the same number of tiles in each box, but the entire tiled pattern scales up and down together.

When using object bounding box units like this, keep in mind the lessons from Chapter 7 about the distorting effect of the coordinate system. If the box is not square, the coordinate system will be non-uniform with horizontal and vertical units of different lengths. Circles, text, and images will all be stretched and rotational angles will be uneven. Also note that *everything* is scaled according to the new units, including stroke widths and font size.

Furthermore, for `patternContentUnits`, unlike for the pattern tile dimensions, percentages are *not* interchangeable with decimals. Instead, the definition of 100% from the user space coordinate system is scaled up proportional to the scaling effect on all other units.

 No matter what scaling method you use, percentages in the pattern content do not refer to the pattern tile.

If the main viewport was 200 units wide (1% is 2 horizontal units) and 150 units high (1% is 1.5 vertical units), 1% will now be twice the box width and 1.5 times the box height in the scaled coordinate system. Inside a different SVG, the ratios would be different.

This is not particularly useful, so percentages are best avoided when using object bounding box units for pattern contents.

What you *can* use are decimal numbers, knowing that they are always a proportion of the bounding box's height or width.

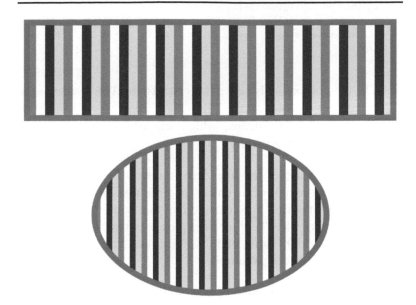

Figure 10-3. Shapes filled with a bounding box scaled repeating stripes pattern

Example 10-3 uses this approach to adapt Example 10-1. The colored stripes now scale in width as well as spacing to fit in the different shapes, as shown in Figure 10-3.

Example 10-3. Filling shapes with a scaled repeating stripes pattern

```
<svg xmlns="http://www.w3.org/2000/svg"
    xmlns:xlink="http://www.w3.org/1999/xlink"
    width="4in" height="3in" >
    <title xml:lang="en">Bounding Box Striped Pattern</title>
    <style type="text/css">
        svg {
            stroke-width: 6px;
        }
    </style>
    <pattern id="stripes2" x="5%" width="10%" height="100%"
            patternContentUnits="objectBoundingBox"
            stroke-width="0.025px" >                        ❶
        <line x1="0.0125" x2="0.0125" y2="1" stroke="maroon" />
        <line x1="0.0375" x2="0.0375" y2="1" stroke="gold" />   ❷
        <line x1="0.0625" x2="0.0625" y2="1" stroke="tomato" />
    </pattern>
```

```
<g stroke="royalBlue" fill="url(#stripes2)">
    <rect x="0.1in" y="0.1in" width="3.8in" height="1in" />
    <ellipse cx="50%" cy="2.1in" rx="1.2in" ry="0.8in" />
</g>
</svg>
```

❶ The pattern explicitly sets `patternContentUnits` to match the default for `patternUnits`. The pattern contents will inherit a `stroke-width` of 0.025px, which will be interpreted in the `objectBoundingBox` scale.

❷ The coordinates of the lines have similarly been transformed into object bounding box units. The lines are spaced 0.025 units apart, with the first line centered half that width from the edge of the pattern tile. The three lines plus an equal-sized gap therefore add up to 0.1 units, or 10% of the bounding box width, the exact width of each pattern tile.

When using decimal bounding box units, it is usually easiest to work solely within the mathematical user units, and not bother with units, which will be divorced from their real-world meaning. However, you can use units, and they will be measured proportional to user unit scale, as demonstrated by the `stroke-width` value.

 Although `px` units should always be interchangeable with SVG user units—in any coordinate system—Firefox (version 40) rounds up the stroke-width when it is specified as 0.025px, to 0.03 units. It renders the stroke correctly if specified as 0.025, without units.

There is an alternative to using progressively smaller decimal numbers for coordinates. The `<pattern>` element can take a `viewBox` attribute to define your own coordinate system for each tile. We will explore `viewBox` patterns—and more uses of object bounding box patterns—in Chapter 11, which focuses on creating fill content that fills up the entire bounding box in a single tile.

For repeating tiles, however, it's more likely that you will use `userSpaceOnUse` units.

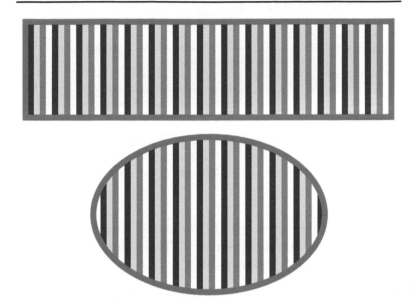

Figure 10-4. Shapes filled with a user-space repeating stripes pattern

Laying Tiles

With `userSpaceOnUse` units for both `patternUnits` and (by default) `patternContentUnits`, you create fixed-size tiles with a fixed-size graphic in each one. The result is something closer to the real-world concept of tiles, such as you might use to cover a floor or wall. The tiles don't change between larger or smaller floor areas, only the number of tiles that can fit in that room.

Example 10-4 adapts the same striped pattern from Example 10-1, but this time keeps the fixed-size lines and adapts the tiles to match. Figure 10-4 shows the result.

Example 10-4. Filling shapes with a user-space repeating stripes pattern

```
<svg xmlns="http://www.w3.org/2000/svg"
    xmlns:xlink="http://www.w3.org/1999/xlink"
    width="4in" height="3in" >
    <title xml:lang="en">UserSpace Striped Pattern</title>
    <style type="text/css">
        svg {
```

```
        stroke-width: 6px;
    }
</style>
<pattern id="stripes3" x="12px" width="24px" height="10px"
        patternUnits="userSpaceOnUse">                          ❶
    <line x1="3" x2="3" y2="10" stroke="maroon" />
    <line x1="9" x2="9" y2="10" stroke="gold" />               ❷
    <line x1="15" x2="15" y2="10" stroke="tomato" />
</pattern>

<g stroke="royalBlue" fill="url(#stripes3)">
    <rect x="0.1in" y="0.1in" width="3.8in" height="1in" />
    <ellipse cx="50%" cy="2.1in" rx="1.2in" ry="0.8in" />
</g>
</svg>
```

❶ This time, the pattern explicitly sets `patternUnits` to match the default for `patternContentUnits`. The pattern tile attributes have all been redefined in px units.

❷ The lines no longer have to stretch until 100% of the SVG height; because we know the tile size, we can draw the lines exactly to match.

The stripes in the rectangle and ellipse are not only the same size; they are also perfectly aligned. The x and y offsets for a user-space pattern tile are calculated relative to the main coordinate system's origin, not the corner of the shape's bounding box. Similar to the user-space gradients we explored in Chapter 7, this creates a continuous flow of paint from one shape to another—unless the shapes themselves are transformed!

With a consistent coordinate system for both the pattern tiles and pattern contents, it becomes possible to create patterns more complex than straight lines stretching to infinity. A circle can be centered in the tile, an icon can be sized to fit, or an `<image>` can be used to exactly fill the tile.

Nonetheless, when you want the pattern to continue smoothly from one tile to the next, like the vertical stripes in Figure 10-4, it is usually best to draw the graphics slightly larger than the pattern tile. In some SVG viewers, you can see the edges of each pattern tiles created by the code in Example 10-4 as either a too-dark or too-light edge, caused by the browser rounding the shapes to the pixel grid. Making each stripe extend from y1="-1" to y2="11" (instead of 0 to

10) can usually fix this; the ends of the lines are clipped at the point where they would overlap.

You can take advantage of this clipping effect to create patterns that do not, at first glance, follow a rectangular repeating tile. You can repeat shapes yourself, overlapping opposite sides of the tile, in such a way that when the tiles are placed side by side, the shapes appear to flow from one to the next.

Figure 10-5 shows a pattern of overlapping scales, like the scales of a tropical fish. Although the smallest repeating unit is a staggered, overlapping circle, you can create a simple rectangular repeating pattern by drawing a square from the center of one scale to the center of the next one directly to the side and directly below, as shown in the bottom half of the figure. Example 10-5 provides the code for the pattern, including the scaled up (if you'll pardon the pun) version of the repeated unit.

Example 10-5. Creating a complex pattern with overlapping shapes

```
<svg xmlns="http://www.w3.org/2000/svg"
    xmlns:xlink="http://www.w3.org/1999/xlink"
    width="4in" height="6.5in" viewBox="0 0 400 650">
    <title xml:lang="en">Fish Scale Pattern</title>
    <style type="text/css"><![CDATA[
        .scale {
            fill: url(#scale-gradient);
            stroke: black;
        }
    ]]> </style>
    <defs>
        <radialGradient id="scale-gradient">          ❶
            <stop stop-color="#004000" offset="0"/>
            <stop stop-color="green" offset="0.85"/>
            <stop stop-color="yellow" offset="1"/>
        </radialGradient>
        <pattern id="scales-pattern" width="20" height="20"
                patternUnits="userSpaceOnUse" >          ❷
            <g id="scales">
                <circle class="scale" cx="0" cy="19" r="10"/>   ❸
                <circle class="scale" cx="20" cy="19" r="10"/>
                <circle class="scale" cx="10" cy="9" r="10"/>    ❹
                <circle class="scale" cx="0" cy="-1" r="10"/>
                <circle class="scale" cx="20" cy="-1" r="10"/>   ❺
            </g>
        </pattern>
    </defs>
    <rect width="400" height="400" fill="url(#scales-pattern)"/>   ❻
```

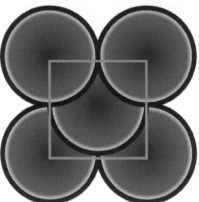

Figure 10-5. A scale pattern used to fill a rectangle (top) and its repeating tile unit (bottom)

```
<g transform="translate(200,525) scale(5) translate(-10,-10)">
    <use xlink:href="#scales" />                              ❼
    <rect width="20" height="20" fill="none"
          stroke="deepSkyBlue" stroke-width="0.5"/>           ❽
</g>
</svg>
```

❶   A <radialGradient> is used to fill each scale in the pattern.

❷   The pattern itself uses userSpaceOnUse values for the patternUnits, meaning that the pattern tile will be 20px square regardless of the size of the shape being filled.

❸   The first two scales are centered *almost* at the bottom corners of the pattern tile.

❹   The next scale, which will be drawn overtop of the previous two, is nearly centered in the tile. However—to avoid clipping the edge of its stroke—it is shifted up by one unit, along with all the other circles.

❺   The final two scales are centered just above the top corners of the tile. They will overlap the middle tile, and will appear to be continuous with the bottom row of scales on the tile above them —and with each other on left and right.

❻   The rectangle in the upper half of the figure displays the scales as a continuous fill pattern.

❼   At the bottom of the figure, a <use> element duplicates the group of five scales. Thanks to the transform attribute on the <g> element, the scales are scaled up, by a factor of 5, and then offset so the tile is centered in the available space.

❽   The blue 20×20 rectangle, drawn in the same scaled-up coordinate system, outlines the boundaries of the pattern tile.

Most patterns can be constructed in this way, but it may require a little extra math to figure out the dimensions. It helps to sketch out the final appearance of a block of pattern, from which you can identify the positions at which the pattern repeats in exact horizontal and vertical shifts. This then becomes the bounds of your pattern tile.

CSS Versus SVG
Repeating Background Images

In CSS layout, repeating patterns can be created using background images. The pattern contents can therefore be created from any valid CSS image data-type: a raster image, an SVG image, or a CSS gradient. By default, the image is repeated horizontally and vertically to create a tiled effect similar to an SVG pattern.

Originally, CSS background images were always drawn at the intrinsic size of the image. Similar to a user-space pattern, changing the size of the element with the background would change the number of repeats, not their scale. This wasn't particularly useful for large image backgrounds which should scale to fit the element, and it wasn't useful at all for gradients (and some SVG images) that do not have an intrinsic size. The CSS Backgrounds and Borders Module Level 3 introduced the `background-size` property that allows each background image to be scaled to either a fixed size or a percentage of the element.

There are a few advantages to CSS backgrounds compared to SVG patterns:

- Backgrounds can be set to only repeat in one direction or the other (or not at all) using the `background-repeat` property.

- The `background-size` property accepts `auto` values to allow the height or width of the pattern tile to scale to match the other value and the content's intrinsic aspect ratio.

- Backgrounds can be layered, with each layer having its own size and repeat options.

As mentioned a few times already, layered paint server fills will become an option for SVG 2. We'll show how they can be imitated, with composite patterns, in Chapter 11. Controlled repeat can be imitated by creating pattern tiles that are taller or wider than the object bounding box.

The main *dis*advantage of using CSS backgrounds to create a patterned effect is that the pattern contents must be in a separate image file (or encoded as a data URI), unless they can be represented as gradients. Although gradients can be used to create blocks and stripes, the rendering quality on some browsers is significantly poorer than SVG shapes.

Transformed Tiles

In the previous section, we showed how you can create non-rectangular patterns by including intricate repeats within each pattern tile. For certain geometric patterns, however, you can simplify your code by using coordinate system transformations to achieve the same effect.

The `patternTransform` attribute allows you to rotate, skew, scale, and translate a pattern. The transformation does not only apply to the pattern's contents, however: it applies to the entire pattern tile, and to the repeating pattern of tiles laid end to end.

> As with `gradientTransform`, the CSS Transformations Module redefines `patternTransform` as a presentation attribute synonym for the `transform` style property—although it isn't yet supported in browsers.

Pattern transformations make it easy to create diagonal lines and other angled patterns, without having to use trigonometry to figure out the exact horizontal or vertical distance between the line repeats. Example 10-6 uses a 45° rotation to create bias-cut pinstripe and grid patterns. The example also demonstrates more ways to use one pattern as a template for another. Figure 10-6 shows the result.

Example 10-6. Creating diagonal patterns with patternTransform

```
<svg xmlns="http://www.w3.org/2000/svg"
    xmlns:xlink="http://www.w3.org/1999/xlink"
    width="4in" height="4in" viewBox="0 0 400 400">
    <title xml:lang="en">Pinstripe Patterns</title>
    <defs fill="#444" stroke="lightSkyBlue">              ❶
        <pattern id="pinstripe" patternUnits="userSpaceOnUse"
                width="30" height="30">                   ❷
            <rect id="r" width="30" height="30"
                stroke="none" />
            <line id="l" x1="15" y="0" x2="15" y2="30"
                fill="none" />
        </pattern>
        <pattern id="diagonals" xlink:href="#pinstripe"
                patternTransform="rotate(45)" />          ❸
        <pattern id="grid" xlink:href="#pinstripe">
            <use xlink:href="#r" />                       ❹
            <use xlink:href="#l" />
```

Figure 10-6. Pinstriped patterns, before and after rotational transformations

```
        <use xlink:href="#l" transform="rotate(90, 15, 15)"/>
    </pattern>
    <pattern id="diagonal-grid" xlink:href="#grid"
            patternTransform="rotate(45)" />                    ❺
</defs>

<rect width="200" height="200"
    fill="url(#pinstripe)" />
<rect width="200" height="200" x="200"
    fill="url(#diagonals)" />
<rect width="200" height="200" y="200"
    fill="url(#diagonal-grid)" />
<rect width="200" height="200" x="200" y="200"
    fill="url(#grid)" />
</svg>
```

❶ The four patterns use the same color scheme, here set on the `<defs>` element. Patterns and other paint servers inherit styles from their surroundings, the same as shapes do.

❷ The core `pinstripe` pattern tile consists of a solid-filled square, with a vertical line stroked down its center. The tile will be a fixed size relative to the user-space coordinate system.

❸ The `diagonals` pattern duplicates the first pinstripe pattern, but rotates it by 45° to create diagonal lines.

❹ The `grid` pattern also uses the `pinstripe` pattern element as a template for the attributes on the `pattern` element, but it replaces the pattern contents with a copy of the solid rectangle and two copies of the line, rotated at 90° to each other. As with gradients, if the `<pattern>` has *any* child content, it replaces all the content from the template.

❺ The final pattern duplicates and rotates the grid pattern.

Example 10-6 also emphasizes how patterns and their contents inherit styles as normal based on their position in the document tree. Patterns do *not* inherit styles from the element being filled by the pattern.

 The combination of `xlink:href` pattern templating and pattern style inheritance suggests that you can create color variations of a pattern by changing the inherited styles, similar to how you can create color variations of an icon by setting styles on a `<use>` element. Unfortunately, the drafters of the SVG specifications did not consider this possibility, and no browsers tested have implemented it this way.

However, neither do the specifications specifically say that duplicated pattern content *shouldn't* inherit from the new pattern, so it might change in the future. For now, ensure that all inherited styles are the same on both the original and duplicate pattern elements.

Diagonal lines such as these could also be created with object bounding box pattern tiles, although the lessons from the section "Gradients, Transformed" on page 100 still apply. Object bounding box units add their own transformation, which distorts rotational angles. A 45° rotation would create lines that follow the diagonal of the bounding box, whether or not that is a 45° angle in an absolute sense.

Future Focus
Shorthand Hatch Patterns

SVG 2 introduces a new type of paint server element that will greatly simplify the creation of stripe patterns like those from Example 10-6. Called *hatches*, they are also intended to remove the possibility of having discontinuities (caused by rounding errors) at the edges of pattern tiles. Instead of tiles repeated in both directions, hatches would consist of *strips*. The strips would tile like patterns in one direction, but they would consist of a continuous path, infinitely long, in the other. Each path would have repeating segments, but it would be painted smoothly as a single element.

A hatch pattern would be defined by a `<hatch>` element, which takes the following attributes:

- `x` and `y` (offsets defining the position of the first strip)
- `pitch` (the spacing between strips)
- `rotate` (the angle of the strips)
- `hatchUnits` and `hatchContentUnits` (one of `userSpaceOnUse` or `objectBoundingBox`, with defaults the same as patterns)
- `transform` (equivalent to `patternTransform`)
- `xlink:href` (a reference to another `<hatch>` element to use as a template)

The hatch element would contain `<hatchPath>` elements, each of which defines a line or path to be drawn. By default, the path would be a straight vertical line (subject to any transformation on the parent `<hatch>`). However, you could also use a `d` attribute to provide a segment of a path definition: the path instructions you specify would be concatenated indefinitely. The following would therefore create a pattern of infinite wavy lines:

```
<hatch hatchUnits="userSpaceOnUse" pitch="6">
    <hatchPath stroke-width="1"
               d="c 0,4 8,6 8,10 8,14 0,16 0,20"/>
</hatch>
```

There is no option to create a background color for a hatch pattern; because of the new layered fill syntax, a background color can be specified when the hatch is used.

Using transformations, you can create pattern tile layouts where the tiles are parallelograms or diamonds instead of simple rectangles. For the most predicatable results, these patterns usually work best with userSpaceOnUse patterns. The uneven scale of object bounding box units might not play nice with the patternTransform values.

Figure 10-7 shows two geometric patterns that can be created through transformations of rectangular tiles. The code to create them is presented in Example 10-7.

Example 10-7. Creating triangular and diamond patterns with patternTransform

```
<svg xmlns="http://www.w3.org/2000/svg"
     xmlns:xlink="http://www.w3.org/1999/xlink"
     width="4in" height="6.5in" viewBox="0 0 400 650">
    <title xml:lang="en">Transformed Patterns</title>
    <pattern id="triangles" patternUnits="userSpaceOnUse"
             width="20" height="17.32"
             patternTransform="skewX(30)">                         ❶
        <rect width="30" height="20" fill="lightGreen" />
        <polygon points="0,0 20,0 0,17.32" fill="forestgreen" />   ❷
    </pattern>
    <pattern id="argyle" patternUnits="userSpaceOnUse"
             width="20" height="20"
             patternTransform="scale(2,4) rotate(45)">             ❸
        <rect fill="mediumPurple" width="20" height="20"/>
        <rect fill="indigo" width="10" height="10"/>              ❹
        <rect fill="navy" width="10" height="10"
              x="10" y="10"/>
        <path stroke="lavender" stroke-width="0.25" fill="none"
              d="M0,5  L20,5  M5,0  L5,20
                 M0,15 L20,15 M15,0 L15,20" />                    ❺
    </pattern>


    <rect width="400" height="325" fill="url(#triangles)" />
```

Figure 10-7. Triangular and argyle patterns created using transformed pattern tiles

```
    <rect width="400" height="325" y="325"
          fill="url(#argyle)" />
</svg>
```

❶ The first pattern uses a 30° skew to turn the pattern tiles into parallelograms. The height of each tile is scaled to equal the height of an equilateral triangle that has a base equal to the width of the pattern tile.

❷ As a result, the `<polygon>` triangle that fills the top left corner of the untransformed tile becomes a perfect equilateral triangle after the 30° skew.

❸ The second pattern uses a nonuniform scale and a 45° rotation to create diamond-shaped pattern tiles.

❹ A checked pattern is created by using two rectangles, each half the width and height of the tile, in opposite corners. The checks will be transformed along with the pattern tile, to create checked diamond shapes.

❺ The final element of the argyle pattern is a `<path>` that draws four separate straight lines, bisecting each of the diamond checks.

Both of the patterns in Example 10-7 do repeat horizontally and vertically, and could have been created without transformations. However, the pattern contents would have been more complex. More coordinates would need to be calculated with trigonometry, and there would be greater risk that rounding errors would introduce discontinuities between adjacent tiles.

CSS Versus SVG
Complex Repeating Patterns

CSS background images cannot be transformed separately from the shape to which they are attached. To create patterns like those in Figures 10-6 or 10-7, you have two options:

- Use a pseudoelement to contain the repeating background, setting its z-index so that it is behind the main content, and then giving it a `transform` property to apply the rotations, skew, or scale. Be sure that the pseudoelement is set to block display and is larger than its parent (so that the transformation does not reveal any empty spots), and also be sure that the parent is set to hide any overflow.

- Draw a larger section of the background, calculated to exactly match the amount of repetition in the horizontal and vertical directions, and include the transformation effects in each background tile. This is similar to the approach used to create the overlapping fish scales pattern in Example 10-5.

CHAPTER 11

Picture-Perfect Patterns

The word *pattern* evokes the repeating designs we explored in Chapter 10. However, the SVG `<pattern>` element is more flexible than this. By defining a pattern tile that fits the object bounding box, you can create a pattern that fills the entire shape without repeating.

Why would you want to do that? One reason is to be able to layer together multiple paint servers. Another is to fill a shape with an image, similar to a CSS background image.

As we have already mentioned briefly, SVG 2 will allow you to layer multiple paint servers in a single `fill` declaration, and use an image as a fill value directly, making these types of pattern redundant. Until those features are available, however, these techniques are essential to create many effects.

This chapter also examines the use of the `viewBox` and `preserveAspectRatio` attributes on the `<pattern>` element. These attributes are particularly important with full-image fills, but they can also be used with repeated patterns.

The Layered Look

In Example 9-8 at the end of Chapter 9, we created the effect of a spotlight on a stage by drawing three separate rectangles, each filled with a different gradient. This approach is fine for a single shape, but isn't very useful if you want to use the same layering effect on multiple shapes. That's where patterns come in. A pattern can contain all the layers, turning them into a single paint server for use by other shapes.

Example 11-1 uses three gradients combined in a `<pattern>` to make a circle and an ellipse appear as unevenly lit colored globes. The same pattern is also used to fill a text heading, as shown in Figure 11-1.

Example 11-1. Layering gradients using a non-repeating pattern

```
<svg xmlns="http://www.w3.org/2000/svg"
    width="4in" height="6.5in" viewBox="0 0 400 650">
  <title xml:lang="en">Multiple gradients</title>
  <defs>
    <linearGradient id="red-blue" y2="1">              ❶
      <stop stop-color="red" offset="0"/>
      <stop stop-color="blue" offset="1"/>
    </linearGradient>
    <linearGradient id="yellow-violet" y1="1" y2="0">  ❷
      <stop stop-color="yellow"
            stop-opacity="0.9" offset="0.1"/>
      <stop stop-color="darkMagenta"
            stop-opacity="0" offset="0.5"/>            ❸
      <stop stop-color="violet"
            stop-opacity="0.9" offset="0.9"/>
    </linearGradient>
    <radialGradient id="flare" fx="0.2" fy="0.2"
                    stop-color="white" >              ❹
      <stop stop-color="inherit"
            stop-opacity="0" offset="0.75"/>
      <stop stop-color="inherit"
            stop-opacity="0.05" offset="0.85"/>
      <stop stop-color="inherit"
            stop-opacity="0.2" offset="1"/>
    </radialGradient>
    <pattern id="gradient-pattern" width="1" height="1"
             patternContentUnits="objectBoundingBox" >  ❺
      <rect width="1" height="1" fill="url(#red-blue)"/>
      <rect width="1" height="1" fill="url(#yellow-violet)"/>
      <rect width="1" height="1" fill="url(#flare)"/>    ❻
    </pattern>
  </defs>
  <g fill="url(#gradient-pattern)">                     ❼
    <circle cx="200" cy="180" r="180" />
    <ellipse cx="110" cy="500" rx="110" ry="145" />
    <text x="400" y="525" text-anchor="end"
          font-size="100px" font-family="serif"
          stroke="indigo">Layers</text>
```

Figure 11-1. Shapes and text filled with a layered gradient pattern

```
    </g>
</svg>
```

❶ The red-blue gradient stretches from the top left to bottom right (remember, x2 is 100% by default) of the bounding box. It uses solid colors and will be at the bottom of the layers.

❷ The yellow-violet gradient stretches from the bottom left to the top right of the bounding box.

❸ This gradient is partially transparent, transitioning to complete transparency (stop-opacity="0") at the mid point, to allow the other layer to show through. The transparent stop still needs a stop-color, otherwise it will default to black and the colors on either side will be given a dark gray tint.

❹ The white radial gradient is mostly transparent, only transitioning to 20% opacity at the very edges. To make it easy to edit or animate, the single color is specified on the gradient element and then explicitly inherited by each stop. Unfortunately, stop-color does not inherit by default.

❺ The <pattern> uses objectBoundingBox units for both the pattern tile (by default) and the content (explicitly). The tile width and height set it to fill the entire box without repeating.

❻ The gradient layers are drawn by filling <rect> elements, which are also scaled to fill the entire bounding box, 1 unit each for width and height.

❼ The layered pattern is assigned to fill the shapes and text by setting the fill presentation attribute on a group. However, each element inherits the fill property independently, and uses its own bounding box to define the gradient layers.

The pattern—and component gradients—in Figure 11-1 stretches to fit each shape (or text element) according to the object bounding box dimensions. For abstract gradients, that isn't a problem. For other pattern contents, the distortion is unacceptable.

One option to avoid distortion would be to use userSpaceOnUse units for the pattern contents. However, the pattern will no longer scale to fit the shape. Furthermore, the positioning of the coordinates are relative to the overall space for the graphic, not the object itself. If you move the object so that its coordinates change, the pattern will remain fixed relative to the background.

You could address the positioning problem by always defining your shapes relative to a fixed point in the coordinate system, and then moving them into place with transformations or the x and y attributes on a <use> element (which have the same effect as a translation). To address the scaling problem, however, you would have to use <symbol> elements or nested SVGs to create a separate coordinate system for each shape, in which it fills the entire width or height. Of course, this all sounds like a lot of extra work and complication.

Luckily, there is one more option for scaling the contents of a <pattern>: define a viewBox and use preserveAspectRatio to ensure that it is not distorted.

Preserved Patterns

You cannot work with SVG—particularly on the Web—without running into the viewBox attribute. On your root <svg> element, it establishes the basic coordinate system and aspect ratio, allowing your graphics to scale to fit any region you set for them. It can also be used on nested <svg> elements and for reused symbols to create local scaling effects.

The viewBox is specified with four numbers: the first two specify the (*x,y*) coordinate of the minimum point you want to include in the graphic, while the third and fourth number specify the number of units to include in the width and height, respectively. Usually, either the first two numbers are zero (so the origin is in the top left corner and all coordinates in the graphic are positive) or they are negative values designed to position the origin in the center of the graphic.

The preserveAspectRatio attribute is easier to overlook, simply because the default value is often all you need. It sets one of three scaling modes:

- meet to scale down your entire viewBox region to just fit in (*meet* the edges of) the available space without distortion
- slice to scale up the viewBox to cover the available space (*slicing* off the extra)

- none to stretch or squish the viewBox as required to exactly fill the available space in both directions.

For the meet and slice options, you must also specify an alignment value of the form xMinYMax that controls which point in the viewBox region is aligned with the equivalent point in the drawing rectangle.

On a <pattern> element, a viewBox attribute overrides the patternContentUnits setting and creates your own coordinate system for the pattern. The coordinate system created by the viewBox will scale to fit the pattern tile, respecting any preserveAspectRatio attribute value.

 In Firefox versions prior to 40 (which was released in mid-2015), the viewBox and any preserveAspectRatio values are applied *after* converting to object bounding box units (regardless of the patternContentUnits value). This results in a distorted pattern for non-square bounding boxes, even if the pattern's aspect ratio perfectly matches the shape.

Because a meet option for preserving aspect ratio scales the content *down* to fit the entire width and height in the available space, this can leave blank space around the pattern contents. This includes the default xMidYMid meet value that applies when a viewBox is specified but not preserveAspectRatio.

One option is to intentionally draw a backdrop element, within your pattern, that is much larger than the viewBox. This backdrop will be clipped to the pattern tile, while the viewBox is scaled to fit. This is used in Example 11-2 to create a padded circular gradient that maintains its circular shape, regardless of the aspect ratio of the shape it fills. The gradient's shape is maintained by drawing it within a square shape (a circle could also be used). That square fills the entire viewBox, but the viewBox will not always fill the entire pattern tile.

Figure 11-2 shows the resulting gradient pattern, filling an oblong rectangle.

Figure 11-2. A circular gradient in a rectangular box, via a fixed-aspect-ratio pattern

Example 11-2. Creating an always-circular gradient using a fixed-aspect-ratio pattern

```
<svg xmlns="http://www.w3.org/2000/svg"
     width="100%" height="100%">                                ❶
    <title xml:lang="en">Always-Circular Gradient</title>
    <defs>
        <radialGradient id="radial">                            ❷
            <stop stop-color="lightYellow" offset="0"/>
            <stop stop-color="yellow" offset="0.2"/>
            <stop stop-color="gold" offset="0.8"/>
            <stop stop-color="orangeRed" offset="1"/>
        </radialGradient>
        <pattern id="circular-gradient" width="1" height="1"
                 viewBox="0 0 1 1">                             ❸
            <rect width="5" height="5" x="-2" y="-2"
                  fill="orangeRed"/>                            ❹
            <rect width="1" height="1"
                  fill="url(#radial)"/>                         ❺
        </pattern>
    </defs>
    <rect height="100%" width="100%" fill="url(#circular-gradient)"/>
</svg>
```

❶ The SVG (and the rectangle it contains) scale to 100% of the available space, so you can test different aspect ratios by re-scaling the browser window.

❷ The radial gradient uses default values for positioning and sizing, so it will be centered in the shape in which it is drawn and scale to fit the bounding box.

❸ The pattern also fills the entire bounding box (`width` and `height` of 1, with the default `patternUnits` setting). The `viewBox` defines the content units, creating an explicit 1:1 aspect ratio, regardless of bounding box dimensions.

❹ A backdrop rectangle is drawn five times the size of the square created by the `viewBox`, centered around it. The backdrop is filled with the same color as the last (padded) gradient stop.

❺ The gradient itself is drawn within a square that just fits to the width and height defined by the `viewBox`.

An important thing to note is that the shapes within the pattern are specified in the scaled user units, not in percentages. Although the `viewBox` creates both a new coordinate system origin and a new scale, it does not create a new viewport for the purposes of defining percentage lengths. Within a pattern, percentage lengths are scaled proportional to the change in scale of individual units, regardless of any `viewBox` values.

As mentioned for object bounding box units, this is not generally useful or predictable, and percentages should be avoided except for `userSpaceOnUse` patterns.

The use of a `viewBox` instead of object bounding box units also removes the codependency between the pattern tile scale and the pattern content scale. A `viewBox` on a pattern is always scaled to fit each individual pattern tile, not the bounding box as a whole. Figure 11-3 shows how the pattern appears after scaling down each pattern tile to 10% of the box width and 25% of its height, using the following attributes:

```
<pattern id="circular-gradient" width="0.1" height="0.25"
         viewBox="0 0 1 1">
```

The width and height used for the `<rect>` elements in the pattern contents have not changed at all.

The oversized-backdrop approach used in Example 11-2 is not ideal. If the aspect ratio of the pattern tile is more extreme than 5:1, the backdrop will not be big enough to fill it. If it's more important

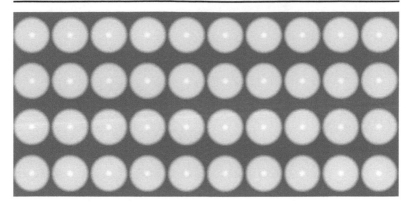

Figure 11-3. A repeating circular gradient pattern

to have the entire tile covered by your pattern than to have your entire pattern content visible, you can use a slice value for preserveAspectRatio. This ensures that the pattern contents always completely cover the tile.

Background Images, SVG-Style

When a slice approach to preserving aspect ratio is combined with a single-tile bounding box pattern, the net effect is very similar to a CSS background images set to background-size: cover. A single graphic fills the entire shape.

Example 11-3 uses a pattern to contain a fanciful SVG graphic of a sunny sky graphic, such as might be used for a backdrop in a slide or poster. The slice effect is demonstrated by using the pattern to fill a series of rectangles of different aspect ratios, with the results shown in Figure 11-4.

Example 11-3. Reusing an SVG graphic as a non-repeating image fill

```
<svg xmlns="http://www.w3.org/2000/svg"
    width="4in" height="6.5in" viewBox="0 0 400 650">
    <title xml:lang="en">Sliced Image Pattern</title>
    <defs>
        <linearGradient id="sky" x2="0" y2="1">            ❶
            <stop stop-color="lightSkyBlue" offset="0"/>
            <stop stop-color="deepSkyBlue" offset="1"/>
        </linearGradient>
        <radialGradient id="sunlight" cx="0" cy="0" >
```

Figure 11-4. Rectangles of different aspect ratios, and text, filled with the same graphic backdrop

```
            <stop stop-color="yellow"
                  stop-opacity="0.9" offset="0.2"/>
            <stop stop-color="lightYellow"
                  stop-opacity="0" offset="1"/>
      </radialGradient>
      <radialGradient id="cloud" fx="0.5" fy="0.15" r="0.6">
            <stop stop-color="oldLace" offset="0.75"/>
            <stop stop-color="lightGray" offset="0.9"/>
            <stop stop-color="darkGray" offset="1"/>
      </radialGradient>
      <pattern id="sky-pattern" width="1" height="1"
               viewBox="0 0 100 50"
               preserveAspectRatio="xMinYMin slice" >       ❷
            <rect width="100" height="50" fill="url(#sky)"/>
            <g fill="url(#cloud)">                           ❸
                <g>
                    <circle cx="10" cy="42" r="5" />
                    <circle cx="6" cy="42" r="3" />
                    <circle cx="16" cy="43" r="3" />
                    <circle cx="14" cy="41" r="4" />
                </g>
                <g>
                    <circle cx="20" cy="22" r="7" />
                    <circle cx="50" cy="22" r="10" />
                    <circle cx="40" cy="18" r="7" />
                    <circle cx="45" cy="25" r="9" />
                    <circle cx="30" cy="25" r="12" />
                </g>
                <g>
                    <circle cx="72" cy="39" r="5" />
                    <circle cx="77" cy="40" r="3" />
                    <circle cx="83" cy="41" r="4" />
                    <circle cx="80" cy="36" r="5" />
                    <circle cx="76" cy="35" r="3" />
                    <circle cx="86" cy="39" r="3" />
                </g>
            </g>
            <rect width="50" height="50" fill="url(#sunlight)"/>
      </pattern>
  </defs>
  <g fill="url(#sky-pattern)">                                ❹
      <rect width="400" height="175" />
      <text x="200" y="280" textLength="390"
            text-anchor="middle" font-family="sans-serif"
            font-size="124px" font-weight="bold"
            stroke-width="2" stroke="deepSkyBlue"
            >Clouds</text>
      <rect y="290" width="250" height="250" />
      <rect x="270" y="290"
            width="130" height="250" />
      <rect x="0" y="550"
```

```
                  width="400" height="100" />
    </g>
</svg>
```

❶ The code includes a number of gradient definitions that will be used by the graphics within the pattern.

❷ The pattern itself has a 2:1 (100×50) aspect ratio defined in its viewBox. No patternUnits or patternContentUnits attribute are required: the patternUnits are the default, and the width and height fill the entire bounding box. Again, content units are not required, as they are replaced by the viewBox. Finally, the preserveAspectRatio sets the slice scale and the alignment.

❸ The pattern contents consists of a rectangle filled with a blue gradient, a collection of gradient-filled circles to create the clouds, and finally another rectangle filled with the gold-to-transparent radial gradient for the sun.

❹ The <rect> elements and text that actually draw the graphic inherit the fill setting from a group. As usual, the bounding box for each fill layer is calculated per element, not for the group.

The pattern uses an xMinYMin alignment option, in addition to the slice scaling mode, so that the top left corner of the graphic is always included within the bounding box—although not necessarily within the shape itself, as demonstrated when the fill is used for the text.

Future Focus
Filling SVG Shapes and Text with Image Files

As mentioned briefly in Chapter 6, SVG 2 will allow CSS image types to be used directly as fill values for SVG shapes and text. This includes the CSS gradient functions, but also URL references to separate image files, whether those files are SVG or raster.

For example, you could create a separate graphic file with your reused backdrop, and apply it to your shapes with a rule like:

```
.slide {
    fill: url(clouds.svg);
}
```

The exact syntax for declaring the size and position of each fill layer has not been finalized at the time of writing, but will likely be similar to the syntax used for CSS background images.

Although you cannot yet use a separate image file *instead* of an SVG paint server, you can use an image file *within* a paint server, using the SVG <image> element.

Example 11-4 creates a pattern out of a photographic image (a composite image of the Earth from space by NASA). The image is scaled up to fill the pattern tile, with the extra sliced off. Figure 11-5 shows the result.

Example 11-4. Filling text with a photographic image inside a pattern

```
<svg xmlns="http://www.w3.org/2000/svg"
    xmlns:xlink="http://www.w3.org/1999/xlink"
    width="400" height="250" viewBox="0 0 800 500">
    <title xml:lang="en">Earth in Space</title>
    <style type="text/css">
        .earth {
            font-family: sans-serif;
            font-weight: bold;
            font-size: 148pt;

            text-anchor: middle;
            fill: url('#photoFill');
            stroke: #205334;
            stroke-width: 3;
            text-decoration: overline underline;
            text-shadow: white 0 0 8px ;                    ❶
        }
        .background {
            fill: url(#background);
        }
    </style>
    <defs>
        <pattern id="photoFill" width="1" height="1"
                viewBox="0 0 1 1"
                preserveAspectRatio="xMidYMid slice">        ❷
            <image x="-0.1" y="-0.1" width="1.2" height="1.2"
                xlink:href="globe_west_1024.jpg" />          ❸
```

```
    </pattern>
    <linearGradient id="background"
                    gradientTransform="rotate(90)">        ❹
        <stop stop-color="black" offset="0"/>
        <stop stop-color="black" offset="0.5"/>
        <stop stop-color="navy" offset="0.80"/>
        <stop stop-color="blue" offset="0.9"/>
        <stop stop-color="lightBlue" offset="0.95"/>
        <stop stop-color="green" offset="0.95"/>
        <stop stop-color="brown" offset="1.2"/>
    </linearGradient>
  </defs>

  <rect width="100%" height="100%" class="background"/>
  <text class="earth" x="400" y="60%">EARTH</text>        ❺

  <metadata>                                                ❻
Image Source: http://visibleearth.nasa.gov/view.php?id=57723
  </metadata>
</svg>
```

❶ Both the font-styles and the SVG styles are set using a CSS class.
   A text-shadow adds a slight glow around the letters in browsers
   that support this property, while paired underline and overline
   decorations add a border effect.

❷ The height and width attributes create a single pattern tile that
   fits the bounding box. The viewBox creates a square aspect ratio
   that will expand to cover the tile, with excess sliced off according to preserveAspectRatio.

❸ The image itself is drawn slightly larger than the viewBox, so
   that the black space around the globe will not be included.

❹ A <linearGradient> provides a horizon-like backdrop effect.

❺ The text is positioned in the middle of the SVG viewBox, with
   the size, font, and text-anchor set by the CSS class.

❻ The <metadata> element holds extra information about the file
   that is neither part of the image nor its alternative text.

The example demonstrates how text-decoration marks (under-
lines, overlines, and strike-throughs) are treated as an intrinsic part
of the text content, and are both filled and stroked with the same

Figure 11-5. Image-filled text using a sliced pattern

styles as the letters. An extra text-specific painting effect is added with `text-shadow` to improve contrast around the letters.

 Although most browsers support `text-shadow` for text laid out with CSS, Internet Explorer does not support it for SVG, nor do many other tools based on the SVG 1.1 specifications. Even web browsers that do support it can be buggy: Chrome does not scale shadows when text is scaled; Firefox does not draw the shadow if the text uses paint servers to fill the text; and Safari creates a shadow around each *em*-box instead of following the shapes of the letters when using paint servers.

In other words, use `text-shadow` for non-essential decoration only. If you do use it, it must be specified using CSS, not as a presentation attribute.

The source image used in Example 11-4 is shown in Figure 11-6 for comparison. It is square, exactly matching the aspect ratio created by the `height` and `width` attributes on the `<image>` element. If it did not match, by default it would scale down to fit, ruining the

*Figure 11-6. The image used to fill the SVG text (photo by NASA God-
dard Space Flight Center/Reto Stöckli with enhancements by Robert
Simmon (http://visibleearth.nasa.gov/view.php?id=57723))*

slice effect on the pattern. For a different image, you would need to
change the image elements dimensions and also the aspect ratio in
the viewBox so that the image would still fill it completely.

If you do not know the aspect ratio of the photograph you're going to use, you can specify a
slice value for preserveAspectRatio on the
element itself. The two slice settings
might slice off more than really necessary, but
that's better than having empty space show
through!

You could describe the effect from Example 11-4 as *clipping* the image to text. You can, in fact, create a very similar effect (minus the strokes and shadow), by including the text inside a `<clipPath>` element and referencing it in the `clip-path` property of an `<image>` element. In that case, however, the `<image>` would be the element on the screen, and the text would be a graphical effect. By using an image fill to a `<text>` element, the text remains selectable and accessible.

Future Focus
Painting Text Decorations

The CSS Text Decoration Module Level 3 extends the **text-decoration** property, making it a shorthand for a series of subproperties. The extended syntax not only allows you to set the type of line (under, over, or through) but also its color and its style, such as dashed or wavy lines.

Most of the new options will apply to SVG, but the color option is complicated by the fact that SVG text has fill and stroke paint, not a single text color. As a result, SVG 2 introduces coordinating **text-decoration-fill** and **text-decoration-stroke** properties.

Browsers have started to implement support for the new text decoration options. However, at the time of writing, none have implemented the SVG-specific control over fill and stroke paint.

The **text-shadow** effect used in Example 11-4 was initially proposed for CSS 2, but did not make it to the final specification; it is now included in the draft CSS Text Decoration Module Level 3. At the time of writing, it has not officially been adopted into SVG as a presentation attribute.

CHAPTER 12

Textured Text

We've now shown a few examples of using patterns to fill text, and we highlighted some other text styling options at the end of Chapter 11. We also used stroked text to demonstrate the `paint-order` property back in Chapter 2.

Throughout, we've emphasized that filling and stroking text in SVG is similar to filling shapes.

For the most part, that's true. However, there are a few differences with respect to paint servers, which stem from the way object bounding boxes are calculated for text. This chapter looks at paint servers and text more closely.

The differences between painting text and painting shapes are especially important if you are considering replacing text with shapes. Most graphics programs offer a text-to-path conversion that can preserve the visual appearance of text in a particular font, without the complications of having to distribute that font with your graphic on the Web, and without the unreliability of many browsers' text rendering bugs (particularly on mobile devices). Depending on how it is implemented, this conversion may create subtle differences or quite significant changes in the way the letterforms are painted.

 Converting text to path also makes it inaccessible to screen readers, or to regular users who want to search for, copy, or translate the text content. Be sure to provide machine-readable alternatives for any text as shapes.

The SVG specifications include numerous options for controlling the layout of text, some of which are borrowed from the original CSS 2 specifications, some of which were new to SVG but have since been adopted by CSS 3, and some of which are uniquely SVG. Some of these options are even reliably implemented in web browsers! Discussing all the text layout options is a book in itself,[1] so the examples in this chapter don't go into too much detail about how the layouts are created, except to indicate when features are poorly supported.

Bounding Text

Every element in SVG that is drawn to the screen has a bounding box. Although they aren't used in painting, bounding boxes are also defined for groups and other container elements such as <use> and <svg>; these container bounding boxes are used for clipping, masking, and filters. The bounding box is always a rectangle aligned with the axes of the coordinate system for that element (including any transformations).

For shapes, the box is always the *tightest* rectangle that can control the basic geometry of the shape. For containers, it is the tightest rectangle that can contain all the child components. For text, it is the tightest rectangle that can contain the *em boxes* for each character.

The *em box* in typography is the region in which each character is drawn. It is always the full em height for the font, and the full width determined by the normal spacing of the letters. In many cases, the actual letter only takes up a small part of this rectangle. For other characters, the letter might extend outside of the rectangle, with swooshes that extend under or over other characters in the row of text. As a result, the region of text that you're filling may not match the object bounding box used to scale your paint server.

Example 12-1 defines a simple striped pattern, scaled to the object bounding box, and uses it to fill four different text elements. Each element takes up a different amount of space within the drawing. Figure 12-1 shows how they are painted.

---

1 Specifically, *SVG Text Layout*, by the same authors and publisher as the book you are reading.

Mixing BLOCK

Three line text

Figure 12-1. Four text elements filled with the same striped pattern

Example 12-1. Filling text with an object bounding box pattern

```
<svg xmlns="http://www.w3.org/2000/svg"
    xmlns:xlink="http://www.w3.org/1999/xlink"
    width="400px" height="300px" viewBox="0 0 400 300"
    xml:lang="en">
    <title>Text Bounding Box</title>
    <style type="text/css">
        text {
            font-size: 50px;
            font-family: sans-serif;
            font-weight: bold;
        }
    </style>
    <pattern id="stripes" width="100%" height="20%"
            patternContentUnits="objectBoundingBox">  ❶
        <rect width="1" height="0.1" fill="indigo" />
        <rect width="1" height="0.1" y="0.1"
            fill="royalBlue" />                        ❷
    </pattern>
    <defs>
        <path id="p" d="M250,150 L350,200 250,270" />
    </defs>

    <g fill="url(#stripes)">                            ❸
```

```
<text x="50%" y="1em" dx="-10"
      text-anchor="end">Mixing</text>
<text x="50%" y="1em" dx="10"
      text-anchor="start">BLOCK</text>                    ❹
<text x="10%" y="3em"
      >Three <tspan x="10%" dy="1.2em"
      >line </tspan><tspan x="10%" dy="1.2em"
      >text</tspan></text>                                ❺
<text><textPath xlink:href="#p"
      >TextPath</textPath></text>                         ❻
    </g>
</svg>
```

❶ Each pattern tile extends the width of the bounding box and one-fifth (20%) of its height.

❷ The pattern contents are also scaled to the bounding box. Each stripe is one-tenth (0.1) of the bounding box height.

❸ A group applies the pattern fill to all of the `<text>` elements. As usual, each element will be filled based on its own bounding box.

❹ The first two elements are aligned horizontally. One has mixed-case letters, the other is all block capitals.

❺ The next element uses positioned `<tspan>` segments to break it across three lines.

❻ The final text element is arranged along a `<textPath>` that takes up approximately the same height on the page as the three-line text.

The first thing to notice in Figure 12-1 is that the stripes are different sizes in the multiline and `<textPath>` text than in the single-line text elements. These elements have larger bounding boxes, which create larger pattern tiles.

If you look specifically at the top row (the two single-line elements), you'll notice that you can't count a full five pairs of stripes from top to bottom of the letters. You'll also notice that the stripes are the same size for both words, despite the fact that the block capitals do not descend below the baseline. This is a consequence of calculating the bounding box based on the full em-height of each character, even if the characters used do not fill that space.

Mixing BLOCK

Three
line
text

Figure 12-2. Individual letterform paths filled with the same striped pattern

The larger elements are likewise slightly smaller than their bounding boxes, although the unused parts make up a smaller proportion of the larger bounding box.

For `<textPath>` and other text elements with rotated characters, many browsers (Blink, WebKit, and Internet Explorer at the time of writing) rotate the pattern along with the letter. For Example 12-1, this results in patchy, discontinuous stripes. Figure 12-1 is based on the rendering in Firefox (v37).

In contrast, if you were to convert the text to paths, the bounding box would be the tight individual bounding box for each `<path>` element. Figure 12-2 shows the result after using the Convert Object to Path feature in the Inkscape editor. Each letter becomes its own `<path>` element; the stripes are therefore scaled and aligned to fit five pairs of blue and indigo stripes from top to bottom within that shape.

Before converting text to path, the SVG code from Example 12-1 first had to be modified to replace all the percentage lengths and em-based units in user coordinates, as neither of these are currently supported natively in Inkscape (version 0.91).

The appearance can be made closer to the original by merging all the individual paths into a single, multipart path for each text block (in Inkscape, this is done by selecting the groups created for each former <text> element and using the Combine Path option). However, the pattern scale would still not be identical to the original <text>. The bounding box of the text extends beyond the bounds of the letters, and therefore of the resulting path.

With all these factors that can affect the scale of your bounding box pattern, it would be convenient to be able to easily adjust the size of each pattern tile. Unfortunately, with the code in Example 12-1, the pattern contents, also measured in object bounding box units, directly depend on the pattern tile size.

A viewBox can be used to define a complete coordinate system for the contents independent of the tile size, even if you do not need the pattern to maintain a fixed aspect ratio. A none setting for preserveAspectRatio stretches that square to fill the full tile, regardless of any changes to the tile size. Like bounding box units, the lack of aspect ratio control creates a distorted coordinate system, but for rectangular stripes that isn't a problem.

As mentioned in Chapter 11, Firefox prior to version 40 does not render patterns with a viewBox correctly.

Example 12-2 shows how this would work for the stripe pattern. To demonstrate the independence between pattern content and pattern tile, two variations of the pattern are created—one with thick stripes and one with thin stripes—by duplicating the pattern content with an xlink:href reference. Figure 12-3 shows the two versions of the pattern.

*Example 12-2. Creating scalable bounding box patterns with viewBox,
without preserving aspect ratio*

```
<svg xmlns="http://www.w3.org/2000/svg"
     xmlns:xlink="http://www.w3.org/1999/xlink"
     width="400px" height="70px" viewBox="0 0 400 70"
     xml:lang="en">
    <title>Adjustable Stripes</title>
    <style type="text/css">
        text {
            font-size: 50px;
            font-family: sans-serif;
            font-weight: bold;
        }
    </style>
    <pattern id="thick-stripes" width="100%" height="40%"
            viewBox="0 0 2 2" preserveAspectRatio="none">
        <rect width="2" height="1" fill="indigo" />
        <rect width="2" height="1" y="1"
            fill="royalBlue" />
    </pattern>
    <pattern id="thin-stripes" height="12.5%"
            xlink:href="#thick-stripes" />

    <text x="50%" y="1em" dx="-10" fill="url(#thick-stripes)"
        text-anchor="end">Stripy</text>
    <text x="50%" y="1em" dx="10" fill="url(#thin-stripes)"
        text-anchor="start">Stripy</text>
</svg>
```

Stripy Stripy

*Figure 12-3. Text elements filled with different-sized variations of a
striped pattern*

Each rectangle within the pattern is half the height of the viewBox
and its full width. The number of horizontal stripes that fit within
the bounding box height is therefore controlled only by the single
height attribute on the pattern, and can easily be overridden in a
second <pattern> element referencing the first.

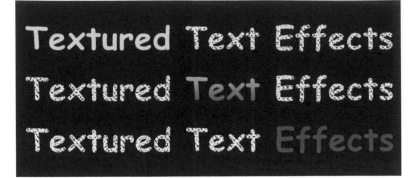

Figure 12-4. Patterned and gradient-filled multiline text

Switching Styles Midstream

Although each `<text>` element in Example 12-1 creates its own object bounding box for painting, the individual `<tspan>` elements in the multiline text do not. This is always true despite the fact that individual `<tspan>` elements can have different `fill` settings from the rest of the text.

 If the fill for a `<tspan>` uses an object bounding box scale, it is based on the scale of the entire `<text>` element, not the individual span.

Example 12-3 demonstrates this effect by using a bounding box gradient to fill three separate `<tspan>` elements within a larger `<text>` element. It also provides a slightly more readable example of using a pattern to fill text; instead of bold stripes, it uses a more subtle texture to re-create the effect of chalk on a blackboard. Figure 12-4 shows the result.

Example 12-3. Filling text with object bounding box patterns and gradients

```
<svg xmlns="http://www.w3.org/2000/svg"
     xmlns:xlink="http://www.w3.org/1999/xlink"
     width="10cm" height="5cm"
     xml:lang="en">
    <title>Chalkboard Text</title>
```

```
<style>
    text {
        font-family: cursive;
        font-weight: bold;
        font-size: 9mm;
        font-size-adjust: 0.54;                        ❶
    }
    .chalk {
        fill: url(#chalk-texture);
    }
    .chalk-marks {
        fill: white;
        fill-opacity: 0.8;
        stroke: silver;
        stroke-width: 0.2px;
    }
    .highlight {
        fill: url(#highlight-gradient);
    }
    .blackboard {
        fill: black;
    }
</style>
<pattern id="chalk1" class="chalk-marks"
        patternUnits="userSpaceOnUse"
        width="9" height="6">                          ❷
    <circle r="1" cx="0" cy="3" />
    <circle r="1" cx="1" cy="5" />
    <circle r="1" cx="2" cy="1" />
    <circle r="1" cx="3" cy="2" />
    <circle r="1" cx="4" cy="5" />
    <circle r="1" cx="5" cy="4" />
    <circle r="1" cx="6" cy="0" />
    <circle r="1" cx="7" cy="6" />
    <circle r="1" cx="8" cy="3" />
</pattern>
<pattern id="chalk2" xlink:href="#chalk1"
        x="2" width="5" height="5"/>                   ❸
<pattern id="chalk3" xlink:href="#chalk1"
        y="4" width="7" height="7"/>
<pattern id="chalk-texture" patternUnits="userSpaceOnUse"
        width="315" height="210">                      ❹
    <rect fill="url(#chalk1)" width="315" height="210"/>
    <rect fill="url(#chalk2)" width="315" height="210"/>
    <rect fill="url(#chalk3)" width="315" height="210"/>
</pattern>

<linearGradient id="highlight-gradient" x2="0" y2="1">
    <stop stop-color="gold" offset="0.3" />            ❺
    <stop stop-color="deeppink" offset="0.7" />
</linearGradient>
```

```
    <rect class="blackboard" width="100%" height="100%" />
    <text y="5mm" class="chalk" textLength="29cm">          ❻
        <tspan x="3mm" dy="1em"><tspan
            class="highlight">Textured</tspan>              ❼
          Text Effects</tspan>
        <tspan x="3mm" dy="1.6em">Textured
            <tspan class="highlight">Text</tspan> Effects</tspan>
        <tspan x="3mm" dy="1.6em">Textured
            Text <tspan class="highlight">Effects</tspan></tspan>
    </text>
</svg>
```

❶ You don't have to use px or pt to size text: the SVG is scaled to use metric units, so the text is as well. A font-size-adjust setting ensures that the apparent font size will remain approximately the same regardless of the actual font used; the 0.54 value is based on Comic Sans MS, the default cursive font for most browsers on a Windows computer.

❷ The basic chalk pattern is created from nine erratically positioned white and gray dots within a small pattern tile. The styling for the circles is set by the chalk-marks class on the <pattern> itself.

❸ To make the pattern denser and more irregular, it is duplicated twice, but with different pattern tile sizes and offsets.

❹ A composite pattern is then created by layering the three chalk mark patterns together. The composite pattern uses userSpaceOnUse units to define a large pattern tile that is just large enough to contain an even number of repeats of each of the layered patterns.

❺ The gradient used for the highlighted spans is a simple vertical linear gradient scaled to the object bounding box (default gradientUnits). Approximately the first third (to offset 0.3) is solid gold—in color, if not in value—and the last third (after offset 0.7) is solid pink, with a transition in between.

❻ The text is contained within a single <text> element. A textLength attribute ensures that the total length of three lines of text is adjusted to slightly less than three times the width of the SVG.

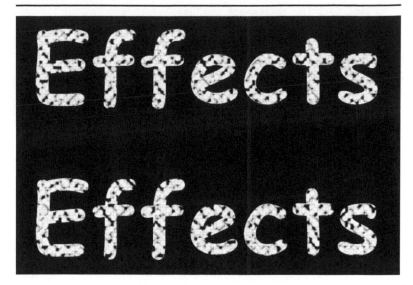

Figure 12-5. Close-up view of the pseudorandom textured pattern

❼ Three `<tspan>` elements break the text into separate lines. Within each line, a `<tspan>` with class `highlight` changes the fill of a single word.

The gradient-filled words within Figure 12-4 most obviously show how the entire `<text>` element is a single bounding box. However, it is also evident in the chalk texture. If each row of text were its own element, filled with the same pattern, the cracks and irregularities in the fill would be positioned at the exact same points. Instead, because each of the component patterns repeats on its own scale—and none of those exactly match the height of a line of text—the result looks appropriately random, as shown in Figure 12-5, which zooms in on the final word in the first two lines.

Example 12-3 uses the browser's default `cursive` font. In general, that isn't recommended, as they can vary so much from one browser or operating system to another. Normally, you would give a list of specific font-family names, or use web fonts to be sure that the correct font was available. However, sometimes those strategies fail, so it is worth paying attention to the other code attributes that encourage a consistent rendering: the `textLength` attribute and the `font-size-adjust` style.

The textLength attribute—which squeezes or stretches text to the given length—is very buggy in browsers, and not supported at all in older SVG tools. The way it is used here (defined on the parent <text> element) is supported in Firefox and Internet Explorer; Blink and WebKit browsers, on the other hand, will not adjust the content in the <tspan> unless a textLength attribute is set on each child element. Firefox ignores textLength on <tspan>, and Internet Explorer does not correctly center or end-justify text with length adjustments.

The font-size-adjust property, which tells the browser to preserve the ex-height of the font instead of the em-height (by specifying the ratio between the two), is currently only supported in Firefox.

In a conforming web browser, these settings ensure that the overall layout is preserved even if a completely different font is used, as shown in Figure 12-6. In other browsers, the text may not fill the full width, or may creep too close to the far edge.

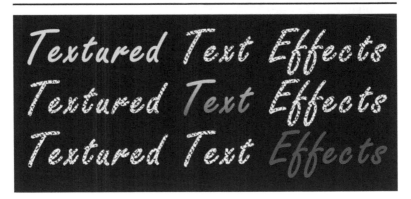

Figure 12-6. Patterned and gradient-filled multiline text, in a different font adjusted to fit

CSS Versus SVG
Filling Text with Graphics

The image-filled text from Example 11-4 and the textured text in Example 12-3 are nice effects for headings and other large text. To create it for non-SVG text, WebKit-based browsers (including Safari, Chrome, and recent Opera versions) support the nonstandard property `-webkit-background-clip` that can be used to create a similar effect.

The standard `background-clip` property allows you to clip backgrounds to the content box, the padding box, or the border box of an element. The experimental WebKit option also supports clipping to the text content of the element. In combination with transparent text (set using the WebKit-specific `-webkit-text-fill-color` so as not to affect other browsers), this creates image-filled text.

At the time of writing, there is no existing or draft web standard to set a fill image or pattern for text outside of SVG. However, there have been repeated discussions in the past about adopting `fill` and `stroke` for all CSS-styled text. It is also possible to achieve similar effects with new options for blending and compositing of elements and background images.

CHAPTER 13

Painting Lines

The gradient and pattern examples so far have nearly all used the fill property to apply that paint to a shape. However, we mentioned early on in the book that paint servers can also be used for the stroke property.

Applying paint servers to strokes introduces new complexities, which is why we have separated the topic into its own chapter. We cover the difficulties here, but also give some examples of unique effects you can create with painted strokes. And we include teasers about some new features proposed for SVG 2 that will make this easier.

Beyond the Edges

Strokes, as we've briefly mentioned, do not have to use solid colors. The stroke property, like the fill property, can use a url() function to reference a paint server—a gradient or pattern—by its id value. You can also include a fallback color in case there is a problem with that paint server, and—as you'll soon see—those fallback colors do get used.

It is when using paint servers that you are most strongly reminded that the stroke is really a secondary shape, built upon the element that defines it, and not a line drawn with a pen or brush. Patterns and gradients currently cannot be painted *along* the path; similar to when painting the fill of a shape, the stroke is cut out of wallpaper-like paint server content.

Figure 13-1. A rectangle stroked with a linear gradient

There are two main areas where designers tend to get frustrated when using paint servers for strokes:

- The `objectBoundingBox` units used by paint servers *do not* include the stroke region.
- All paint servers create a rectangle region of paint that is unaffected by the shape or direction of the stroke.

These complications aren't always impenetrable obstacles. For many shapes, a gradient or patterned stroke works just fine. Example 13-1 uses the basic horizontal red-blue gradient from Chapter 6 to paint a thick-stroked rectangle, as displayed in Figure 13-1.

Example 13-1. Using gradients as stroke paint on a rectangle

```
<svg xmlns="http://www.w3.org/2000/svg"
     width="4in" height="1.5in" >
    <title xml:lang="en">Gradient on a Stroke</title>
    <linearGradient id="red-blue" >
        <stop stop-color="red" offset="0"/>
        <stop stop-color="lightSkyBlue" offset="1"/>
    </linearGradient>
    <rect width="80%" height="50%" x="10%" y="25%"
          stroke-width="20%" stroke="url(#red-blue)"
          fill="none" />
</svg>
```

The gradient vector may be sized based on the rectangle's geometric dimensions, rather than the stroke's dimensions, but with a smooth gradient such as this it is hard to tell. If you change the `spreadMethod` to `repeat`, it becomes much more obvious, as shown

Figure 13-2. A rectangle stroked with a repeating linear gradient

in Figure 13-2. Half of the stroke on each side is beyond the gradient vector, in the repeat region.

Future Focus
Multiple Strokes

We have mentioned how SVG will allow you to layer multiple fills, to create multiple stacked gradients or patterns that accent an independently set solid color. The same possibility will also be supported with strokes, but with even greater potential. Because each stroke can have a different width or dash patterns, even solid-colored strokes can be effectively layered.

The exact details have not all been finalized at the time of writing, but SVG 2 will likely adopt a syntax similar to that used for CSS layered backgrounds. Any of the properties would be specifiable as a list of values, and if the list for one property was not as long as the list for the main (**stroke**) property, it would be repeated as necessary. So, if you wanted all the layers to have 0.5 opacity, you would only need to specify that value once.

Another new addition for strokes, similar to **fill**, would be to support CSS image data types—gradient functions and references to other image files— directly within the **stroke** property. As with SVG gradients, the result would be as if the stroke region was cut from a rectangle filled with the gradient, not a gradient that followed the direction of the stroke.

The sharp repeat edges in Figure 13-2 are not something you're likely to create by accident. You therefore might assume that objectBoundingBox units are not a big obstacle after all. They aren't, until you start stroking lines instead of shapes.

The Empty Box

Example 13-2 uses the same red-blue linear gradient to stroke a series of straight lines in different orientations. Because a straight line cannot be filled, using a thick gradient stroke is often a desired effect.

Example 13-2. Using gradients as stroke paint on straight lines

```
<svg xmlns="http://www.w3.org/2000/svg"
    width="4in" height="3in" >
    <title xml:lang="en">Gradient on Straight Lines</title>
    <linearGradient id="red-blue" >
        <stop stop-color="red" offset="0"/>
        <stop stop-color="lightSkyBlue" offset="1"/>
    </linearGradient>
    <g fill="none" stroke-width="0.5in"
        stroke="url(#red-blue) purple" >           ❶
        <line x1="10%" x2="90%" y1="10%" y2="10%" />  ❷
        <line x1="90%" x2="90%" y1="25%" y2="75%" />
        <line x1="90%" x2="10%" y1="90%" y2="90%" />
        <line x1="10%" x2="10%" y1="75%" y2="25%" />
        <line x1="30%" x2="70%" y1="25%" y2="75%" />  ❸
        <line x1="70%" x2="30%" y1="25%" y2="75%" />
    </g>
</svg>
```

❶ Style properties are applied as presentation attributes on a group containing the individual lines. The stroke value includes both the reference to the gradient and a fallback solid color.

❷ The first four lines outline the drawing region: straight across the top, down the right side, back horizontally across the bottom, then vertically up the left.

❸ The final two lines are diagonal, one going down left to right and the other angled down right to left.

The code seems simple, but as Figure 13-3 shows, the result isn't often what is desired.

Figure 13-3. Lines stroked with a linear gradient—or its fallback color

Why are so many of the lines stroked in solid purple? Because pure horizontal or vertical lines have no bounding box region. And no bounding box region means no bounding box gradient. If we had not specified a fallback color, the strokes would not have been visible at all.

Instinctively, this seems rather extreme for gradients. After all, even if the horizontal lines do not have any height, they still have width. Shouldn't that be enough for a horizontal linear gradient? And the vertical lines, couldn't they at least be padded red on one side and blue on the other?

The difficulty comes from the way paint servers are implemented, as rectangular sheets of paint that are transformed to fit the bounding box. Transformations that result in any dimension collapsing to zero cause division-by-zero errors in the browser's internal math. To avoid them, the SVG specifications treat zero-width or zero-height bounding boxes as an error for bounding box paint servers. The browser responds to the error the same way it would if it couldn't find the paint server at all—by using the fallback color.

Figure 13-4. Lines stroked with linear gradients that match the line direction

In contrast, the diagonal lines are painted with the gradient—even though the lines still have no fill region—because the bounding box is the tightest rectangle that can contain the object *aligned with the coordinate system axes*. For an angled line, that is the rectangle of which it is the diagonal. Although the two diagonal lines are drawn in opposite directions, they have the same bounding box, and so the gradient is continuous between the two.

When most people think of a gradient on a line, they are usually thinking of something more like Figure 13-4. Each gradient goes from one end of the line to the other, in the direction that the line is drawn.

As you probably guessed, Figure 13-4 can be created with SVG. However, it requires considerably more markup than Example 13-2. You cannot use gradients with object bounding box units, so you need to use a userSpaceOnUse gradient. Then you need to match the gradient vector to the position, direction, and length of the line.

There are two ways to do this. Example 13-3 shows the code used for Figure 13-4. It creates a separate <linearGradient> element for each `<line>`, and sets all the gradient vector positioning attributes to match the line's positioning attributes.

Example 13-3. Matching linear gradients with straight lines

```
<svg xmlns="http://www.w3.org/2000/svg"
     xmlns:xlink="http://www.w3.org/1999/xlink"
     width="4in" height="3in" >
    <title xml:lang="en">Gradients Made to Measure
                    for Straight Lines</title>
    <linearGradient id="red-blue"
                    gradientUnits="userSpaceOnUse">     ❶
        <stop stop-color="red" offset="0"/>
        <stop stop-color="lightSkyBlue" offset="1"/>
    </linearGradient>
    <g fill="none" stroke-width="0.5in" >               ❷
        <linearGradient xlink:href="#red-blue" id="g1"
            x1="10%" x2="90%" y1="10%" y2="10%" />      ❸
        <line x1="10%" x2="90%" y1="10%" y2="10%"
            stroke="url(#g1) purple"/>                  ❹
        <linearGradient xlink:href="#red-blue" id="g2"
            x1="90%" x2="90%" y1="25%" y2="75%" />
        <line x1="90%" x2="90%" y1="25%" y2="75%"
            stroke="url(#g2) purple"/>
        <linearGradient xlink:href="#red-blue" id="g3"
            x1="90%" x2="10%" y1="90%" y2="90%" />
        <line x1="90%" x2="10%" y1="90%" y2="90%"
            stroke="url(#g3) purple"/>
        <linearGradient xlink:href="#red-blue" id="g4"
            x1="10%" x2="10%" y1="75%" y2="25%" />
        <line x1="10%" x2="10%" y1="75%" y2="25%"
            stroke="url(#g4) purple"/>
        <linearGradient xlink:href="#red-blue" id="g5"
            x1="30%" x2="70%" y1="25%" y2="75%" />
        <line x1="30%" x2="70%" y1="25%" y2="75%"
            stroke="url(#g5) purple"/>
        <linearGradient xlink:href="#red-blue" id="g6"
            x1="70%" x2="30%" y1="25%" y2="75%" />
        <line x1="70%" x2="30%" y1="25%" y2="75%"
            stroke="url(#g6) purple"/>
    </g>
</svg>
```

❶ The basic gradient containing the color stops is used as a template. It has `userSpaceOnUse` set for `gradientUnits`, which will be inherited by the gradients that reference it.

❷ There's no use setting the stroke value on the group; each element will need a separate stroke property referencing its custom-made gradient.

❸ The <linearGradient> elements each have an xlink:href attribute referencing the template gradient, a unique id, and x1, x2, y1, and y2 attributes that directly match those on the corresponding <line>.

❹ The lines each have the correct stroke gradient set as a presentation attribute. The fallback color is included just in case, but won't be used unless we made a typo!

The main downside of the code in Example 13-3 is that it is rather repetitive. For example, the duplicated attributes between the <line> and <linearGradient> elements mean that you have to update everything twice if you want to reposition anything. However, this structure is quite effective if you're using a data-based script to generate the lines in the first place. You could create a function that sets these attributes on an element based on the data, and then run it twice, once for the line and once for the gradient.

 If your <line> elements make use of default values for some positioning attributes, remember that <linearGradient> has a different default for x2 (100% instead of 0).

Another limitation of the approach used in Example 13-3 is that it significantly increases the number of elements in your DOM. If you have a very large number of lines and gradients in a dynamic graphic, this could slow down your web page.

An alternative approach to aligning gradients and lines is to use a single gradient, and draw all your lines along it; then, use transformations to size and position the lines where you want them. We use this approach in Example 13-4. Because SVG 1.1 transformations must be specified in user units, not percentages, the drawing has been redefined with a viewBox and the numbers have been adjusted. As a result, the final SVG shown in Figure 13-5 is not an exact match for Figure 13-4, but it is close.

Figure 13-5. Lines stroked with a gradient, then transformed into place

Example 13-4. Transforming lines drawn to match a linear gradient

```
<svg xmlns="http://www.w3.org/2000/svg" xml:lang="en"
    width="4in" height="3in" viewBox="0 0 100 75">              ❶
    <title xml:lang="en">Userspace Gradient on
                        Transformed Straight Lines</title>
    <linearGradient id="red-blue" gradientUnits="userSpaceOnUse">❷
        <stop stop-color="red" offset="0"/>
        <stop stop-color="lightSkyBlue" offset="1"/>
    </linearGradient>
    <g fill="none" stroke-width="12"
        stroke="url(#red-blue) purple" >                        ❸
        <line x2="100%"
            transform="translate(10,7.5) scale(0.8,1)" />       ❹
        <line x2="100%"
            transform="translate(90,18.75)
                        rotate(90) scale(0.375,1)" />           ❺
        <line x2="100%"
            transform="translate(90,67.5) scale(-0.8,1)" />     ❻
        <line x2="100%"
            transform="translate(10,56.25)
                        rotate(-90) scale(0.375,1)" />
        <line x2="100%"
            transform="translate(30,18.75)
                        rotate(45) scale(0.5315,1)" />
```

```
<line x2="100%"
      transform="translate(70,18.75)
                 rotate(135) scale(0.5315,1)" />
  </g>
</svg>
```

❶ The `viewBox` uses a 100-unit width, so that the horizontal percentages can be directly converted to user unit values. However, vertical percentages will need to be scaled to the 70-unit height.

❷ There is only one gradient, which uses `userSpaceOnUse` units. The gradient vector uses the default arrangement: horizontally from 0 to 100%.

❸ A single `stroke` value is applied to the group containing all the lines. Again, the fallback color is only just-in-case; the user-space gradient should always provide valid results.

❹ Each `<line>` element has the exact same positioning attributes: a single `x2="100%"` to match the default attributes on the `<linearGradient>`. The actual size and position of the line is controlled by the `transform` attribute.

❺ The transformations are arranged in a particular order that ensures they do not interact in unexpected ways: first, the origin (and start of the line) is translated into place, then it is rotated into the correct orientation, and finally it is scaled along its length (which is the x-axis in its transformed coordinate system).

❻ As an alternative to a 180° rotation, the right-to-left gradient is created with a negative x-scaling factor.

With this approach, you do not create any extra elements. However, you must completely redefine the geometry of the graphic. If you know in advance that the gradients are an essential part of your graphic, and can plan ahead, this might not be a big obstacle. In contrast, rewriting a graphic like this—converting code that was defined with positioning attributes to use transformations instead—is usually more hassle than it's worth.

Using the Coordinate Space

User-space stroke gradients have more applications than as imperfect substitutes for gradients along a line. In data visualizations, they can be used to change the appearance of a data line according to its value. Example 13-5 demonstrates this effect. It creates a generic status monitor dashboard, with a line that marks a changing value that should not reach 100%: as the line gets closer to maximum, it turns from green to yellow to red.

The basic framework for the graphic—including the gradient—is defined in the markup, while the data is inserted via a script. In practice, the data would come from a web server of some sort; in the example, the data is randomly generated. Figure 13-6 shows one possible data pattern.

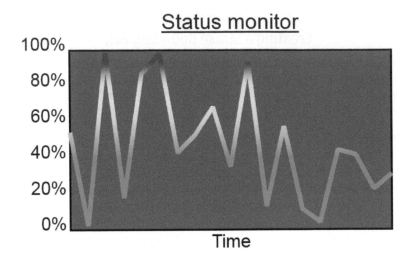

Figure 13-6. A data chart using a stroked gradient to emphasize changing values

Example 13-5. Using a gradient to add information to a line chart

```
<svg xmlns="http://www.w3.org/2000/svg"
     width="4in" height="3in"
     xml:lang="en">
    <title>Stroked Gradient as Status Indicator</title>
    <svg x="0.6in" y="0.5in" width="3.6in" height="2in"
         viewBox="0 0 180 100"
         style="overflow: visible; font: 10px sans-serif;">      ❶
        <linearGradient id="status" y1="100%" y2="0%" x2="0%"
                        gradientUnits="userSpaceOnUse">            ❷
            <stop stop-color="limegreen" offset="0.4"/>
            <stop stop-color="yellow"    offset="0.8"/>           ❸
            <stop stop-color="red"       offset="0.95"/>
        </linearGradient>

        <rect stroke="black" fill="dimGray"
            width="100%" height="100%" />
        <g text-anchor="end" dominant-baseline="middle"
           transform="translate(-2,0)">                           ❹
            <desc>Y-axis tick labels</desc>
            <text y="100">0%</text>
            <text y="80">20%</text>
            <text y="60">40%</text>
            <text y="40">60%</text>
            <text y="20">80%</text>
            <text y="0">100%</text>
```

```
        </g>
        <g text-anchor="middle">
            <text x="50%" dy="-1em" font-size="12px"
                  text-decoration="underline"
                  >Status monitor</text>
            <text x="50%" y="100%" dy="1em">Time</text>
        </g>

        <polyline id="dataline" stroke="url(#status)"
                  stroke-linejoin="bevel"
                  stroke-width="2.5" fill="none" />         ❺
    </svg>
    <script><![CDATA[
(function(){
    var n = 19,
        dx = 10,
        maxY = 100;                                         ❻

    var data = new Array(n),
        points = new Array(n);
    for (var i=0; i<n; i++) {
        data[i] = [i, Math.random()];
        points[i] = [i*dx, maxY * (1 - data[i][1])];        ❼
    }

    var dataline = document.getElementById("dataline");
    dataline.setAttribute("points", points.toString() );    ❽
})()
]]> </script>
</svg>
```

❶ A nested <svg> is used to create a user-space coordinate system
    that exactly matches the size of the data region in the chart. A
    viewBox applies a custom coordinate system, including a 100-
    unit height that will convert easily to percentage values.

❷ The <linearGradient> is drawn within a user-space coordinate
    system, with a vector that goes from bottom to top.

❸ The first 40% of the gradient is solid green; it then transitions
    through yellow until being solid red after 95%.

❹ A solid background fills the data region, while text labels are
    offset *outside* of the data region (which has visible overflow). By
    including the labels inside the nested SVG, they can be posi-
    tioned using the viewBox coordinate system, even though they
    are printed outside of its width and height region.

❺ The data line is a `<polyline>` element. Its presentation styles—including the gradient stroke—are specified in the markup, but it does not have a `points` attribute, so will not be drawn until the script runs. An `id` attribute makes it easy to access from the script.

❻ Inside the script, a set of initialization variables control the scale between the data and the coordinate system: `n` is the number of data values that will fit in the graphic, `dx` is the horizontal spacing (in user units) between them, `maxY` is the number of vertical units into which the range (0%–100%) should be scaled to fit.

❼ The `data` array contains the raw data (here, an index number followed by a random value between 0 and 1). The `points` array contains the scaled coordinates for those data points, using the control variables to scale the data and invert the *y*-coordinates, so that 0% is at the bottom and 100% is at the top.

❽ The `points` array-of-arrays is converted to a comma-separated string with its default `toString()` method, and used as the `points` attribute of the polyline.

The key to effectively using a `userSpaceOnUse` gradient to convey data was to precisely control the user-space coordinate system to match the data region. Nested coordinate systems allowed the `viewBox` to exactly match the data region, while still leaving room outside it for the labels.

 To correctly scale the gradient to the data region in Internet Explorer and WebKit/Blink browsers, the `<linearGradient>` *must* be a child of the nested SVG. As already mentioned, these browsers use the paint server's parent coordinate system as the `userSpaceOnUse` instead of the one associated with the painted shape.

The visual effect of the user-space painted stroke is similar to having a continous rectangular gradient that is then masked by the line, to only show those regions. However, just as with the image-filled text we discussed in Chapter 11, there is an important structural difference between a gradient clipped to a line and a line painted with a

---

gradient. If you have any interactive effects in your data graph, you want the line to be the object they interact with, not a mostly invisible rectangle.

Nonetheless, the effect need not be restricted to practical data graphics. You could also use a textured pattern or an image as the revealed content that shines through the stroked areas.

Patterned Lines

Patterned strokes work much the same way as gradient strokes. However, because patterns repeat in strict vertical and horizontal tiles, it can become even more obvious when the stroke orientation does not align with the paint server's.

As with gradients, a userSpaceOnUse approach is recommended to avoid problems with objectBoundingBox units. You *can* still use bounding box patterns if your shape is sure to have a valid bounding box (i.e., it isn't a horizontal or vertical straight line), but the scale of the pattern will be based on the scale of the fill region, not the scale of the stroke.

Example 13-6 uses various patterns from Chapters 10 and 11 to stroke some basic shapes—with varying degrees of effectiveness, as shown in Figure 13-7.

Example 13-6. Using a gradient to add information to a line chart

```
<svg xmlns="http://www.w3.org/2000/svg"
    width="4.3in" height="4.3in" viewBox="0 0 400 400">
    <title>Patterned Strokes</title>
    <defs>
        <!-- pattern definitions clipped -->              ❶
    </defs>
    <g style="stroke-width: 40px; fill: lightSkyBlue;" >   ❷
        <rect x="20" y="20" width="360" height="360"
                stroke="url(#pinstripe) gray" />            ❸
        <polygon points="200,30 370,200 200,370 30,200"
                stroke="url(#scales-pattern) green"/>       ❹
        <circle cx="200" cy="200" r="90"
                stroke="url(#gradient-pattern) peachPuff"/> ❺
    </g>
</svg>
```

Figure 13-7. Shapes stroked with various patterns

❶ The patterns (and their constituent gradients) are copied directly from Examples 10-5, 10-6, and 11-1, so they are not reprinted here.

❷ All the shapes will have a thick, 40px-wide stroke over top of a light blue fill.

❸ The rectangle uses the pinstripe pattern from Example 10-6.

❹ The diamond-shaped `<polygon>` uses the fish scale pattern from Example 10-5.

❺ The circle uses the layered gradients from Example 11-1. Along with the other shapes, it is given an appropriate fallback color, just in case.

The small, repeated pattern of the fish scales looks quite effective on the wide strokes. The pinstripes may or may not have the effect you want: the vertical stripes go across the horizontal strokes of the square, but down the length of the vertical strokes. The layered gradients create quite an unusual effect. The gradients were compiled using a bounding box pattern; because that bounding box doesn't fill up the entire stroke region, it is tiled on each side, creating sharp changes in color.

As with gradients, there are ways to work around the problems. For example, some striped stroke effects can be created with dashed strokes. To avoid tiling when using an object bounding box pattern for stroke, you can set the x, y, width, and height attributes to define a pattern tile that is large enough to include the stroke region (i.e., x and y are negative, while width and height are greater than 100%). All of this will become easier in the future with multiple strokes and stroke bounding boxes.

CHAPTER 14

Motion Pictures

SVG colors, gradients, and patterns may be collectively referred to as paint, but there is one important difference from oils or watercolors: SVG paint can move.

SVG within a web browser is dynamic. It can be animated, either on a continuous loop or in response to user interactions.

Animation complicates the discussion of SVG painting properties and paint servers in a few ways. This chapter sums up the major issues and approaches to address them. It starts with a review of the different ways in which SVG can be animated, using animated fill colors as an example. It then addresses the animation of paint servers under two situations: synchronized animations of many painted elements, or animation of a single element without affecting others.

Screenshots have been included for the animation examples, but a full appreciation will require running the code in a web browser.

A complete discussion of SVG animation is worth several books on its own, so this chapter does not attempt to exhaustively describe all the options and syntax. Instead, it focuses on the aspects that are unique to working with colors and paint servers. If you're not already comfortable with CSS, SMIL, and JavaScript animations, you may need to consult other references to fully understand how the code creates the final effect.

Animation Options

There are three different methods you can use to animate SVG graphics:

- Including animation elements within the markup (`<animate>`, `<set>`, `<animateTransform>`, and `<animateMotion>`) to modify other elements.
- Adding CSS animation or transition properties to your graphics' styles.
- Using JavaScript to sequentially manipulate the styles or attributes of your graphics.

All three methods offer at least a limited potential for interactive animations. Animation elements can be triggered or modified to start or end on user events such as click or mouseover. CSS animations and transitions can be triggered by interactive pseudoclasses (`:hover`, `:focus`, `:active`). And JavaScript can of course be used for all sorts of user interactions and programming.

Which strategy you use to animate the SVG will depend a lot on how you plan to use that SVG. JavaScript will not run if the SVG is embedded in another web page as an image, either with the `<img>` tag or using CSS `background-image` or similar properties; the SVG code must either be included inline or embedded as an interactive `<object>`. JavaScript may also be intentionally disabled by the user for security or performance reasons.

The declarative methods (animation defined with markup or CSS properties) *will* run in SVG used as an image, provided all the styles are defined in the same SVG file. The animation will not be interactive, however, as no user events will be passed to the SVG document.

Browser support for the declarative animation methods is currently poorer than for scripted animation, although support for CSS animation is increasing. For scripted animation, most limitations in browser support can be patched over with additional code (with compromises in performance); there are also various code libraries that can make designing efficient animations easier.

Finally, when it comes to animating `fill` and `stroke`, the type of paint content will affect your animation options. Colors can be animated by directly changing the style property on the element using

---

the style. Paint servers, however, must be animated by modifying styles and attributes on the pattern, gradient, or stop elements.

The examples in this chapter will show multiple ways of coding the same effect, and emphasize the benefits and limitations of each—including both limitations in the specifications and limitations in browser support.

For animation elements, the following factors should affect your decision:

- Limited browser support, which is currently expected to decline.

- Ability to animate nearly any style property or attribute (although there are important browser support limitations).

- Interaction uses DOM events to start and stop animations. The animation runs until it completes or is explicitly ended by another event; the end state can also be "frozen," but it will immediately revert if the animation restarts.

- For interaction, the element being animated and the element receiving user input can be completely independent.

- Animations can be chained together or staggered by using the begin and end events of one animation element to trigger another.

- Multiple animations on the same property and element can be set to add together (for most properties) or to replace one another.

- Timed animation (noninteractive) will run in an SVG used as an image.

For CSS animation, consider these factors:

- Limited browser support is expected to improve.

- Restricted to animating style properties only.

- Limited interaction tied to pseudoclasses. The animation will be cut off if the pseudoclass no longer applies, although transitions can smooth out the effect.

- For interaction, the element with the pseudoclass must be able to influence the target element using descendent or sibling CSS selectors. This is particularly problematic when animating paint servers.

- Chained animations are difficult; either a single keyframes sequence must include all the stages, or multiple animations must have delay values hardcoded to match the duration of the previous animations.

- Multiple animations on the same property and element always replace one another.

- Timed animation (noninteractive) will run in an SVG used as image.

Finally, for JavaScript animation, the relevant factors are as follows:

- Optimal browser support, particularly with polyfills for older browsers. However, users may disable JavaScript.

- Ability to animate any style property, attribute, text content, or even DOM structure.

- Interaction is possible using any information passed through DOM events, affecting any element in the document.

- Multistage and chained animations can be difficult to code, but JavaScript libraries are available to simplify your work (at the cost of extra downloads for users).

- Will not run in images; external SVG files must be embedded with `<object>`.

The options are not always exclusive. In particular, you can use JavaScript to trigger CSS animations (by changing element classes) or animation elements (using the animation element's `.beginElement()` method). This allows you to integrate the logic and control of scripted animation with the simplicity of declarative animations.

A Unified Web Animations Model

The Web Animations specification provides an overarching description of all timed animations in web pages. Its unified model describes the implementation of both SVG animation elements and CSS animation features. It also defines a script API for dynamically creating animation effects. These effects would be created by specifying the start and end values and timing parameters, without having to directly set the intermediary values at each frame yourself. This will combine the control of scripted animation with the simplicity and performance benefits of declarative animation syntaxes.

The web animation API is in the process of being implemented in most browsers at the time of writing. There are JavaScript polyfills for other browsers, which convert API instructions into frame-by-frame animations. However, the polyfills are generally not as performance-optimized as other JavaScript animation libraries.

Regardless of how you animate your SVG, it is usually straightforward to manipulate simple color values for fill and stroke. The same is true for most other presentation attributes including fill-opacity or stroke-opacity.

Example 14-1 showcases the basic syntax of animation elements, used to cycle through different fill colors in an image of three stars. The color cycle lasts 3 seconds, but repeats indefinitely. The same sequence of colors is used for each star, but offset to start at different times. Figure 14-1 shows a single instant in the cycle.

Example 14-1. Animating fill colors with animation elements

```
<svg xmlns="http://www.w3.org/2000/svg"
    xmlns:xlink="http://www.w3.org/1999/xlink"
    width="4in" height="2in" viewBox="0 0 200 100">
    <title xml:lang="en">Simple SMIL Animation</title>
    <symbol id="star" viewBox="0 0 200 200">
        <path d="M100,10 L150,140 20,50 180,50 50,140 Z" />
    </symbol>
    <rect height="100%" width="100%" fill="#222"/>
    <g fill="gold">
        <use xlink:href="#star" width="50" height="50"
            transform="translate(10,20) rotate(-10)">
```

Figure 14-1. Still from an animation sequence of color-changing stars

```
        <animate attributeName="fill"
                values="gold;lightYellow;gold;tomato;gold"
                dur="3s" repeatDur="indefinite" />
    </use>
    <use xlink:href="#star" width="40" height="40"
        transform="translate(140,10) rotate(20)">
        <animate attributeName="fill" begin="-1s"
                values="gold;lightYellow;gold;tomato;gold"
                dur="3s" repeatDur="indefinite" />
    </use>
    <use xlink:href="#star" width="35" height="35"
        transform="translate(80,60) rotate(-5)">
        <animate attributeName="fill" begin="-2s"
                values="gold;lightYellow;gold;tomato;gold"
                dur="3s" repeatDur="indefinite" />
    </use>
  </g>
</svg>
```

The colors transition according to their RGB values. The intermediary values are calculated using the same rules as for gradients. The only difference is that the transition happens in time, instead of across space.

 The color animation should be affected by the `color-interpolation` property. However, as mentioned in Chapter 3, this property is not well supported in web browsers.

The SVG animation elements use a syntax developed for the Synchronized Multimedia Integration Language (SMIL), which was intended for coordinating audio, video, and XHTML content. As you can imagine, the syntax includes a number of options for synchronizing one animation with another, either simultaneously or one after the other. It can therefore be used to schedule complicated sequences of animation. However, these complicated animation sequences do not combine well with the interactive features. The declarative format of SMIL animations does not have any way to include decision logic that would alter the response to a user event based on the current state of the animation.

Another limitation of the animation element syntax is its verbosity. Each element being animated requires its own animation element. There is no way to quickly apply variations on the same animation to many graphical components, such as the three stars in Example 14-1.

Nonetheless, the most significant limitation to widespread use of SVG animation elements is poor browser support.

 Internet Explorer has no support for animation elements. The Chromium team has, at the time of writing, announced plans to deprecate the feature. In the short term, that means printing warnings to the developer's console for web pages that use the animation syntax. In the long term, the animations may cease to work.

For simple animations of presentation styles, CSS animations provide a more concise and flexible syntax. Example 14-2 creates the exact same twinkling star effect, but with CSS animation keyframes. A class is used to apply the same animation sequence to all three stars, and then `nth-of-type` selectors are used to alter the start time on individual shapes.

Example 14-2. Animating fill colors with CSS keyframes

```
<svg xmlns="http://www.w3.org/2000/svg"
    xmlns:xlink="http://www.w3.org/1999/xlink"
    width="4in" height="2in" viewBox="0 0 200 100">
    <title xml:lang="en">Simple CSS Animation</title>
    <style type="text/css">
        .star {
```

```
        fill: gold;
        animation: twinkle 3s infinite;
    }
    .star:nth-of-type(3n+2){
        animation-delay: -1s;
    }
    .star:nth-of-type(3n+3){
        animation-delay: -2s;
    }
    @keyframes twinkle {
        25% {fill: lightYellow;}
        50% {fill: gold; }
        75% {fill: tomato;}
    }
</style>
<symbol id="star" viewBox="0 0 200 200">
    <path d="M100,10 L150,140 20,50 180,50 50,140 Z" />
</symbol>
<rect height="100%" width="100%" fill="#222"/>
<use xlink:href="#star" width="50" height="50" class="star"
    transform="translate(10,20) rotate(-10)"/>
<use xlink:href="#star" width="40" height="40" class="star"
    transform="translate(140,10) rotate(20)"/>
<use xlink:href="#star" width="35" height="35" class="star"
    transform="translate(80,60) rotate(-5)"/>
</svg>
```

The main limitation of CSS animations of SVG are that only presentation attributes can be manipulated. Geometric attributes (that are only specificied in the XML) cannot be animated with CSS rules. The SVG 2 specifications are redefining a number of layout attributes as presentation attributes, but many features of SVG will remain inaccessible to CSS animation.

CSS animations are also not well suited to long sequences of consecutive animations, and can only respond to a limited set of user actions.

 CSS animations are not supported in some older browsers that are still in use. In all but the latest WebKit browsers, CSS animations require the -webkit- experimental prefix, which means you'll need to duplicate your animation properties and your keyframe rules. Internet Explorer does not support CSS animation of SVG elements; however, support is expected to be added in the Edge browser.

For more universal support of animation, you can manipulate your DOM with JavaScript. For simple linear animations, it is fairly straightforward to cycle through all the intermediary values, using the `requestAnimationFrame` method to only update the graphic when the browser is able to update the display. For more complex, multistage animations (e.g., the staggered color changes), you may want to use a dedicated JavaScript animation library, which converts your declarative statements (of which attributes to animate and by how much) into optimized frame-by-frame adjustments.

Coordinated Animation

Animating color values for `fill` and `stroke` is straightforward. With either animation elements or CSS animations, the browser transitions between the colors for you. But what about paint servers? That gets more complicated. The actual value used in the `fill` and `stroke` properties is a URL. The browser cannot generate intermediary values in between two URLs.

 The specifications do allow URL values to be modified by animations, in discrete steps. However, browser support is poor, restricted to SMIL animations in Firefox at the time of writing.

What *can* be animated, however, are the paint server elements themselves. Gradient stop colors and opacity values can be animated with CSS, as can presentation styles on the contents of a pattern. In the future, gradient and pattern transformations will also be affected by CSS animations of the `transform` property. These and many more structural attributes can be animated with SVG markup or with JavaScript.

Animating a paint server has an important difference from animating a `fill` or `stroke` paint property. The animation automatically affects *all* elements using that paint server, changing them all simultaneously.

Whether this feature is desired or not really depends on the particulars of your graphic. "Animated Interactions" on page 251 will explore alternative approaches for when you *don't* want every element to change simultaneously. In particular, that section will focus on using animation to highlight a particular element the user is interacting with. In contrast, for many decorative animations, it is acceptable or even desirable to have synchronized animations.

Example 14-3 uses synchronized animations in an adaptation of the twinkling stars animation. Now, instead of animating the `fill` colors on the stars themselves, the animation is applied to the `stop-color` values in a series of `<stop>` elements. Otherwise, the animation code looks quite similar. Figure 14-2 shows a screenshot of the gradient-filled stars, but you'll need to run the code to get the full twinkling effect.

Example 14-3. Animating gradient stop colors with CSS

```
<svg xmlns="http://www.w3.org/2000/svg"
    xmlns:xlink="http://www.w3.org/1999/xlink"
    width="4in" height="2in" viewBox="0 0 200 100">
    <title xml:lang="en">CSS-Animated Gradient</title>
    <style type="text/css">
        .star {
            fill: url(#shine);
        }
        #shine stop {
            stop-color: gold;
            animation: twinkle 3s infinite;
        }
        #shine stop:nth-of-type(3n+2){
            animation-delay: -1s;
        }
        #shine stop:nth-of-type(3n+3){
            animation-delay: -2s;
        }
        @keyframes twinkle {
            25% {stop-color: lightYellow;}
            50% {stop-color: gold; }
            75% {stop-color: tomato;}
        }
    </style>
    <symbol id="star" viewBox="0 0 200 200">
        <path d="M100,10 L150,140 20,50 180,50 50,140 Z" />
    </symbol>
    <linearGradient id="shine" gradientTransform="rotate(20)">
        <stop offset="0" />
        <stop offset="0.25" />
        <stop offset="0.5" />
        <stop offset="0.75" />
        <stop offset="1" />
    </linearGradient>
    <rect height="100%" width="100%" fill="#222"/>
    <use xlink:href="#star" width="50" height="50" class="star"
```

Figure 14-2. Still from an animation sequence of stars with oscillating gradients

```
              transform="translate(10,20) rotate(-10)"/>
    <use xlink:href="#star" width="40" height="40" class="star"
          transform="translate(140,10) rotate(20)"/>
    <use xlink:href="#star" width="35" height="35" class="star"
          transform="translate(80,60) rotate(-5)"/>
</svg>
```

The oscillating color stops could also be created with SMIL-style animation elements, by adding an `<animate>` element within each `<stop>`. However, it is more useful to use animation elements for something that CSS animations cannot do: modifying the geometric attributes.

Example 14-4 uses two animations to modify the x1 and y2 attributes of the `<linearGradient>` element. A still screenshot of the graphic would look quite similar to Figure 14-2, but the dynamic effect is quite different: instead of having each color twinkle in place, they stretch and shift like gentle waves.

Example 14-4. Animating the gradient vector with animation elements

```
<svg xmlns="http://www.w3.org/2000/svg"
      xmlns:xlink="http://www.w3.org/1999/xlink"
      width="4in" height="2in" viewBox="0 0 200 100">
    <title xml:lang="en">SMIL-Animated Gradient</title>
    <style type="text/css">
        .star {
            fill: url(#shine);
```

```
            }
        </style>
        <symbol id="star" viewBox="0 0 200 200">
            <path d="M100,10 L150,140 20,50 180,50 50,140 Z" />
        </symbol>
        <linearGradient id="shine" spreadMethod="repeat"
                        gradientTransform="rotate(20)" >
            <animate attributeName="y2" values="1;1.5;1;0.75;1"
                    dur="2s" repeatDur="indefinite" />
            <animate attributeName="x1" values="0;0.5;0"
                    dur="3s" repeatDur="indefinite" />
            <stop offset="0" stop-color="gold" />
            <stop offset="0.25" stop-color="lightYellow" />
            <stop offset="0.5" stop-color="gold" />
            <stop offset="0.75" stop-color="tomato" />
            <stop offset="1" stop-color="gold" />
        </linearGradient>
        <rect height="100%" width="100%" fill="#222"/>
        <use xlink:href="#star" width="50" height="50" class="star"
            transform="translate(10,20) rotate(-10)"/>
        <use xlink:href="#star" width="40" height="40" class="star"
            transform="translate(140,10) rotate(20)"/>
        <use xlink:href="#star" width="35" height="35" class="star"
            transform="translate(80,60) rotate(-5)"/>
</svg>
```

Neither Firefox nor WebKit browsers currently update the painted graphics when the gradient is animated with SMIL (i.e., it only works in Blink browsers).

Greater browser support for this effect could be created by using JavaScript instead of SMIL to modify the gradient attributes. However, all three stars would still animate in perfect synchronization, because they all use the same gradient.

For some graphics, you may be able to disrupt the repetition by using a repeating userSpaceOnUse graphic that is slightly different under each shape. For the three stars, that approach does not have an effect: each star is drawn in the same position within its own <symbol> coordinate system, so each star would be drawn at the exact same point of a user-space gradient.

Future Focus
Transitioning Between Gradients

CSS gradient functions can be animated (with CSS animations) in some browsers, following the latest draft versions of the CSS Image Values and Replaced Content Module Level 3. To transition in between two gradients, they must be of the same type (e.g., `repeating-linear-gradient`) and must have the same number of stops. The stop offsets and colors are then transitioned individually.

Browsers that do not support the interpolation of gradients will ignore any values set within an `@keyframes` rule, and will apply other changes immediately without transitions.

A proposed version of the CSS transitions specification would recommend that URL references to SVG gradients be transitioned in the same way. In other words, if both gradients are of the same type and have the same number of stops, the browser would generate all the in-between values when switching between paint servers with CSS animations or transitions. At the time of writing, this has not been implemented in browsers, and there is opposition to including it in the final specification. The Level 4 specification includes an alternative transition mode, cross-fading, which would allow any image to dissolve into another; this is more easily adapted to SVG paint server content.

Animated Interactions

One of the most important uses of animation in modern websites is to provide user feedback and continuity. Content should visibly change when users interact with it, but it should do so in a smooth way so the user can intuitively understand the connection between the old and new states.

If you are using animations to represent the user's interaction with a particular element, you clearly cannot have the same animation happening simultaneously on all similar elements in the web page. One solution is to have a dedicated paint server element (or elements) that applies the animation effects and is only used when needed. Other paint servers render the static states of the element.

Animating one element (a paint server) when the user interacts with another (a graphical icon) is difficult-to-impossible with CSS animations. It can sometimes be done with sibling and child selectors, but only if you rearrange your markup into a rather messy structure! Therefore, we'll start with a SMIL-based approach to describe what we are trying to achieve, then show how to create the same effect—with more work but more flexibility and good browser support—in JavaScript.

The SMIL animation approach takes advantage of timing attributes for synchronizing multiple animations. It uses the <set> element to switch the paint server from the shared, static gradient to an animatable paint server, and then uses <animate> elements to implement the effect. Finally, another <set> element switches the graphic to the final state, which is again a shared paint server.

 Blink and WebKit browsers will not correctly animate URL references to paint servers, even with a <set> element; the fill is replaced with transparent (WebKit) or solid (Blink) black. Given the Chromium project's plan to deprecate SMIL support, this is not expected to be fixed. The example therefore only works on Firefox.

Example 14-5 uses this method to implement a click effect on star icons, such as might be used to indicate favorite or bookmarked elements. It uses the silver and gold linear gradients we saw previously in the star-rating icon example from Chapter 8, plus an additional radial gradient for the transition effect.

The stars begin filled with the silver-gray gradient. Upon activation, a gold fill radiates out from the center of the element, before fading into a gold-shine linear gradient. The animated effect involves all three gradients, layered within a <pattern> element; in addition to animating the radius of the radial gradient, the opacity of the pattern layers are modified for smooth transitions.

Figure 14-3 shows a screenshot in which one icon is in the final gold state, one is in the initial silver state, and the other has just been clicked and is partway through the radiating animation.

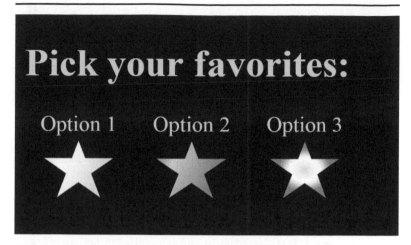

Figure 14-3. Screenshot of an interactive animated web page, shortly after the final icon has been selected

Example 14-5. Animating a single element's paint upon user interaction, with animation elements

HTML MARKUP:

```html
<!DOCTYPE html>
<html lang="en">
<head>
    <meta charset="utf-8" />
    <title>Interactive Animated Gradient with SMIL</title>
    <style type='text/css'>
        /* styles must be in the same document */
    </style>
</head>
<body>
    <svg class="defs-only"
        aria-hidden="true" focusable="false" width="0" height="0" >
        <linearGradient id="silver-shine" spreadMethod="repeat"
                    gradientTransform="rotate(20)" >
            <stop offset="0" stop-color="gray" />
            <stop offset="0.35" stop-color="silver" />
            <stop offset="1" stop-color="gray" />
        </linearGradient>
        <linearGradient id="gold-shine" spreadMethod="repeat"
                    gradientTransform="rotate(20)" >
            <stop offset="0" stop-color="gold" />
            <stop offset="0.35" stop-color="lightYellow" />
            <stop offset="1" stop-color="gold" />
        </linearGradient>
```

```
    <radialGradient id="gold-ripple" r="0.2">                    ❶
        <animate id="ripple"
                attributeName="r" from="0.1" to="1"
                dur="0.7s" fill="freeze"
                begin="reaction.begin + 0.1s" />
        <stop offset="0" stop-color="gold" />
        <stop offset="0.5" stop-color="lightYellow" />
        <stop offset="0.75" stop-color="silver" />
        <stop offset="1" stop-color="gray" />
    </radialGradient>
    <pattern id="turn-gold" width="1" height="1"
            patternContentUnits="objectBoundingBox">            ❷
        <rect fill="url(#gold-shine)" width="1" height="1" />
        <rect fill="url(#silver-shine)" width="1" height="1" >
            <set attributeName="opacity" to="0"
                begin="reaction.begin + 0.5s" />                ❸
        </rect>
        <rect fill="url(#gold-ripple)" width="1" height="1" >
            <animate id="reaction"
                    attributeName="opacity"
                    values="0;1;1;0"
                    keyTimes="0;0.2;0.8;1"
                    dur="1s"
                    begin="switch1.begin;
                    switch2.begin; switch3.begin" />
        </rect>
    </pattern>

    <symbol id="star" viewBox="0 0 200 200">
        <path d="M100,10 L150,140 20,50 180,50 50,140 Z" />
    </symbol>
</svg>
<h1>Pick your favorites:</h1>
<div>
    <figure id="opt1" role="checkbox" tabindex="0">            ❹
        <figcaption>Option 1</figcaption>
        <svg><use class="star" xlink:href="#star">
            <set id="switch1"
                attributeName="fill" to="url(#turn-gold)"
                dur="1s" begin="opt1.click; opt1.activate"/>
            <set attributeName="fill" to="url(#gold-shine)"
                dur="indefinite" begin="switch1.end" />       ❺
        </use></svg>
    </figure>
    <figure id="opt2" role="checkbox" tabindex="0">
        <figcaption>Option 2</figcaption>
        <svg><use class="star" xlink:href="#star">
            <set id="switch2"
                attributeName="fill" to="url(#turn-gold)"
                dur="1s" begin="opt2.click; opt2.activate"/>
            <set attributeName="fill" to="url(#gold-shine)"
```

```
                    dur="indefinite" begin="switch2.end" />    ❻
            </use></svg>
        </figure>
        <figure id="opt3" role="checkbox" tabindex="0">
            <figcaption>Option 3</figcaption>
            <svg><use class="star" xlink:href="#star">
                <set id="switch3"
                    attributeName="fill" to="url(#turn-gold)"
                    dur="1s" begin="opt3.click; opt3.activate"/>
                <set attributeName="fill" to="url(#gold-shine)"
                    dur="indefinite" begin="switch3.end" />
            </use></svg>
        </figure>
    </div>
    <script>
        /* do something based on the selected options */
    </script>
</body>
</html>
```

❶ The first two linear gradients are unremarkable. The new radial gradient, however, has an <animate> element that will manipulate the r attribute. The animation is timed to begin one-tenth of a second after another animation with id reaction begins.

❷ A <pattern> element contains all the layers that will need to be animated for the transition, as a single tile that completely fills the shape bounding box.

❸ Two more animation elements are nested within the pattern: a <set> element that switches the underlying layer from silver to gold, and an <animate> element that first increases then decreases the opacity of the radiating gradient. This latter animation has the reaction ID value, and is used to drive the other two transition animations. The reaction animation itself is started any time one of the three switch animations begins.

❹ In the main web-page markup, the <figure> elements that contain the animated SVG are the functional equivalent of a checkbox, so they are identified by the ARIA role="checkbox" attribute. Each SVG contains a <use> element, as usual for inline icons. However, each <use> element then contains two animation elements.

❺ The switch1 animation is a <set> element that responds to a click or activation event on the checkbox <figure>, switching the relevant icon from the silver gradient to the transition pattern, which will then begin to animate. A second <set> element switches the fill again to the final gold state after the animation completes.

❻ The other icons use the same animation structure, but with unique ID values.

CSS STYLES:

```css
html {
    background-color: #222;
    color: lightSkyBlue;
}
svg.defs-only {
    display: block;
    position: absolute;
    height: 0; width: 0;
    overflow: hidden;
}

figure[role="checkbox"] {
    display: inline-block;
    max-width: 33%;
    min-width: 5em;
    padding: 0; margin: 0;
    font-size: larger;                    ❶
}
figcaption {
    display: block;
    text-align: center;
}
figure[role="checkbox"] > svg {
    display: block;
    margin: auto;
    width: 4em;
    height: 4em;
}
.star {
    fill: url(#silver-shine);
    cursor: pointer;                      ❷
}
```

❶ The checkbox role is used instead of a class in the CSS selectors that control the layout.

❷ The CSS also sets the default fill for the star icons, using the silver-gray gradient. The `pointer` cursor will let mouse users know the content is interactive.

There are other limitations to this approach beyond the poor browser support:

- If the user selects two items less than 1 second apart, the first animation will be reset, synchronizing with the second one.

- The animation element that drives the main reaction must reference all events that could trigger it in its `begin` attribute. Example 14-5 simplifies it somewhat by having that animation respond to the `<set>` animations, rather than the original user events. However, adding new interactive icons to the web page would still require new values in the `begin` attribute.

- The selection does not toggle and the animation does not reverse the next time the icon is clicked; subsequent clicks restart the same animation sequence, but do not de-select the item. If you wanted to implement a reverse animation, you would need to add a separate transparent SVG element that appears overtop of the main icon when it is selected (using another `<set>` animation) and catches all user events (using `pointer-events:all`). This element would then be used to trigger the de-selection.[1] You would also need new `<animate>` and `<set>` elements to control the reverse animation sequence.

- Although the icons have been given the ARIA role of `checkbox`, so that screen reader users can activate them, the checked state of that element is not currently updated when the icon is selected. This would need to be implemented within the script, as SMIL animations cannot modify attributes on HTML elements in any browser.

These issues are solved by Example 14-6, which uses JavaScript to control the animations with sensible logic for the checkboxes. It also integrates keyboard support and adds a new feature: when an icon is activated based on a mouse click or tap, the radial gradient spreads

---

1 If you are interested in creating toggled SMIL animations (for other types of animation, such as shape morphing, that have better browser support), Michael J. Harris has written a good tutorial (*http://codepen.io/mikemjharris/blog/svg-toggling*).

outward from the touch point. This type of subtle reaction to user events is recommended by many interaction design guidelines, including Google's Material Design style guide.

Example 14-6. Animating a single element's paint upon user interaction, with JavaScript

HTML MARKUP:

```html
<!DOCTYPE html>
<html lang="en">
<head>
    <meta charset="utf-8" />
    <title>Interactive Animated Gradient with JavaScript</title>
    <style type='text/css'>
        /* styles unchanged */                              ❶
    </style>
</head>
<body>
    <svg class="defs-only"
        aria-hidden="true" focusable="false" width="0" height="0" >
        <linearGradient id="silver-shine" spreadMethod="repeat"
                        gradientTransform="rotate(20)" >
            <stop offset="0" stop-color="gray" />
            <stop offset="0.25" stop-color="silver" />
            <stop offset="1" stop-color="gray" />
        </linearGradient>
        <linearGradient id="gold-shine" spreadMethod="repeat"
                        gradientTransform="rotate(20)" >
            <stop offset="0" stop-color="gold" />
            <stop offset="0.25" stop-color="lightYellow" />
            <stop offset="1" stop-color="gold" />
        </linearGradient>
        <radialGradient id="gold-ripple" r="0.2">
            <stop offset="0" stop-color="gold" />
            <stop offset="0.5" stop-color="lightYellow" />
            <stop offset="0.75" stop-color="silver" />
            <stop offset="1" stop-color="gray" />
        </radialGradient>
        <pattern id="turn-gold" width="1" height="1"
                patternContentUnits="objectBoundingBox">     ❷
            <rect class="transition"
                fill="url(#gold-ripple)" width="1" height="1" />
            <rect class="on"
                fill="url(#gold-shine)" width="1" height="1" />
            <rect class="off"
                fill="url(#silver-shine)" width="1" height="1" />
        </pattern>
        <symbol id="star" viewBox="0 0 200 200">
            <path d="M100,10 L150,140 20,50 180,50 50,140 Z" />
```

```
    </symbol>
  </svg>
  <h1>Pick your favorite:</h1>
  <div>
      <figure id="opt1" role="checkbox">
          <figcaption>Option 1</figcaption>
          <svg><use xlink:href="#star"/></svg>        ❸
      </figure>
      <figure id="opt2" role="checkbox">
          <figcaption>Option 2</figcaption>
          <svg><use xlink:href="#star"/></svg>
      </figure>
      <figure id="opt3" role="checkbox">
          <figcaption>Option 3</figcaption>
          <svg><use xlink:href="#star"/></svg>
      </figure>
  </div>
  <script>
      /* Script included at end of file
         or as an async-loaded external resource */
  </script>
</body>
</html>
```

❶ The basic style rules are the same as in Example 14-5.

❷ The gradients and pattern are almost the same. The animation
elements have been removed, and the pattern layers reshuffled
to make the animation code simpler.

❸ The web page markup is also the same, except for the removal
of the animation elements.

JAVASCRIPT:

```
(function(){
    var toggles = document.querySelectorAll("[role='checkbox']");
    var selectGraphic = ".star";
    var svg = document.querySelector("svg");
        //arbitrary <svg> element so that
        //we can access SVG dom methods
    var paint = {
                off: "url(#silver-shine)",
                animate: "url(#turn-gold)",
                on: "url(#gold-shine)"
            };                                          ❶
    var animating = false,
        animatingOption,
        nextFrame;
```

```
    for (var i=0, n=toggles.length; i<n; i++){                    ❷
        toggles[i].setAttribute("aria-checked", false);
        toggles[i].querySelector(selectGraphic).style.fill
            = paint.off;
        toggles[i].addEventListener("click", toggleState);
        toggles[i].addEventListener("keyup", checkKey);

        //tell Internet Explorer not to focus <svg>
        toggles[i].querySelector("svg")
                .setAttribute("focusable", false);
}
function checkKey(e) {                                            ❸
    //check for spacebar or Enter key,
    //using both the new standard syntax
    //and the old keycode syntax
    if ( (e.key == " ")||(e.key == "Enter") ||
        (e.keyCode == 32 )||(e.keyCode == 13) )
        toggleState.apply(this, arguments);
}
function toggleState(e){                                          ❹
    var currentlyChecked =
            (this.getAttribute("aria-checked")
                    === true.toString() );

    //update the actual state
    this.setAttribute("aria-checked", !currentlyChecked);
        /* maybe do something based on the selected options */

    if (currentlyChecked) {
        //animate turning off quickly
        animateStar(this, e, 300, true);                         ❺
    }
    else {
        //animate turning on, more slowly
        animateStar(this, e, 1000);
    }
}

function animateStar(option, event, dur, reverse) {
    if ((!dur)||isNaN(dur)) return;
        //must have a valid animation duration

    /* animation parameters */
    var effects = [                                              ❻
                {selector:"#gold-ripple", attr:"r",
                 from:0.1, to:1, t1:0.1, t2:0.8},
                {selector:"#turn-gold .on", attr:"opacity",
                 from:0, to:1, t1:0.8, t2:1},
                {selector:"#turn-gold .off", attr:"opacity",
                 from:1, to:0, t1:0, t2:0.2}
```

```
                        ];
    var selectTracker = "#gold-ripple";
    var star = option.querySelector(selectGraphic);
    var startTime = 0;

    if (reverse) {
        //swap the order of each effect
        effects.forEach(function(effect){
            var swap = effect.from;
            effect.from = effect.to;
            effect.to = swap;

            swap = effect.t1;
            effect.t1 = 1 - effect.t2;
            effect.t2 = 1 - swap;
        });
    }

    if (animating){                                          ❼
        //abort current animation
        cancelAnimationFrame(nextFrame);

        if (animatingOption != option) {
            //tidy up the current animation by setting
            //it to the correct end state
            animatingOption.querySelector(selectGraphic)
                .style.fill =
                (animatingOption.getAttribute("aria-checked")
                    === true.toString() ) ?
                paint.on : paint.off;
        }
        else {
            //set the new animation to start
            //from the current state
            effects.forEach(function(effect){
                effect.from = parseFloat(
                        document.querySelector(effect.selector)
                            .getAttribute(effect.attr) );
            });
        }
    }

    var track = document.querySelector(selectTracker);
    if (event instanceof MouseEvent) {                       ❽
        //recenter the radial gradient
        //to track the mouse event
        //by converting mouse coordinates first to
        //userSpace coordinates for the star,
        //and then to bounding box coordinates
        var bbox = star.getBBox(),
            CTM = star.getScreenCTM().inverse(),
```

```
              p = svg.createSVGPoint(),
              p2, newCx, newCy;
        p.x = event.clientX;   //NOT screenX and screenY
        p.y = event.clientY;
        p2 = p.matrixTransform(CTM);
        newCx = (p2.x - bbox.x)/bbox.width;
        newCy = (p2.y - bbox.y)/bbox.height;
        if (!animating ||(animatingOption != option)) {
            //start immediately at the mouse point
            track.setAttribute("cx", newCx);
            track.setAttribute("cy", newCy);
        }
        else {
            //create an animated shift in the gradient center
            var oldCx = parseFloat(track.getAttribute("cx"));
            var oldCy = parseFloat(track.getAttribute("cy"));
            effects.push(
                {selector: selectTracker, attr:"cx",
                 from: oldCx, to: newCx,
                 t1: 0, t2: 0.2
                } );
            effects.push(
                {selector: selectTracker, attr:"cy",
                 from: oldCy, to: newCy,
                 t1: 0, t2: 0.2
                } );
        }
    }
    else {
        //center gradient if triggered by keyboard event
        track.setAttribute("cx", 0.5);
        track.setAttribute("cy", 0.5);
    }

    //set overall animation parameters and initialize
    animating = true;
    animatingOption = option;
    requestAnimationFrame(function(t){
        startTime = t;
        star.style.fill = paint.animate;              ❾
    });


    //create a function to transform a time point
    //into a position in the animation effects
    var getProgress = function(t){ return (t-startTime)/dur; };

    //determine which element will be animated for each effect
    //and the total amount of change
    effects.forEach(function(effect){
        effect.node = document.querySelector(effect.selector);
```

```
            effect.by = effect.to - effect.from;
    });

    function applyEffects(t){                                    ❿
        var a = getProgress(t),
            val;
        effects.forEach(function(effect){
            if(a <= effect.t1) {
                val = effect.from;
            }
            else if (a >= effect.t2) {
                val = effect.to;
            }
            else {
                val = effect.from + effect.by*(
                    (a - effect.t1)/(effect.t2 - effect.t1) );
            }
            effect.node.setAttribute(effect.attr, val);
        });

        if ( a < 1 ) {
            //loop
            nextFrame = requestAnimationFrame(applyEffects);
        }
        else {
            //animation is complete
            star.style.fill = reverse? paint.off : paint.on;
            animating = false;
        }
    }
    //start updating
    nextFrame = requestAnimationFrame(applyEffects);
    }
})();
```

❶ The script starts by declaring constants and variables that will
    be persistent between function calls. This includes the set of
    checkbox-like elements, the selector to identify the graphic we
    will change, a random <svg> element that we'll need for some
    SVG utility methods, and the references to the specific fill val-
    ues that will be used, so they can be easily updated.

❷ The for loop initializes each toggle (checkbox-like element) to
    the unchecked state, and adds the event listeners.

❸ The checkKey helper function responds to keyboard events, and
    determines whether or not the state of the toggle should be

changed; if so, it calls the main event handler function with the current context and arguments.

❹ The `toggleState` function is either triggered directly by a `click` event or indirectly by a keyboard event; it updates the current state of the `aria-checked` attribute, and starts the transition animation.

❺ The `animateStar` function does all the calculations required to start the animation; parameters indicate how long the animation should last and whether the animation should run backward from checked to unchecked.

❻ The overall animation is defined as an array of distinct effects; each effect object describes which element will be modified (as a CSS `selector` value), which attribute will be changed (`attr`), what the initial (`from`) and final (`to`) values should be, and when the animation should start (`t1`) and end (`t2`) as a proportion of the overall animation duration. The hardcoded values describe the forward animation; the values are then swapped if the animation should run in reverse.

❼ The `if(animating)` block contains cleanup code required to prevent two animations from conflicting, as they modify the same paint server elements.

❽ The next block tests whether the animation was triggered by a pointer click on screen, and if so adjusts the radiating or collapsing gradient to center around the touch point.

❾ A one-time call to `requestAnimationFrame` is used to save a timestamp for the beginning of the animation, and to swap the paint server to the animated pattern.

❿ The rest of the animation uses `requestAnimationFrame` to repeatedly call the `applyEffects` function, which updates all the transitioning attributes without a lot of extra calculations to slow it down.

The markup is almost the same as Example 14-5, minus the animation elements. The one change is to the ordering of the layers within the `<pattern>`—this change allows each animation effect to be described by a single-direction animation, from one value to another. Instead of having the animated radial gradient layer fade in and then out, it is drawn as the bottom layer and the two linear gradient layers are faded in or out over top.

The overall pattern of actions after a user event is as follows:

1. Determine whether the action is toggling on or off, and update the ARIA state (the `toggleState` function). This would also be where any other behavior related to checking and unchecking options would be added.

2. Call the animation set-up function (`animateStar`), to either run a 1,000ms turn-on animation or a 300ms turn-off animation. Times are in milliseconds because most JavaScript and DOM timing methods use milliseconds. The turn-off animation runs more quickly because we want to very clearly respond to the user's dismissal of the selection.

3. Check if another animation is running, and if so cancel the pending animation request. If the running animation was on a different star, immediately switch that star to its final state. Otherwise, if it was on the same star, adjust the parameters for the current animation so that it smoothly continues from the current state.

4. If this was a mouse event (which includes clicks created by taps on a touch screen), center the radial gradient on the mouse point. This section uses a number of methods unique to the SVG DOM:

   - `element.getBBox()` returns the bounding box of an object in its local coordinate system as an object with properties x, y, width, and height.

   - `element.getScreenCTM()` returns the cumulative transformation matrix (CTM) between that element's coordinate system and the root coordinate system for the page. Despite the unfortunate name, this is not the *screen* coordinates used in mouse events, but instead the *client* coordinate system.

   - `matrix.inverse()` returns a new transformation matrix that exactly reverses the transformation created by the original matrix.

- *svg*.createSVGPoint() generates an SVG data object that can hold x and y numerical values. SVGPoint objects are used when accessing the points of a polygon or polyline. The only reason to create your own is for the next method.

- *point*.matrixTransform(*matrix*) calculates the position of the given point after applying the specified matrix transformation.

Using these methods, the mouse coordinates from the event are converted to the coordinate system used for the star, and then the star's bounding box is used to convert to object bounding box coordinates for the gradient's cx and cy attributes. If altering an in-progress animation, the shift in center is applied as additional animation effects, by adding new objects to the effects array. In contrast, if the toggle was triggered by a keyboard event, cx and cy are reset to the center of the element.

5. Call a one-time animation function to initialize the animation, changing the fill property of the star to the animating pattern, and recording the start time for the animation loop.

6. Define a function (getProgress) to convert document timestamps into a fraction of the time between the start and end of the animation effect. If you wanted to use an easing function to slow down or speed up the animation as it progresses, this would be the place to incorporate it.

7. Identify which element will be animated for each effect, and store it in a variable for quick access. Also convert the from-to animation syntax into from-by format for faster math at each frame of the animation.

8. Finally, apply the changing effects at each stage of the animation, according to the timestamp passed to the callback function (applyEffects) by the browser in response to an animation frame request. The effects are defined using an array of data objects; each object has the same structure so that it can be applied using a single function that calculates the current value and updates the corresponding attribute of a specified element.

The method used here only supports the interpolation of simple numerical values, and only supports changes to attributes (including presentation attributes). If you wanted to animate colors, complex lists of data, or animate style values, additional code would be required.

9. Within the animation callback, check whether the animation is complete. If it hasn't yet completed, request another animation frame; if it has, switch the star to its final gradient state.

The only limitation remaining is that the animation on one star is aborted if another star is interacted with. This is necessary to avoid conflict, as there is only a single paint server used to draw the animation states of all the stars. In order to work around this, you would need to dynamically create separate copies of the paint servers (the `<radialGradient>` and the `<pattern>` that references it) for each element being animated. These DOM manipulations would have performance impacts, so you would need to decide if they were worth the small chance of overlapping interactions. Of course, the likelihood of two interactions overlapping will depend on how long each animation lasts. A 1-second animation is actually considered quite long for user interaction animations.

This is all a lot of code for a subtle interaction effect. For this reason, it is rare to write a complete custom animation script for each project. JavaScript libraries such as Snap.svg (*http://snapsvg.io/*), D3.js (*http://d3js.org/*), or the GreenSock Animation Platform, GSAP (*https://greensock.com/*) provide methods to efficiently control the timing of animation and interpolation of values. As browser support increases for the Web Animations API, that will become the preferred method of defining specific animation effects.

Nonetheless, the overall strategy of creating an animation by switching between paint servers and animating the paint server components would still apply when using those tools. That said, this particular effect will get much easier when there is good browser support for layered fills, CSS gradients as a fill value, and CSS transitions of gradient functions.

Color Keywords and Syntax

Colors within SVG and CSS may be specified either as exact numerical values or by using predefined color keywords.

Custom solid colors can be specified in any of the following formats:

- *#RRGGBB*, six hexidecimal digits, with each pair representing a value between 0 (00) and 255 (FF) for each color channel

- *#RGB*, three hexadecimal digits, equivalent to the six-digit version with every digit duplicated

- rgb(*r*,*g*,*b*), with either three integers between 0 and 255, or three percentage values

- hsl(*h*,*s*,*l*), where the first (hue) parameter is a number representing an angle in degrees on the color wheel (relative to red), and the saturation and lightness values are percentages

Custom partially transparent colors can be specified with one of two functions:

- rgba(*r*,*g*,*b*,*a*), where the first three values may either be percentages or integers and the *a* value is a decimal between 0 and 1

- hsla(*h*,*s*,*l*,*a*), where the parameters are a number, two percentages, then a decimal alpha value between 0 and 1

The named solid colors are listed in Table A-1 along with their equivalents in hexadecimal, RGB, and HSL formats. The percentage

RGB values and HSL values have been rounded to whole numbers. In addition, the keyword transparent represents rgba(0,0,0,0) or hsla(0,0%,0%,0).

Table A-1. Named colors in SVG and CSS

Keyword	Hex value	RGB decimal			RGB percent			HSL		
		R	G	B	R	G	B	H	S	L
AliceBlue	#f0f8ff	240	248	255	94%	97%	100%	208	6%	97%
antiqueWhite	#faebd7	250	235	215	98%	92%	84%	34	14%	91%
aqua	#00ffff	0	255	255	0%	100%	100%	180	100%	50%
aquamarine	#7fffd4	127	255	212	50%	100%	83%	160	50%	75%
azure	#f0ffff	240	255	255	94%	100%	100%	180	6%	97%
beige	#f5f5dc	245	245	220	96%	96%	86%	60	10%	91%
bisque	#ffe4c4	255	228	196	100%	89%	77%	33	23%	88%
black	#000000	0	0	0	0%	0%	0%	0	0%	0%
blanchedAlmond	#ffebcd	255	235	205	100%	92%	80%	36	20%	90%
blue	#0000ff	0	0	255	0%	0%	100%	240	100%	50%
blueViolet	#8a2be2	138	43	226	54%	17%	89%	271	81%	53%
brown	#a52a2a	165	42	42	65%	16%	16%	0	75%	41%
burlywood	#deb887	222	184	135	87%	72%	53%	34	39%	70%
cadetBlue	#5f9ea0	95	158	160	37%	62%	63%	182	41%	50%
chartreuse	#7fff00	127	255	0	50%	100%	0%	90	100%	50%
chocolate	#d2691e	210	105	30	82%	41%	12%	25	86%	47%
coral	#ff7f50	255	127	80	100%	50%	31%	16	69%	66%
cornflowerBlue	#6495ed	100	149	237	39%	58%	93%	219	58%	66%
cornsilk	#fff8dc	255	248	220	100%	97%	86%	48	14%	93%
crimson	#dc143c	220	20	60	86%	8%	24%	348	91%	47%

Keyword	Hex value	RGB decimal			RGB percent			HSL		
		R	G	B	R	G	B	H	S	L
cyan	#00ffff	0	255	255	0%	100%	100%	180	100%	50%
darkBlue	#00008b	0	0	139	0%	0%	55%	240	100%	27%
darkCyan	#008b8b	0	139	139	0%	55%	55%	180	100%	27%
darkGoldenrod	#b8860b	184	134	11	72%	53%	4%	43	94%	38%
darkGray	#a9a9a9	169	169	169	66%	66%	66%	0	0%	66%
darkGreen	#006400	0	100	0	0%	39%	0%	120	100%	20%
darkGrey	#a9a9a9	169	169	169	66%	66%	66%	0	0%	66%
darkKhaki	#bdb76b	189	183	107	74%	72%	42%	56	43%	58%
darkMagenta	#8b008b	139	0	139	55%	0%	55%	300	100%	27%
darkOliveGreen	#556b2f	85	107	47	33%	42%	18%	82	56%	30%
darkOrange	#ff8c00	255	140	0	100%	55%	0%	33	100%	50%
darkOrchid	#9932cc	153	50	204	60%	20%	80%	280	75%	50%
darkRed	#8b0000	139	0	0	55%	0%	0%	0	100%	27%
darkSalmon	#e9967a	233	150	122	91%	59%	48%	15	48%	70%
darkSeaGreen	#8fbc8f	143	188	143	56%	74%	56%	120	24%	65%
darkSlateBlue	#483d8b	72	61	139	28%	24%	55%	248	56%	39%
darkSlateGray	#2f4f4f	47	79	79	18%	31%	31%	180	41%	25%
darkSlateGrey	#2f4f4f	47	79	79	18%	31%	31%	180	41%	25%
darkTurquoise	#00ced1	0	206	209	0%	81%	82%	181	100%	41%
darkViolet	#9400d3	148	0	211	58%	0%	83%	282	100%	41%
deepPink	#ff1493	255	20	147	100%	8%	58%	328	92%	54%
deepSkyBlue	#00bfff	0	191	255	0%	75%	100%	195	100%	50%
dimGray	#696969	105	105	105	41%	41%	41%	0	0%	41%

Keyword	Hex value	RGB decimal			RGB percent			HSL		
		R	G	B	R	G	B	H	S	L
dimGrey	#696969	105	105	105	41%	41%	41%	0	0%	41%
dodgerBlue	#1e90ff	30	144	255	12%	56%	100%	210	88%	56%
firebrick	#b22222	178	34	34	70%	13%	13%	0	81%	42%
floralWhite	#fffaf0	255	250	240	100%	98%	94%	40	6%	97%
forestGreen	#228b22	34	139	34	13%	55%	13%	120	76%	34%
fuchsia	#ff00ff	255	0	255	100%	0%	100%	300	100%	50%
gainsboro	#dcdcdc	220	220	220	86%	86%	86%	0	0%	86%
ghostWhite	#f8f8ff	248	248	255	97%	97%	100%	240	3%	99%
gold	#ffd700	255	215	0	100%	84%	0%	51	100%	50%
goldenrod	#daa520	218	165	32	85%	65%	13%	43	85%	49%
gray	#808080	128	128	128	50%	50%	50%	0	0%	50%
green	#008000	0	128	0	0%	50%	0%	120	100%	25%
greenYellow	#adff2f	173	255	47	68%	100%	18%	84	82%	59%
grey	#808080	128	128	128	50%	50%	50%	0	0%	50%
honeydew	#f0fff0	240	255	240	94%	100%	94%	120	6%	97%
hotPink	#ff69b4	255	105	180	100%	41%	71%	330	59%	71%
indianRed	#cd5c5c	205	92	92	80%	36%	36%	0	55%	58%
indigo	#4b0082	75	0	130	29%	0%	51%	275	100%	25%
ivory	#fffff0	255	255	240	100%	100%	94%	60	6%	97%
khaki	#f0e68c	240	230	140	94%	90%	55%	54	42%	75%
lavender	#e6e6fa	230	230	250	90%	90%	98%	240	8%	94%
lavenderBlush	#fff0f5	255	240	245	100%	94%	96%	340	6%	97%
lawnGreen	#7cfc00	124	252	0	49%	99%	0%	90	100%	49%

Keyword	Hex value	RGB decimal			RGB percent			HSL		
		R	G	B	R	G	B	H	S	L
lemonChiffon	#fffacd	255	250	205	100%	98%	80%	54	20%	90%
lightBlue	#add8e6	173	216	230	68%	85%	90%	195	25%	79%
lightCoral	#f08080	240	128	128	94%	50%	50%	0	47%	72%
lightCyan	#e0ffff	224	255	255	88%	100%	100%	180	12%	94%
lightGoldenrodYellow	#fafad2	250	250	210	98%	98%	82%	60	16%	90%
lightGray	#d3d3d3	211	211	211	83%	83%	83%	0	0%	83%
lightGreen	#90ee90	144	238	144	56%	93%	56%	120	39%	75%
lightGrey	#d3d3d3	211	211	211	83%	83%	83%	0	0%	83%
lightPink	#ffb6c1	255	182	193	100%	71%	76%	351	29%	86%
lightSalmon	#ffa07a	255	160	122	100%	63%	48%	17	52%	74%
lightSeaGreen	#20b2aa	32	178	170	13%	70%	67%	177	82%	41%
lightSkyBlue	#87cefa	135	206	250	53%	81%	98%	203	46%	75%
lightSlateGray	#778899	119	136	153	47%	53%	60%	210	22%	53%
lightSlateGrey	#778899	119	136	153	47%	53%	60%	210	22%	53%
lightSteelBlue	#b0c4de	176	196	222	69%	77%	87%	214	21%	78%
lightYellow	#ffffe0	255	255	224	100%	100%	88%	60	12%	94%
lime	#00ff00	0	255	0	0%	100%	0%	120	100%	50%
limeGreen	#32cd32	50	205	50	20%	80%	20%	120	76%	50%
linen	#faf0e6	250	240	230	98%	94%	90%	30	8%	94%
magenta	#ff00ff	255	0	255	100%	0%	100%	300	100%	50%
maroon	#800000	128	0	0	50%	0%	0%	0	100%	25%
mediumAquamarine	#66cdaa	102	205	170	40%	80%	67%	160	50%	60%
mediumBlue	#0000cd	0	0	205	0%	0%	80%	240	100%	40%

Keyword	Hex value	RGB decimal			RGB percent			HSL		
		R	G	B	R	G	B	H	S	L
mediumOrchid	#ba55d3	186	85	211	73%	33%	83%	288	60%	58%
mediumPurple	#9370db	147	112	219	58%	44%	86%	260	49%	65%
mediumSeaGreen	#3cb371	60	179	113	24%	70%	44%	147	66%	47%
mediumSlateBlue	#7b68ee	123	104	238	48%	41%	93%	249	56%	67%
mediumSpringGreen	#00fa9a	0	250	154	0%	98%	60%	157	100%	49%
mediumTurquoise	#48d1cc	72	209	204	28%	82%	80%	178	66%	55%
mediumVioletRed	#c71585	199	21	133	78%	8%	52%	322	89%	43%
midnightBlue	#191970	25	25	112	10%	10%	44%	240	78%	27%
mintCream	#f5fffa	245	255	250	96%	100%	98%	150	4%	98%
mistyRose	#ffe4e1	255	228	225	100%	89%	88%	6	12%	94%
moccasin	#ffe4b5	255	228	181	100%	89%	71%	38	29%	85%
navajoWhite	#ffdead	255	222	173	100%	87%	68%	36	32%	84%
navy	#000080	0	0	128	0%	0%	50%	240	100%	25%
oldLace	#fdf5e6	253	245	230	99%	96%	90%	39	9%	95%
olive	#808000	128	128	0	50%	50%	0%	60	100%	25%
oliveDrab	#6b8e23	107	142	35	42%	56%	14%	80	75%	35%
orange	#ffa500	255	165	0	100%	65%	0%	39	100%	50%
orangeRed	#ff4500	255	69	0	100%	27%	0%	16	100%	50%
orchid	#da70d6	218	112	214	85%	44%	84%	302	49%	65%
paleGoldenrod	#eee8aa	238	232	170	93%	91%	67%	55	29%	80%
paleGreen	#98fb98	152	251	152	60%	98%	60%	120	39%	79%
paleTurquoise	#afeeee	175	238	238	69%	93%	93%	180	26%	81%
paleVioletRed	#db7093	219	112	147	86%	44%	58%	340	49%	65%

Keyword	Hex value	RGB decimal			RGB percent			HSL		
		R	G	B	R	G	B	H	S	L
papayaWhip	#ffefd5	255	239	213	100%	94%	84%	37	16%	92%
peachPuff	#ffdab9	255	218	185	100%	85%	73%	28	27%	86%
peru	#cd853f	205	133	63	80%	52%	25%	30	69%	53%
pink	#ffc0cb	255	192	203	100%	75%	80%	350	25%	88%
plum	#dda0dd	221	160	221	87%	63%	87%	300	28%	75%
powderBlue	#b0e0e6	176	224	230	69%	88%	90%	187	23%	80%
purple	#800080	128	0	128	50%	0%	50%	300	100%	25%
rebeccaPurple	#663399	102	51	153	40%	20%	60%	270	67%	40%
red	#ff0000	255	0	0	100%	0%	0%	0	100%	50%
rosyBrown	#bc8f8f	188	143	143	74%	56%	56%	0	24%	65%
royalBlue	#4169e1	65	105	225	25%	41%	88%	225	71%	57%
saddleBrown	#8b4513	139	69	19	55%	27%	7%	25	86%	31%
salmon	#fa8072	250	128	114	98%	50%	45%	6	54%	71%
sandyBrown	#f4a460	244	164	96	96%	64%	38%	28	61%	67%
seaGreen	#2e8b57	46	139	87	18%	55%	34%	146	67%	36%
seashell	#fff5ee	255	245	238	100%	96%	93%	25	7%	97%
sienna	#a0522d	160	82	45	63%	32%	18%	19	72%	40%
silver	#c0c0c0	192	192	192	75%	75%	75%	0	0%	75%
skyBlue	#87ceeb	135	206	235	53%	81%	92%	197	43%	73%
slateBlue	#6a5acd	106	90	205	42%	35%	80%	248	56%	58%
slateGray	#708090	112	128	144	44%	50%	56%	210	22%	50%
slateGrey	#708090	112	128	144	44%	50%	56%	210	22%	50%
snow	#fffafa	255	250	250	100%	98%	98%	0	2%	99%

Keyword	Hex value	RGB decimal			RGB percent			HSL		
		R	G	B	R	G	B	H	S	L
springGreen	#00ff7f	0	255	127	0%	100%	50%	150	100%	50%
steelBlue	#4682b4	70	130	180	27%	51%	71%	207	61%	49%
tan	#d2b48c	210	180	140	82%	71%	55%	34	33%	69%
teal	#008080	0	128	128	0%	50%	50%	180	100%	25%
thistle	#d8bfd8	216	191	216	85%	75%	85%	300	12%	80%
tomato	#ff6347	255	99	71	100%	39%	28%	9	72%	64%
turquoise	#40e0d0	64	224	208	25%	88%	82%	174	71%	56%
violet	#ee82ee	238	130	238	93%	51%	93%	300	45%	72%
wheat	#f5deb3	245	222	179	96%	87%	70%	39	27%	83%
white	#ffffff	255	255	255	100%	100%	100%	0	0%	100%
whiteSmoke	#f5f5f5	245	245	245	96%	96%	96%	0	0%	96%
yellow	#ffff00	255	255	0	100%	100%	0%	60	100%	50%
yellowGreen	#9acd32	154	205	50	60%	80%	20%	80	76%	50%

Elements, Attributes, and Style Properties

This guide to SVG paint server elements provides a quick reference to the available attributes, with their default and allowed values.

\<linearGradient>

A gradient in which color stops are drawn as parallel lines, extending perpendicularly (in the gradient's coordinate system) from a gradient vector.

id

>   the value used to reference this gradient
>
>   - same restrictions as for any other element id

x1

>   horizontal position of the gradient vector's start point
>
>   - a length (in user coordinates or with units) or percentage (of coordinate system width)
>   - default 0.

y1

>   vertical position of the gradient vector's start point

- a length (in user coordinates or with units) or percentage (of coordinate system height)
- default 0.

x2

    horizontal position of the gradient vector's end point

- a length (in user coordinates or with units) or percentage (of coordinate system width)
- default 100%.

y2

    vertical position of the gradient vector's end point

- a length (in user coordinates or with units) or percentage (of coordinate system height)
- default 0.

gradientUnits

    the coordinate system to use

- either userSpaceOnUse or objectBoundingBox
- default objectBoundingBox

gradientTransform

    transformations to apply to the gradient content, independent of the shape it fills

- a list of whitespace-separated transformation functions: translate(*tx*,*ty*), scale(*s*), scale(*sx*,*sy*), rotate(*a*), rotate(*a*,*cx*,*cy*), skewX(*a*), and skewY(*a*)
- each transformation parameter is specified as a number without units (in the SVG 1 syntax); lengths are interpretted as user units (px), angles are interpretted as degrees
- default is no transformation

spreadMethod

    the strategy to use for filling content beyond the start and end of the gradient vector

- one of pad, reflect or repeat
- default pad

xlink:href

a reference to another gradient that should be used as a template for this one

- a URL with a target fragment which must match the ID of a `<linearGradient>` or `<radialGradient>` element in the same document
- all attributes on the referenced element become the default values for the current element
- if the current element does *not* contain any `<stop>` elements, then the stops from the referenced element will be used
- in XML documents (including SVG), the xlink prefix must be attached to the XLink namespace, *http://www.w3.org/1999/xlink*, using an xmlns:xlink attribute

`<radialGradient>`

A gradient in which color stops are drawn along rays from a starting point to an ending circle.

id

the value used to reference this gradient

- same restrictions as for any other element id

cx

horizontal position of the center point

- a length (in user coordinates or with units) or percentage (of coordinate system width)
- default 50%

cy

vertical position of the center point

- a length (in user coordinates or with units) or percentage (of coordinate system height)
- default 50%

r

radius of the circle

- a length (in user coordinates or with units) or percentage (proportional to the coordinate system diagonal length, such that the diagonal is always $\sqrt{2}\times100\%$)
- default 50%
- negative values are an error.

fx

horizontal position of the focal point

- a length (in user coordinates or with units) or percentage (of coordinate system width)
- default is to match cx

fy

vertical position of the focal point

- a length (in user coordinates or with units) or percentage (of coordinate system height)
- default is to match cy

gradientUnits

the coordinate system to use

- either userSpaceOnUse or objectBoundingBox
- default objectBoundingBox

gradientTransform

transformations to apply to the gradient content, independent of the shape it fills

- syntax and options are the same as for <linearGradient>

`spreadMethod`
> the strategy to use for filling content beyond the ending circle
>
> - syntax and options are the same as for `<linearGradient>`

`xlink:href`
> a reference to another gradient that should be used as a template
> for this one
>
> - syntax and options are the same as `<linearGradient>`

`<stop>`

A fixed value within a gradient.

`offset`
> The distance along the gradient vector or ray at which to posi-
> tion this value
>
> - a number between 0 and 1, or a percentage
> - values will be clamped to the range [0–1] or [0%–100%]
> - stops must be listed in order of increasing offsets; if not, the
>   offset will be adjusted to match the previous maximum
>   value
> - no official default in SVG 1.1; default 0 in SVG 2 and in
>   most web browsers

`stop-color` *(presentation attribute)*
> The color to use at this stop point
>
> - any valid color definition supported by the browser
> - default `black`

`stop-opacity` *(presentation attribute)*
> The alpha value to use at this stop point
>
> - a number between 0 and 1
> - default 1

<pattern>

A paint server that defines a region of custom SVG content that should be used to fill other elements, repeating it as necessary in a rectangular grid.

id
> the value used to reference this gradient
>
> - same restrictions as for any other element id

x
> horizontal offset of the top left corner of the reference pattern tile
>
> - a length (in user coordinates or with units) or percentage (of coordinate system width)
> - default 0

y
> vertical offset of the top left corner of the reference pattern tile
>
> - a length (in user coordinates or with units) or percentage (of coordinate system height)
> - default 0

width
> width of each pattern tile
>
> - a length (in user coordinates or with units) or percentage (of coordinate system width)
> - default 0, which disables rendering of the pattern
> - negative values are an error

height
> height of each pattern tile
>
> - a length (in user coordinates or with units) or percentage (of coordinate system height)
> - default 0, which disables rendering of the pattern
> - negative values are an error

`patternUnits`
> the coordinate system to use for x, y, `width`, and `height`
>
> - either `userSpaceOnUse` or `objectBoundingBox`
> - default `objectBoundingBox`

`patternContentUnits`
> the coordinate system to use for drawing the child content of the pattern
>
> - either `userSpaceOnUse` or `objectBoundingBox`
> - default `userSpaceOnUse`
> - has no effect if a `viewBox` is specified
> - a value of `objectBoundingBox` is implemented as a non-uniform scale to the user units; it does not create a new reference definition for percentage lengths

`viewBox`
> declaration of a custom coordinate system to use for the pattern contents
>
> - a list of four numbers, separated by whitespace or commas
> - the numbers represent, in order: minimum x, minimum y, width, and height
> - the width and height values must be positive
> - by default, the coordinate system is controlled by `patternContentUnits`
> - the `viewBox` is implemented as a scaling transformation, and does not create a new reference definition for percentage lengths

`preserveAspectRatio`
> the scaling and alignment strategy that should be used when the aspect ratio defined by the `viewBox` does not match the aspect ratio of the pattern tile
>
> - Either `none` or an alignment value followed by `meet` or `slice`

- The alignment value is a single word of the form x*Mxx*Y*Mxx* where *Mxx* is one of Min, Mid, or Max

- default is xMidYMid meet

- has no effect unless a viewBox attribute is specified

patternTransform

transformations to apply to the pattern tiles and their content, independent of the shape it fills

- syntax and options are the same as for the gradientTransform attribute for \<linearGradient\>

- default is no transformation

xlink:href

a reference to another pattern that should be used as a template for this one

- a URL with a target fragment which must match the ID of a \<pattern\> element in the same document

- all attributes on the referenced element become the default values for the current element

- if the current element does *not* contain any child elements, then the pattern content from the referenced element will be used

- in XML documents (including SVG), the xlink prefix must be attached to the XLink namespace, *http://www.w3.org/ 1999/xlink*, using an xmlns:xlink attribute

Index

A

Adobe Illustrator, ix, 161
AJAX (Asynchronous JavaScript and
    XML), 66, 126
alpha, 54
    (see also opacity)
    blending compared with gradi-
        ents, 60
    compositing, 58
animate element, 240
    (see also animation)
animateMotion element, 240
    (see also animation)
animateTransfrom element, 240
    (see also animation)
animation, 5, 239-267
    CSS, 241, 245, 248
    elements, 241, 245, 249, 252
    scripted, 242, 257
        common libraries, 267
    user interaction, 251
animation style properties, 240, 245
    (see also animation)
Apache Batik SVG viewer, ix, 51, 70
ARIA attributes
    aria-checked, 257, 265
    aria-hidden, 120
    aria-labelledby, 119, 126
    aria-owns and aria-flowto, 26
    aria-readonly, 126
    aria-valuenow, aria-valuemin, and
        aria-valuemax, 126

B

background style properties
    fixed attachment versus user-
        space gradients, 100
    for pattern effects, 180
    for repeated gradients effects, 117
    simulating transformed patterns,
        187
base element (HTML), impact on rel-
    ative URLs, 66
Batik (see Apache Batik SVG viewer)
blending, 58
    comparison with gradients, 60
    mix-blend-mode, 59
    sRGB color model and, 49
Blink rendering engine (see Chrome)
bump map, 151
    (see also filter elements)

C

calc CSS function, for gradient stops,
    83
Chrome web browser and Chromium
    project, ix
    color-interpolation support, 51
    CSS gradient rendering quality,
        100
    CSS repeating gradients appear-
        ance, 140
    display:none for paint servers, 120
    external asset support, 65, 119,
        126
    focus control, 121

font-size-adjust support, 218
gradient transitions at 0 or 1 offset, 97
paint-order support, 18
rotated text paint appearance, 211
SMIL animation of paint servers,
250, 252
SMIL animation support, 245
spreadMethod support, 137
text-shadow on SVG text, 203
textLength support, 218
userSpaceOnUse errors, 98, 120,
234
zero-length linear gradient vector
appearance, 86
clipping paths, versus image fills, 205
CMYK color model, 39
color, 31-52
additive versus subtractive mixing, 38
alpha component of, 53
custom values, 40
hexadecimal notation, 40
hsl CSS function, 44
HSL model, 41
(see also HSL color model)
hsla CSS function, 53
keywords, 31
capitalization, 32
perception of, 37, 48
physics of, 36
reference, 269
rgb CSS function, 40
RGB model, 39, 49
(see also RGB color model)
(see also sRGB color model)
rgba CSS function, 53
web safe, 40
color style property, 9
color-interpolation style property, 50,
58
for animation, 244
interaction with color-rendering
hint, 29
color-interpolation-filters style property, 51
color-rendering style property, 28
conic gradients, 161

createSVGPoint method, 266
crisp-edges keyword, image-
rendering, 29
crispEdges keyword, shape-
rendering, 26
CSS (Cascading Style Sheets), 4, 65
CSS 3 modules
Colors, 53
Compositing and Blending, 59
Image Values and Replaced Content Level 3
gradient functions, 83
image-rendering hint, 29
transitioning gradients, 251
Image Values and Replaced Content Level 4, 161, 251
Text Decoration, 205
Transforms, 101
currentColor keyword, 9
cx and cy attributes, radialGradient
element, 141, 279

D
desc element, 119, 119

E
Edge web browser (see Internet
Explorer/Edge)
evenodd keyword, for fill-rule, 10

F
fallback colors, for fill and stroke, 66
fill style property, 9
fallback colors, 66
fill-opacity style property, 10, 53
fill-rule style property, 10
filter elements, 51, 59, 149-152
Firefox web browser, ix
color-interpolation support, 51
CSS gradients with transparent
stops, 155
CSS repeating gradients appearance, 140
display:none for paint servers, 120
external asset support, 65, 119
focus control, 121
font-size-adjust support, 218

paint-order support, 18
rotated text paint appearance, 211
rounding fractional units, 174
SMIL animation of paint servers,
250, 252
spreadMethod support, 113, 137
text-shadow on SVG text, 203
textLength support, 218
viewBox and pattern errors, 194,
212
focal point, in radial gradients, 134,
141, 144
simulating with CSS gradients,
152
focusable attribute, 120
font-size-adjust style property, 217
fr attribute, in SVG 2, 147
fx and fy attributes, radialGradient
element, 144, 280

G

gamut, of color model, 40
Gecko rendering engine (see Firefox)
geometricPrecision keyword
shape-rendering, 26
text-rendering, 27
getBBox method, 265
getScreenCTM method, 265
gradient vector, 85
in CSS gradients, 100, 110
normal (perpendicular) vectors,
92
reflected/repeated gradients, 111,
114, 116
transformations of, 106
zero length, 86
gradients, 75-82
comparison with blending, 60
layering with a pattern, 189
linear, 85-108
(see also linearGradient element)
radial, 133-152
(see also radialGradient element)
repeating/reflecting, 111-116
as a solid color paint server, 68
gradientTransform attribute, 100, 278

comparison with shape transformations, 102
interaction with object bounding
box units, 106
for linear gradients, 101
for radial gradients, 147
gradientUnits attribute, 94, 278
gzip compression, 2, 161

H

hatch and hatchPath elements, SVG
2, 184
height attribute, pattern element, 164,
282
hexadecimal color notation, 40
HSL color model, 41
conversion from RGB, 42
gradient interpolation and, 80
hsl CSS function, 44
hsla CSS function, 53, 84
HTML
SVG within, 2, 9, 59, 118-132
XML versus, 2

I

ICC (International Color Consortium) color profiles, 49
Illustrator, software by Adobe, ix
image element, 3, 167, 201
image-rendering style property, 28
images, SVG embedded as, 3, 240
Inkscape, ix, 161, 211, 212
Internet Explorer/Edge web browsers, ix
color-interpolation support, 51
CSS 3 color support, 44
CSS animation support, 246
CSS repeating gradients appearance, 140
display:none for paint servers, 120
external asset support, 65, 119
focus control, 121
font-size-adjust support, 218
paint-order support, 18
rotated text paint appearance, 211
SMIL animation support, 245
text-shadow on SVG text, 203

textLength support, 218
userSpaceOnUse errors, 98, 120, 234
zero-length linear gradient vector appearance, 86
inverse method, matrix object, 265
iOS (see WebKit)
isolation style property, 59

L

line element
  comparison with linearGradient, 85
  default styles, 12
linear-gradient CSS function, 83
  angle parameters, 109
  animations and transitions, 251
  position keywords, 98
linearGradient element, 70, 76, 85-108
  positioning attributes, 85
  reference, 277
  reflected/repeated gradients, 111-116
linearRGB keyword, for color-interpolation hints, 50
luminance
  in filters and masking, 51
  versus lightness, 42

M

matrixTransform method, 266
media queries, for print color profiles, 71
meet keyword, for preserveAspectRatio, 193
Microsoft Edge (see Internet Explorer/Edge)
mix-blend-mode style property, 59

N

nonzero keyword, for fill-rule, 10
normal vector, 93
  (see also gradient vector)
nth-of-type CSS selector, 126, 245

O

objectBoundingBox units, 90
  distorted scale, 92, 184
  for linear gradients, 91
  for pattern contents, 166, 172
  for pattern tile dimensions, 165
  for radial gradients, 137
  in stroke paint, 222, 224
  text element bounding box, 208, 214
  and transformations, 106, 147
offset attribute, 76, 281
  creating stripes with, 77
  for radial gradients, 134
  reflected/repeated gradients, 116
  sharp transitions at 0 or 1, 97
  valid range and order, 77
opacity, 53-61
  in CSS gradients, 84
  in gradient stops, 78
  multiplicative effect, 58
opacity style property, 53
  comparison with other forms of transparency, 54
  hardware-accelerated animation, 58
  impact on isolation, 59
  stacking context created by, 54
optimizeLegibility keyword, text-rendering, 27
optimizeQuality keyword
  color-rendering, 28
  image-rendering, 28
optimizeSpeed keyword
  color-rendering, 28
  image-rendering, 28
  shape-rendering, 26
  text-rendering, 27
overflow style property, for patterns, 166

P

pad keyword, for spreadMethod, 111
paint servers, 9, 63-72
  external file assets, 65, 87, 119
  versus CSS image data type, 84
paint-order style property, 18-24
painter's model

for fill and stroke, 17
for overlapping elements, 24
strokes as a single shape, 57
pattern element, 163-187, 189-205
reference, 282
for strokes, 235
style inheritance, 183
patternContentUnits attribute, 166,
171, 283
patternTransform attribute, 181, 284
patternUnits attribute, 165, 171, 283
pigments
printing, 38
retinal, 37
pixelated keyword, image-rendering,
29
polyline element, 14
default fill behavior, 12
presentation attribute
new geometric presentation
attributes for CSS control, 5,
101, 246
presentation attributes, 4
overriding with CSS, 65, 70
preserveAspectRatio attribute, 4, 33,
193, 283
image element, 204
pattern element, 212
pseudoclasses (CSS), for animation,
240
px unit, 8, 92

R

r attribute, radialGradient element,
141, 280
radial-gradient CSS function, 139,
142
animations and transitions, 251
radialGradient element, 133-152
comparison with filter effects, 149
reference, 279
reflect keyword, for spreadMethod,
112, 113
repeat keyword, for spreadMethod,
112, 114
repeating-linear-gradient CSS function, 116
animations and transitions, 251

repeating-radial-gradient CSS function, 140, 142
animations and transitions, 251
RGB color model, 39
(see also sRGB color model)
conversion to HSL, 42
rgb CSS function or hexadecimal
notation, 40
rgba CSS function, 53, 84
rotate transformation function, 100

S

Safari web browser (see WebKit)
scale transformation function, 100
set element, 240
(see also animation)
shape-rendering style property, 26,
171
skewX and skewY transformation
functions, 100
slice keyword, for preserveAspectRatio, 193
SMIL (Synchronized Multimedia
Integration Language), 245
(see also animation)
solidcolor element and solid-color
style property, 72
spreadMethod attribute, 111, 278
for radial gradients, 137
sRGB color model, 49
color-interpolation options, 50
gradient interpolation and, 80
and opacity, 58
stop element, 70, 76, 134
duplicated with xlink:href, 87
reference, 281
stop-color style property, 70, 281
stop-opacity style property, 70, 78,
281
stroke style property, 12, 221
(see also strokes)
fallback colors, 66
stroke-dasharray style property, 13
stroke-dashoffset style property, 14
stroke-linecap style property, 13
stroke-linejoin style property, 13
stroke-miterlimit style property, 13
stroke-opacity style property, 13, 53

stroke-width style property, 13
strokes, 221-237
    as a secondary shape, 12
    default paint order, 17
    geometry, 12, 57
    impact on text legibility, 18
    line-joins versus caps, 16
    and object bounding boxes, 90
style element, 65
    (see also CSS)
@supports CSS rule, 19, 25
SVG 2 specification
    changes to fill options, 11
    changes to stroke options, 17, 223
    CSS gradients in fill or stroke, 84
    fr attribute, radialGradient ele-
        ment, 147
    hatches, 184
    images in fill or stroke, 200
    layered fill and stroke, 67, 189
    mesh gradients, 161
    new geometric presentation
        attributes for CSS control, 5,
        246
    paint-order style property, 18
    solidcolor element, 72
    stroke bounding boxes, 231
    text decoration fill and stroke, 205
    z-index style property, 25
SVGPoint object, 266
svgz (file extension), 2
    (see also gzip compression)
symbol element, 4, 118, 250

T
tabindex attribute, 121
text, 207-218
    converting to paths, 207, 211
    filling with image, 201
    strokes and paint-order, 18
text element, 208
text-decoration style property, 202
    new features in CSS 3 and SVG 2,
        205
text-rendering style property, 27
text-shadow style property, 203
textLength attribute, 217
textPath element, 211

title element, 33, 119, 119, 131
    in inline SVG, 131
transformation functions, 47, 100
    repositioning a user-space gradi-
        ent, 228
transformation matrix, 265
transition style properties, 240
    (see also animation)
translate transformation function,
    100
transparency (see opacity)
transparent color keyword, 54, 155
tspan element, 214

U
units, for defining lengths, 8
    objectBoundingBox scaling
        effects, 92
url CSS function, 65
    relative URLs and CSS files, 65
use element, 118
userSpaceOnUse units
    coloring by value in a data chart,
        231
    for gradients, 94
    for pattern contents, 166, 175
    for pattern tile dimensions, 165
    percentages in pattern contents,
        172
    to stroke gradients on straight
        lines, 226
    with SVG icon systems, 120
    and transformations, 107

V
viewBox attribute, 4, 193, 283
    pattern element, 174, 194, 212
    percentage units and patterns, 196

W
Web Animations API, 6, 243
web safe colors, 40
    (see also color)
WebKit project, ix
    color-interpolation support, 51
    CSS animation support, 246

CSS repeating gradients implementation, 116, 140
display:none for paint servers, 120
DOM order limitations on reused content, 82, 120
external asset support, 65, 119, 126
focus control, 121
font-size-adjust support, 218
gradient transitions at 0 or 1 offset, 97
lighting filter support, 151
paint-order support, 18
rotated text paint appearance, 211
SMIL animation of paint servers, 250, 252
spreadMethod support, 113, 137
text-shadow on SVG text, 203
textLength support, 218
userSpaceOnUse errors, 98, 120, 234
zero-length linear gradient vector appearance, 86
-webkit-background-clip, to simulate image-filled text, 219
width attribute, pattern element, 164, 282

X
x attribute, pattern element, 164, 282
x1 and x2 attributes, linearGradient element, 85, 277
X11, as source of color keywords, 31
xlink:href attribute, 279, 284
    for gradients, 86
    linking radial and linear gradients, 134
    pattern element, 183
XML
    HTML versus, 2
    SVG as, 2
xml:base attribute, impact on relative URLs, 66
XMLHttpRequest, 33
    (see also AJAX)

Y
y attribute, pattern element, 164, 282
y1 and y2 attributes, linearGradient element, 85, 277

Z
z-index style property, 25

About the Authors

Amelia Bellamy-Royds is a freelance writer specializing in scientific and technical communication. She is best known in web design circles for her writings about SVG. Amelia is an Invited Expert on the W3C's SVG Working Group, and is also active in the SVG Accessibility Task Force. She helps promote web standards and design through participation in online communities such as Web Platform Docs, Stack Exchange, and Codepen.

Amelia's interest in SVG stems from work in data visualization, and builds upon the programming fundamentals she learned while earning a B.Sc. in bioinformatics. From there, she moved to work in science, health, and environment policy research, and then to a master's degree in journalism. Amelia currently lives in Edmonton, Alberta. If she isn't at a computer, she's probably digging in her vegetable garden or out enjoying live music.

Kurt Cagle worked as a member of the SVG Working Group, and wrote one of the first SVG books on the market in 2004. Currently an Invited Expert with the W3C Xforms working group, Kurt is also an XML Data Architect for the Library of Congress, after having worked in that role for the US National Archives. He has been a regular contributor to O'Reilly Media since 2003, and was an online editor in 2008–2009.

Colophon

The animal on the cover of *SVG Colors, Patterns & Gradients* is a Tibetan blood pheasant (*Ithaginis cruentus tibetanus*). These small, partridge-like pheasants maintain a stable population in forest areas throughout the mountains of eastern Bhutan and southern Tibet. During the summer they can be found at high elevations, retreating to the valleys in fall and winter when the snowfall increases.

The blood pheasant's upper body plumage is blue-gray, with apple-green feathers underneath. The species' common name refers to the feathers on their breast, which are tipped in bright crimson and resemble specks of blood. These birds are also distinguished by their red feet and red-ringed eyes.

Males typically measure 1.5 feet long; females are slightly smaller, with more muted, uniform coloring. Their strong bills are used to snatch up food—mostly green plants such as moss, ferns, and pine shoots.

Not particularly adept at flying, blood pheasants build their nests on the ground beginning in late April and early May. The male stands guard while the female incubates the eggs (usually six or seven in number). If the clutch is thought to be at risk, the nest will be moved to a new location, or possibly deserted. The chicks appear in mid-June and remain with their mother until winter.

Many of the animals on O'Reilly covers are endangered; all of them are important to the world. To learn more about how you can help, go to *animals.oreilly.com*.

The cover animal art is by Karen Montgomery based on an engraving from *Wood's Natural History*. The cover fonts are URW Typewriter and Guardian Sans. The text font is Adobe Minion Pro; the heading font is Adobe Myriad Condensed; and the code font is Dalton Maag's Ubuntu Mono.

Have it your way.

Get even more for your money.

Join the O'Reilly Community, and register the O'Reilly books you own. It's free, and you'll get:

- $4.99 ebook upgrade offer
- 40% upgrade offer on O'Reilly print books
- Membership discounts on books and events
- Free lifetime updates to ebooks and videos
- Multiple ebook formats, DRM FREE
- Participation in the O'Reilly community
- Newsletters
- Account management
- 100% Satisfaction Guarantee

Signing up is easy:

1. Go to: oreilly.com/go/register
2. Create an O'Reilly login.
3. Provide your address.
4. Register your books.

Note: English-language books only

To order books online:
oreilly.com/store

For questions about products or an order:
orders@oreilly.com

To sign up to get topic-specific email announcements and/or news about upcoming books, conferences, special offers, and new technologies:
elists@oreilly.com

For technical questions about book content:
booktech@oreilly.com

To submit new book proposals to our editors:
proposals@oreilly.com

O'Reilly books are available in multiple DRM-free ebook formats. For more information:
oreilly.com/ebooks

Milton Keynes UK
Ingram Content Group UK Ltd.
UKHW021100060324
438918UK00009B/68